T0340119

HANDBOOK OF MOBILITY
DATA MINING

VOLUME ONE

HANDBOOK OF MOBILITY
DATA MINING
DATA PREPROCESSING AND
VISUALIZATION

Edited by

HAORAN ZHANG

School of Urban Planning and Design, Peking University,
Shenzhen, China

ELSEVIER

Elsevier
Radarweg 29, PO Box 211, 1000 AE Amsterdam, Netherlands
The Boulevard, Langford Lane, Kidlington, Oxford OX5 1GB, United Kingdom
50 Hampshire Street, 5th Floor, Cambridge, MA 02139, United States

Notices
Knowledge and best practice in this field are constantly changing. As new research and
experience broaden our understanding, changes in research methods, professional
practices, or medical treatment may become necessary.

Practitioners and researchers must always rely on their own experience and knowledge in
evaluating and using any information, methods, compounds, or experiments described
herein. In using such information or methods they should be mindful of their own safety
and the safety of others, including parties for whom they have a professional
responsibility.

To the fullest extent of the law, neither the Publisher nor the authors, contributors, or
editors, assume any liability for any injury and/or damage to persons or property as a
matter of products liability, negligence or otherwise, or from any use or operation of any
methods, products, instructions, or ideas contained in the material herein.

ISBN: 978-0-443-18428-4

For information on all Elsevier publications visit our
website at https://www.elsevier.com/books-and-journals

Publisher: Joseph P. Hayton
Acquisitions Editor: Kathryn Eryilmaz
Editorial Project Manager: Ali Afzal-Khan
Production Project Manager: Swapna Srinivasan
Cover Designer: Greg Harris

Typeset by TNQ Technologies

Working together
to grow libraries in
developing countries

www.elsevier.com • www.bookaid.org

Contents

List of contributors   ix
Preface   xi
Acknowledgments   xiii

1. **An overview of urban data variety and respective value to urban computing**   **1**

   Hang Yin
   1. Introduction   1
   2. Urban data variety and value   3
   3. Conclusion   9
   References   10

2. **Quality assessment for big mobility data**   **15**

   Yuhao Yao and Haoran Zhang
   1. Introduction   15
   2. Trajectory similarity   16
   3. Travel pattern similarity   26
   4. Origin-destination matrix similarity   27
   5. Conclusion and future directions   31
   References   31

3. **Noise filter method for mobile trajectory data**   **35**

   Defan Feng, Haoran Zhang and Xuan Song
   1. Introduction   35
   2. Simple data cleaning   37
   3. Mean filter and median filter   37
   4. Kalman filter   39
   5. Particle filter   42
   6. Road network matching   44
   7. An example of mobile trajectory data noise filter   45
   References   46

4. **Modifiable areal unit problem in grided population density map**   **51**

   Yuhao Yao and Haoran Zhang
   1. Introduction   51
   2. Error analysis   55

3. Real case experiment   63
4. Conclusion   64
References   64

5. Few-shot count estimation of mobility dynamics by scaling GPS   67
Xiaodan Shi, Haoran Zhang, Quanjun Chen and Ryosuke Shibasaki
1. Introduction   67
2. Related works   69
3. Methodology   71
4. Experiments   75
5. Conclusion   94
References   94
Further reading   96

6. Trip segmentation and mode detection for human mobility data   97
Yuhao Yao, Haoran Zhang and Qi Chen
1. Introduction   97
2. Hidden Markov Model   98
3. Model training   100
4. Decoding   102
5. Application   103
References   114

**7. Benchmark of travel mode detection with smartphone
   GPS trajectories   117**
Jinyu Chen, Wenjing Li, Qing Yu, Ryosuke Shibasaki and Haoran Zhang
1. Introduction   117
2. Ground truth data collection   118
3. Method for travel mode detection   121
4. Case study   127
5. Conclusion   132
References   133

8. Trajectory super-resolution methods   139
Xudong Shen, Dou Huang, Peiran Li and Ning Xu
1. Introduction   139
2. Related work   142
3. Preliminary   144
4. Data description   145
5. Baseline methods   148

6. Experiments and results 152
7. Conclusion and discussion 154
References 154

9. **Map-matching for low accuracy trajectory data** 157
Yuhao Yao and Haoran Zhang
1. Introduction 157
2. Traditional map-matching method 158
3. Multi-steps least cost algorithm 159
4. Real world application 168
References 174

10. **Social information labeling for individual mobile phone user** 177
Chen Zhiheng
1. Background 177
2. Data description 177
3. Framework and case study 178
4. Methodology 179
5. Evaluation metrics 181
6. Result 181
References 184

11. **Web-based spatio-temporal data visualization technology for urban digital twin** 185
Qing Yu, Wen-Long Shang, Jinyu Chen and Haoran Zhang
1. Introduction 185
2. Web-based data visualization technology 186
3. Visualization of data 191
4. Case of web-based urban digital twin application: 3D UrbanMOB 195
5. Conclusion 198
References 199

Index 203

List of contributors

Jinyu Chen
Center for Spatial Information Science, The University of Tokyo, Kashiwa-shi, Chiba, Japan

Qi Chen
School of Geography and Information Engineering, China University of Geosciences (Wuhan), Wuhan, Hubei, China

Quanjun Chen
Center for Spatial Information Science, The University of Tokyo, Kashiwa-shi, Chiba, Japan

Defan Feng
SUSTech-UTokyo Joint Research Center on Super Smart City, Department of Computer Science and Engineering, Southern University of Science and Technology (SUSTech), Shenzhen, China

Dou Huang
Center for Spatial Information Science, The University of Tokyo, Kashiwa-shi, Chiba, Japan

Peiran Li
Center for Spatial Information Science, The University of Tokyo, Kashiwa-shi, Chiba, Japan

Wenjing Li
Center for Spatial Information Science, The University of Tokyo, Kashiwa-shi, Chiba, Japan

Wen-Long Shang
Beijing Key Laboratory of Traffic Engineering, College of Metropolitan Transportation, Beijing University of Technology, Beijing, People's Republic of China

Xudong Shen
Center for Spatial Information Science, The University of Tokyo, Kashiwa-shi, Chiba, Japan

Xiaodan Shi
Center for Spatial Information Science, The University of Tokyo, Kashiwa-shi, Chiba, Japan

Ryosuke Shibasaki
Center for Spatial Information Science, The University of Tokyo, Kashiwa-shi, Chiba, Japan

Xuan Song
SUSTech-UTokyo Joint Research Center on Super Smart City, Department of Computer Science and Engineering, Southern University of Science and Technology (SUSTech), Shenzhen, China

Ning Xu
Beijing Key Laboratory of Urban Oil and Gas Distribution Technology, China University of Petroleum Beijing, Beijing, China

Yuhao Yao
Center for Spatial Information Science, The University of Tokyo, Kashiwa-shi, Chiba, Japan

Hang Yin
LocationMind Inc., Chiyoda-ku, Tokyo, Japan

Qing Yu
Research Institute of Trustworthy Autonomous Systems, Southern University of Science and Technology, Shenzhen, Guangdong, China

Qing Yu
The Key Laboratory of Road and Traffic Engineering, Ministry of Education, Tongji University, College of Transportation Engineering, Shanghai, China

Haoran Zhang
School of Urban Planning and Design, Peking University, Shenzhen, China

Chen Zhiheng
Center for Spatial Information Science, The University of Tokyo, Kashiwa-shi, Chiba, Japan

Preface

In recent times, the smartphone is becoming more and more potent in both computing and storage aspects. The data generated by the smartphone provide a means to get new knowledge about various aspects like usage, movement of the user, etc. Increasingly, application and service providers collect data through sensors embedded in smartphones, such as GPS receivers, while mobile operators collect them through the cellular infrastructure. This information is precious for marketing applications and has an incredible potential to benefit society.

Mobility Data Mining (MDM) is a novel research and business field supported by the growth in smartphone use. MDM can help breed new digital, data-driven services that use several technological capabilities associated with intelligent mobility innovation. It relies on building an ecosystem of stakeholders that agree to manage the supply and demand of the services that travelers want, such as intelligent transportation systems, smart emergency management, sustainability development innovates, etc.

MDM is an emerging topic both in academic and industrial aspects. Currently, all studies about mobile big data mining are fragmented. Few works have summarized the systemic knowledge on this field. Specifically, there is no book focusing on introducing how to screen and process the potential value from "deluge" of unverified, noisy, and sometimes incomplete information of mobile big data. Also, few works comprehensively summarized frontier applications of MDM technologies. However, the above knowledge is significant for stakeholders, such as researchers, engineers, operators, company administrators, and policymakers in related fields, to comprehensively understand current technologies' infra-knowledge structure and limitations. Therefore, we planned to write a series of books mainly focusing on these issues.

The readers of this book can find the knowledge of how to preprocess mobile big data, visualize urban mobility, simulate and predict human travel behavior, and assess the urban mobility characteristics and their matching performance as conditions and constraints in transport, emergency management, and sustainability development systems that are undergoing automation and are highly dependent on software, navigation systems, and connectivity. Further, this book will focus on introducing how to design MDM platforms that adapt to the evolving mobility environment, new types of transportation, and users based on an integrated solution that utilizes the sensing and communication capabilities to tackle the significant challenges that the MDM field faces.

The handbook includes three volumes:

Volume 1: *Data Preprocessing and Visualization* focuses on how to efficiently preprocess mobility big data to extract and utilize critical feature information of high-dimensional city people flow. It first provides a conceptual theory and framework, then goes on to discuss data sources, trajectory map matching, noise filtering, trajectory data segmentation, data quality assessment, and more. It concludes with a chapter on mobility big data visualization.

Volume 2: *Mobility Analytics and Prediction* provides a basis for how to simulate and predict mobility data. After an introductory theory chapter, it then covers crucial topics such as long-term mobility pattern analytics, mobility data generators, user information inference, grid-based population density prediction, and more. It concludes with a chapter on graph-based mobility data analytics.

Volume 3: *Mobility Data-driven Applications* looks at various case studies to illustrate and explore the methods introduced in the first two volumes. It begins with a set of chapters on intelligent transportation management, using cases of bicycle-sharing, ride-hailing, travel time prediction, railway usage analysis, mobility data-driven service, and dynamic road pricing. It concludes with chapters on urban sustainability development, including road emission and living environment inequity analysis.

To help to utilize book outcomes by fellow researchers and developers, all book outcomes will be offered as Open Source Code. Please see the open project, OpenMob, https://github.com/openmob/openmob.

Acknowledgments

I want to thank all lab team members: Zhiling Guo, Dou Huang, Xiaodan Shi, Peiran Li, Jinyu Chen, Yuhao Yao, Qing Yu, Wenjing Li, Zhiheng Chen, Xudong Shen, Wenyi Lu, and Ning Xu, for their efforts, and would also like to thank lab leaders Prof. Ryosuke Shibasaki and Prof. Xuan Song for their support for this book.

CHAPTER ONE

An overview of urban data variety and respective value to urban computing

Hang Yin
LocationMind Inc., Chiyoda-ku, Tokyo, Japan

1. Introduction

The rapid progress of urbanization has led to many big cities, which benefits the lives of residents but also causes some big challenges, such as traffic congestion, environmental pollution, and energy consumption. Nowadays, based on sensing technologies and large-scale computing infrastructures, we can get various urban data from different sources, which implies rich knowledge about a city and can help solve these challenges. Meanwhile, urban anomalies concerning traffic, environment, and crowds may result in loss of life or property if not handled properly. Recently, urban data-driven anomaly analysis frameworks have been forming, which utilize urban big data and machine learning algorithms to detect and predict urban anomalies, thus reducing the losses or mitigating impact. These processes based on urban data collection and computer analysis belongs to the field of urban computing [3].

1.1 Definition of big data

Big data is a buzzword that permeates much of the discussion surrounding the use of digital information in business and government. However, there is almost no consensus on the concept definition of the term. Therefore, we provide some alternative views about what constitutes big data.

- Volume: Big data is often characterized by its huge size, often in petabytes or more. Urban data collected from smartphones is a typical example of a huge size in the concept of time, space, and quantity.
- Velocity: Big data is often generated continuously, in or near real time.

Handbook of Mobility Data Mining, Volume 1
ISBN: 978-0-443-18428-4
https://doi.org/10.1016/B978-0-443-18428-4.00001-3

1

- Variety: Big data can be of any type, so its analysis methodologies need to be flexible enough to deal with any type or, increasingly, a mix of these.

1.2 Definition of urban data

Nowadays, smart devices and various kinds of sensors widely located in cities collect the data produced in urban areas, satisfying the basic views of big data but also being of some unique qualities [1].

- Huge volume: Many urban activities leave a rich digital footprint, such as vehicle tracks and posts on social media platforms, which contain a large amount of urban data.
- Various forms: Different sources usually produce different forms of urban data, including structured data such as human trip records and unstructured data such as surveillance videos.
- Unique dimension: Urban data are associated with time stamps and location labels: Therefore, urban data often contains rich contextual information and brings complex spatio-temporal associations and dependencies between different data points [4].

1.3 Urban computing and challenges

As Fig. 1.1 shows, urban computing is the process of acquiring, integrating, and analyzing urban data generated from different sources (such as sensors, devices, vehicles, buildings, and humans) in urban range to solve major problems concerning about city (such as traffic congestion, air pollution, crowd gathering) [5]. The goal of urban computing is to improve the urban environment, human life quality, and city operation systems. Urban computing is an interdisciplinary field fusing the computing science field with traditional fields, including transportation, environment, economy, etc. [6], which can help us not only in the city management field but also understand urban phenomenon and improve the concept of the city development [7].

However, the goal of urban computing and its data-driven methodologies result in the following challenges:

- Data acquisition technology can continuously collect data unobtrusive across the city. It's easy to monitor traffic flow in sections, but it's a challenge to continuously detect citywide traffic because we don't have sensors on every section. This could be achieved by building a larger sensor infrastructure but would, in turn, increase the burden on the city,

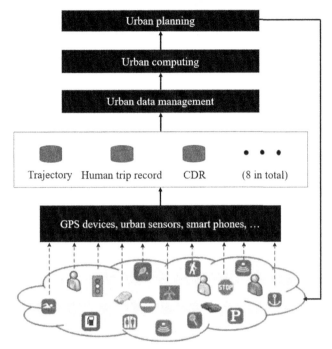

Figure 1.1 Relation among Urban Planning, Urban Computing, Urban Data, and Urban Area. *Credit: original.*

including the energy consumption, sensor expense, and post of the observer.

- For data collection methods that require user participation, privacy protection is an issue that cannot be ignored. In the perception process, users contribute their personal data (usually from smartphones), which is collected by the system to the cloud for analysis. In this process, an necessary balance should be kept among energy consumption, privacy protection, and the efficiency of sharing data.
- The data generated by traditional sensors are generally well structured, easy to understand, and of relatively little missing data. However, the data provided by users usually have great uncertainty and noise, such as data formats with great freedom like text and image.

2. Urban data variety and value

Urban data is the basis of all due to the data-driven methodologies of the urban computing field. Nowadays, various data can be collected from electronic devices. One of the most important sources is smartphones. For example, when a user makes a phone call or connects to a cellular network, the location will be recorded in real time and can be used to track the user's mobility. The information posted by smartphones on social media is also one of the sources of information that can be accepted or analyzed by the system. In addition, electronic sensors distributed around urban areas are also an important source of high-quality urban data. For example, surveillance cameras can record and store the surrounding scene, and traffic sensors can provide real-time traffic conditions. In this section, we divide urban data sets into eight categories based on data types and attributes. Six structured urban data contains trajectory, human trip record, CDR (mobile phone call detail record), event record, urban sensor record and environmental monitoring data, and two unstructured data contains social media data and surveillance camera data.

2.1 Trajectory

The trajectory is a track consisting of a series of time and position records that are recorded and reported by a GPS device. The trajectory data set provides the most detailed and comprehensive record of object movements [8]. A trajectory:

$$T = \left\{ (s, t_s), (l_1, t_{l_1}), (l_2, t_{l_2}), \dots, (l_n, t_{l_n}), (d, t_d) \middle| s, l_i, d \in R \right\}$$

represents a trip of a moving object with a sequence of location and time pairs. s and t_s are the origin location and start time of the trip, while d and t_d are the destination location and arrival time of the trip. The location of the rest of the points l_i in the trajectory are called via locations of T. The R means a range of urban trajectory data correction, all locations of s, d and l_i should be contained in this range [9].

Vehicles equipped with GPS devices provide an important type of movement, given that public and private vehicles are the main transportation means for urban human mobility [10]. People use vehicles for commuting to and from work, for regular and irregular chores, and for leisure activities. By analysis of the observed movements, researchers strive to better understand the demographics of a city, the distribution of services around a city, the effectiveness of the various transportation networks, the dynamics of traffic conditions, the different driving behaviors, etc [11,12].

Take trajectory data collected by taxi with GPS devices as an example. As one of the most important of urban transportation, taxi is ubiquitous in urban areas and operates almost 24 hours a day. The taxi service equipped with a GPS device is driven by the diverse needs of a large number of people, and the movement trajectory of the taxi is not limited by the fixed-route [13,14]. A taxi's GPS trajectory can tell us quite precisely where a passenger got on, off, which route to take, and what steps a driver took to find a new passenger before picking up a passenger. With the diverse needs of passengers and the nature of the service in continuous operation, taxi GPS tracking provides rich and detailed data for the analysis of the motivation and behavior of the urban floating population [15,16].

Through urban computing on trajectory data, researchers are interested in the destination of people during the day, popular places around the city, what functions those popular places have, and what are the connections between those popular places. Also, human mobility described by trajectory is driven by different needs and influenced by external factors such as weather and traffic [17−19]. A deep understanding of social dynamics is essential for the management, design, maintenance, and advancement of urban infrastructure, which is not just limited to the field of urban computing [9].

2.2 Human trip record

Human trip records (origin-destination records) are usually collected from taxi and sharing bike system, which often contains the start location, end location, trip distance, and trip duration [2] and might be able to be generated from trajectory data by segmentation and distance computing algorithm to some extent. A human trip record is often a tuple in the form:

$$TR = \langle u, (o, d), \ t_o, t_d \rangle \ o, d \in R$$

Each tuple contains the user id u, the trip origin o, and trip destination d, the time stamp t_o when user u enters the trip origin o and the time stamp t_d when user u enters the trip destination d. The R means a range of urban human trip record data correction, all locations of o and d should be contained in this range [20].

Vehicles equipped with GPS devices can be one of the most common sources of trip record data, which can help researchers understand human mobility in urban areas. For example, the number of taxi trips recorded from one region to another region reflects the number of people moving from one area to another area approximately [21].

Take overcrowding research and prediction as an example [22,23]. For people traveling using public transport, overcrowding is one of the major causes of discomfort and even accidents, so it is meaningful to understand the pattern of human mobility mode and predict potential overcrowding for preparation in advance. In tradition, some common ideas for overcrowding are widely adapted, such as different fare policies depending on time. Transport operators often attempt to discourage peak-time travel by means of fare differentiation. However, these solutions cannot deal with real-time changes in human mobility patterns. Based on human trip record data, transforming the raw trip record data from a per-user basis to a per-station basis as follow: each tuple u, (o, d), t_o, t_d was split in two, one recording origin and time of origin o, t_o, while another one recording destination and time of destination d, t_d, the real-time population density in city region can be estimated and future changes in population density can be predicted based on trained models, so potential overcrowding can be predicted and prevented by targeted policies [24].

2.3 CDR

Mobile phone CDR includes the time and location information of phone calls. In most countries of the developed world, mobile phone coverage reaches 100% of the population, and even in remote villages of developing countries, it is not unusual to cross paths with someone in the street talking on a mobile phone. Due to the ubiquity of mobile phone users, mobile phones have stimulated the creativity of scientists to use them as millions of potential sensors of the urban environment [25]. According to sources of CDR, it often uses the positions of the associated base stations as user locations and is different from traditional trajectory GPS data in these aspects [26,27]:

- Temporal sparseness: CDR data only records the user location when a call or text message is made or received, thus is temporally sparse since the call or message frequency of users is usually low and unpredictable.
- Spatial sparseness: The location information of users when they make a call or message is recorded as the location of the antenna, which brings the spatial sparseness of CDR data.

CDR data is often in the form:

$$CDR = \{call_1, call_2, \ldots, call_n\}$$

which denotes the set of all calls collected from a mobile phone network. And the all the calls can be defined as a tuple:

$$call_i = \langle u_i, l_j, t_k \rangle, u_i \in U, l_j \in R$$

which means a user u_i makes or receives a call at location l_j at timestamp t_k, where all users u_i belong to set of all users U, and all locations l_j belong to a range of CDR data correction [28,29].

Having such kind of data, researchers can study the behavior of an individual or build a network between different users. The similarity between users can also be inferred, thus offering some personalized service to different user groups. Moreover, using a triangle positioning algorithm, a mobile phone's location can be roughly computed based on three or more base stations [30]. This usage of CDR data can denote citywide human mobility, which can be used for detecting urban anomalies and guiding the urban plan in the long run.

2.4 Event record

In target range, there are some datasets comprehensively recording the event time, locations, and event descriptions [3]. When researching urban anomalies or setting some analysis threshold or limitation for urban computing, researchers often need event record data. Due to the various form of the urban data set, symbols and formulas will not be used to show the urban data format [31,32].

The commonest example of an event record is a traffic accident record provided by the traffic management department [33,34], which is usually used for detection or prediction result validation. When research deals with urban anomalies, crime records provided by police play a close role in urban anomaly appearances, thus often being adopted for the prediction and prevention of urban anomalies [35,36].

2.5 Urban sensor record

Different from urban data generated from user groups by GPS devices or other smart devices, there are many sensors distributed around urban areas to collect urban data, which is called urban sensor record data.

The urban sensor record data can be of various forms, and commonest sensors are the loop detectors on the road, which are installed underneath pavements at around half a mild interval and can record the vehicles passing that location [37]. The record can be utilized to evaluate vehicle speeds and road conditions [38,39]. Moreover, some automatic billing systems often appear in the subway, bus, or highway entrance and exit in the form of card reading machines as an example, which are other important user sensors that record the volume of flow [40]. These various sensors can reflect the urban dynamics of one location from different perspectives. With urban sensor record data, researchers can know the real-time condition and make predictions of the future condition of locations monitored by sensors, evaluate the risk of location, and supplement essential information when concerning urban mobility patterns [41].

2.6 Environmental monitoring data

Urban computing dealing with Environmental monitoring data is often interdisciplinary to some extent. There are various sources of environmental monitoring data. Meteorological data include humidity, temperature, barometer pressure, wind speed, and weather conditions, which can be crawled from public websites [42,43]. Air quality data, such as the concentration of $PM_{2.5}$, NO_2, and SO_2, can be obtained from air quality monitoring stations. Some gasses like CO_2 and CO can even be detected by portable sensors. Noise data are another kind of environmental data that have a direct impact on people's mental and physical health [44]. The environment monitoring data are often influenced by multiple complex factors, such as traffic flow, land use condition, population density, location, etc [45].

In previous research cases concerning environmental monitoring data, the air humidity can be used to evaluate fire risk in urban areas [46–48], the water quality can be used to evaluate the degree of industrialization [49], and the noise data can be used to evaluate the population density in urban areas. The consequences of such evaluation research have close relation with the daily lives of urban residents [50,51], which is also meaningful in the urban computing field [19,52].

2.7 Social media data

Social network data consists of two parts. One is the social structure, which is often used to represent the relationship network between users [53,54]. The other is the information uploaded by users to social media, which is generally in the form of texts, photos, videos, etc., and contains information about user behaviours or interests [22,55,56]. When adding user locations to social media, researchers can use this data to simulate the mobility of people in urban areas, which also helps detect and understand urban anomalies [57].

2.8 Surveillance camera data

Surveillance camera plays a vital role in capturing and monitoring human mobility. Surveillance cameras are widely deployed in urban areas, constantly generating a large number of images and videos reflecting the conditions in the areas monitored by themselves. The form of these data can provide researchers with intuitive information such as traffic conditions, people's behaviors, and environmental conditions in the urban area [58]. However, automatically converting images and videos into formatted data needed by researchers, such as specific traffic volumes, driving speeds, weather conditions, etc., remains a challenging task. Furthermore, it is difficult for researchers to apply machine learning models trained for one urban region to other regions because of differences in region structure and how surveillance cameras are set up, including height, angle, and focus [59]. Therefore, monitoring urban area conditions through this method and then converting it into formatted data that can be accepted by urban computing-related algorithms requires human intervention to some extent [60].

3. Conclusion

Effective planning is essential for building smart cities, and developing urban plans requires evaluating a wide range of factors, which are complex and rapidly evolving, making urban planning an extremely challenging task. As the basis of data-driven methodology, we list the common forms of urban data widely used in urban computing supporting urban planning and analyze their forms and the application values. Table 1.1 shows urban data features. The column "Structured" means whether the urban data is structured and no-needed to be converted to an acceptable form before urban computing. The column "Continuous" means whether the urban data is temporal continuous. The column "Aggregative" means whether the urban data is overall statistic form which describes the condition from a holistic perspective.

Table 1.1 Urban data features.

Urban data	Structured	Continuous	Aggregative
Trajectory	√	√	×
Human trip record	√	√	×
CDR	√	×	×
Event record	√	×	√
Urban sensor record	√	√	√
Environmental monitoring data	√	×	/
Social media data	×	×	/
Surveillance camera data	×	√	/

References

[1]   R. Barkham, S. Bokhari, S. Albert, Urban Big Data: City Management and Real Estate Markets, GovLab Digest, New York, NY, 2018.

[2]   M. Zhang, L. Tong, Y. Yue, Y. Li, H. Pan, Y. Zheng, Urban Anomaly Analytics: Description, Detection, and Prediction, IEEE Transactions on Big Data, 25 Apr 2020.

[3]   Y. Zheng, L. Capra, O. Wolfson, H. Yang, Urban computing: concepts, methodologies, and applications, ACM Transactions on Intelligent Systems and Technology (TIST) 5 (3) (2014) 38.

[4]   X. Song, H. Zhang, R.A. Akerkar, H. Huang, S. Guo, L. Zhong, Y. Ji, A.L. Opdahl, H. Purohit, A. Skupin, Big Data and Emergency Management: Concepts, Methodologies, and Applications, IEEE Transactions on Big Data, 2020.

[5]   R. Li, H. He, R. Wang, Y. Huang, J. Liu, S. Ruan, T. He, J. Bao, Y. Zheng, Just: JD Urban Spatio-Temporal Data Engine, ICDE. IEEE, 2020.

[6]   P. Kalnis, N. Mamoulis, S. Bakiras, On discovering moving clusters in spatio-temporal data, in: Proceedings of the 9th International Conference on Advances in Spatial and Temporal Databases, SSTD'05, Springer-Verlag, Berlin, Heidelberg, 2005, pp. 364–381.

[7]   Y. Yao, H. Zhang, F. Defan, J. Chen, W. Li, R. Shibasaki, X. Song, Modifiable Areal Unit Problem on Grided Mobile Crowd Sensing: Analysis and Restoration, IEEE Transactions on Mobile Computing, 2022.

[8]   M.-F. Chiang, E.-P. Lim, W.-C. Lee, A.T. Kwee, BTCI: a new framework for identifying congestion cascades using bus trajectory data, in: Big Data (Big Data), 2017 IEEE International Conference on, IEEE, 2017, pp. 1133–1142.

[9]   F. Giannotti, M. Nanni, F. Pinelli, D. Pedreschi, Trajectory pattern mining, in: ACM SIGKDD'07, ACM, New York, NY, 2007, pp. 330–339.

[10] Q. Yu, H. Zhang, W. Li, Y. Sui, X. Song, D. Yang, R. Shibasaki, W. Jiang, Mobile phone data in urban bicycle-sharing: market-oriented sub-area division and spatial analysis on emission reduction potentials, Journal of Cleaner Production (2020) 119974.

[11] Y. Sui, H. Zhang, X. Song, F. Shao, X. Yu, R. Shibasaki, R. Sun, M. Yuan, C. Wang, S. Li, GPS data in urban online ride-hailing: a comparative analysis on fuel consumption and emissions, Journal of Cleaner Production (2019) 495–505.

[12] H. Zhang, X. Song, Y. Long, T. Xia, K. Fang, J. Zheng, D. Huang, R. Shibasaki, Y. Liang, Mobile phone GPS data in urban bicycle-sharing: layout optimization and emissions reduction analysis, Applied Energy (2019) 138–147.

[13] P. Samuel Castro, D. Zhang, C. Chen, S. Li, G. Pan, From taxi GPS traces to social and community dynamics: a survey, ACM Computing Surveys 46 (2) (2013) 17.

[14] C. Chen, D. Zhang, P. Samuel Castro, N. Li, L. Sun, S. Li, Real-time detection of anomalous taxi trajectories from GPS traces, in: International Conference on Mobile and Ubiquitous Systems: Computing, Networking, and Services, Springer, 2011, pp. 63–74.

[15] W. Zhang, G. Qi, G. Pan, H. Lu, S. Li, Z. Wu, City-scale social event detection and evaluation with taxi traces, ACM Transactions on Intelligent Systems and Technology (TIST) 6 (3) (2015) 40.

[16] Q. Yu, W. Li, H. Zhang, J. Chen, GPS data in taxi-sharing system: analysis of potential demand and assessment of fuel consumption based on routing probability model, Applied Energy (2022) 118923.

[17] W. Jiang, H. Zhang, Y. Long, J. Chen, Y. Sui, X. Song, R. Shibasaki, Q. Yu, GPS data in urban online ride-hailing: the technical potential analysis of demand prediction model, Journal of Cleaner Production (2021) 123706.

[18] H. Zhang, X. Song, T. Xia, M. Yuan, Z. Fan, R. Shibasaki, Y. Liang, Battery electric vehicles in Japan: human mobile behavior based adoption potential analysis and policy target response, Applied Energy (2018) 527−535.

[19] H. Zhang, J. Chen, W. Li, X. Song, R. Shibasaki, Mobile phone GPS data in urban ride-sharing: an assessment method for emission reduction potential, Applied Energy (2020) 115038.

[20] I. Ceapa, C. Smith, L. Capra, Avoiding the crowds: understanding tube station congestion patterns from trip data, in: Proceedings of the ACM SIGKDD International Workshop on Urban Computing, ACM, 2012, pp. 134−141.

[21] X. Li, Z. Li, J. Han, J.-G. Lee, Temporal outlier detection in vehicle traffic data, in: IEEE International Conference on Data Engineering, IEEE, 2009, pp. 1319−1322.

[22] Y. Zheng, H. Zhang, Y. Yu, Detecting collective anomalies from multiple spatiotemporal datasets across different domains, in: Proceedings of the 23rd SIGSPATIAL International Conference on Advances in Geographic Information Systems, ACM, 2015, p. 2.

[23] C. Lin, Q. Zhu, S. Guo, Z. Jin, Y.-R. Lin, N. Cao, Anomaly detection in spatiotemporal data via regularized non-negative tensor analysis, Data Mining and Knowledge Discovery (2018) 1−18.

[24] X. Song, R. Guo, T. Xia, Z. Guo, Y. Long, H. Zhang, X. Song, S. Ryosuke, Mining urban sustainable performance: millions of GPS data reveal high-emission travel attraction in Tokyo, Journal of Cleaner Production (2020) 118396.

[25] Y. Dong, F. Pinelli, Y. Gkoufas, Z. Nabi, F. Calabrese, V.N. Chawla, Inferring Unusual Crowd Events from Mobile Phone Call Detail Records, ECML PKDD 2015: Machine Learning and Knowledge Discovery in Databases, 2015, pp. 474−492.

[26] D. Zhang, J. Huang, L. Ye, F. Zhang, C. Xu, H. Tian, Exploring human mobility with multi-source data at extremely large metropolitan scales, in: Proceedings of the 20th Annual International Conference on Mobile Computing and Networking, ACM, 2014, pp. 201−212.

[27] I. Trestian, S. Ranjan, A. Kuzmanovic, A. Nucci, Measuring serendipity: connecting people, locations and interests in a mobile 3G network, in: Proceedings of the 9th ACM SIGCOMM Conference on Internet Measurement, ACM, 2009, pp. 267−279.

[28] D.B. Vincent, A. Decuyper, K. Gautier, A survey of results on mobile phone datasets analysis, EPJ Data Science 4 (1) (2015) 10.

[29] F. Calabrese, F. Pereira, G. Lorenzo, L. Liu, C. Ratti, The geography of taste: analyzing cell-phone mobility and social events, in: Pervasive Computing'10, 2010, pp. 22−37.

[30] G. Ranjan, H. Zang, Z.-L. Zhang, B. Jean, Are call detail records biased for sampling human mobility? ACM SIGMOBILE-Mobile Computing and Communications Review 16 (3) (2012) 33−44.

[31] M.M. Chong, A. Abraham, M. Paprzycki, Traffic Accident Analysis Using Decision Trees and Neural Networks. arXiv Preprint Cs/0405050, 2004.

[32] Q. Chen, X. Song, H. Yamada, R. Shibasaki, Learning deep representation from big and heterogeneous data for traffic accident inference, in: Thirtieth AAAI Conference on Artificial Intelligence, 2016.

[33] L. Zhu, F. Guo, R. Krishnan, J.W. Polak, A deep learning approach for traffic incident detection in urban networks, in: 2018 21st International Conference on Intelligent Transportation Systems (ITSC), IEEE, 2018, pp. 1011−1016.

[34] H. Wang, D. Kifer, C. Graif, Z. Li, Crime rate inference with big data, in: Proceedings of the 22nd ACM SIGKDD International Conference on Knowledge Discovery and Data Mining, ACM, 2016, pp. 635−644.

[35] C. Huang, J. Zhang, Y. Zheng, N.V. Chawla, Deepcrime: attentive hierarchical recurrent networks for crime prediction, in: Proceedings of the 27th ACM International

Conference on Information and Knowledge Management, ACM, 2018, pp. 1423–1432.

[36] C. Huang, C. Zhang, J. Zhao, X. Wu, N. Chawla, D.Y. Mist, A multiview and multi-modal spatial-temporal learning framework for citywide abnormal event forecasting, in: The World Wide Web Conference, ACM, 2019, pp. 717–728.

[37] S. Nawaz, C. Mascolo, Mining users' significant driving routes with low-power sensors, in: ACM SenSys '14, ACM, 2014, pp. 236–250.

[38] C. Xu, A.P. Tarko, W. Wang, L. Pan, Predicting crash likelihood and severity on freeways with realtime loop detector data, Accident Analysis & Prevention 57 (2013) 30–39.

[39] C. Oh, J.-S. Oh, S.G. Ritchie, Real-time hazardous traffic condition warning system: framework and evaluation, IEEE Transactions on Intelligent Transportation Systems 6 (3) (2005) 265–272.

[40] C. Xu, W. Wang, L. Pan, A genetic programming model for real-time crash prediction on freeways, IEEE Transactions on Intelligent Transportation Systems 14 (2) (2013) 574–586.

[41] H. Wang, X. Chen, S. Qiang, H. Zhang, Y. Wang, J. Shi, Y. Jin, Early warning of city-scale unusual social event on public transportation smartcard data, in: Ubiquitous Intelligence & Computing, Advanced and Trusted Computing, Scalable Computing and Communications, Cloud and Big Data Computing, Internet of People, and Smart World Congress (UIC/ATC/ScalCom/CBDCom/IoP/SmartWorld), 2016 Intl IEEE Conferences, IEEE, 2016, pp. 188–195.

[42] H. Zhang, J. Chen, J. Yan, X. Song, R. Shibasaki, J. Yan, Urban power load profiles under ageing transition integrated with future EVs charging, Advances in Applied Energy (2021) 100007.

[43] J. Chen, Q. Zhang, N. Xu, W. Li, Y. Yao, P. Li, Q. Yu, C. Wen, X. Song, R. Shibasaki, Roadmap to hydrogen society of Tokyo: locating priority of hydrogen facilities based on multiple big data fusion, Applied Energy (2022) 118688.

[44] E. Potash, J. Brew, L. Alexander, S. Majumdar, A. Reece, J. Walsh, E. Rozier, E. Jorgenson, R. Mansour, R. Ghani, Predictive modeling for public health: preventing childhood lead poisoning, in: Proceedings of the 21th ACM SIGKDD International Conference on Knowledge Discovery and Data Mining, ACM, 2015, pp. 2039–2047.

[45] Y. Jin, H. Zhang, S. Bharule, Modular Metacognitive Digital Twin Technologies for Greener Cities & Cleaner Mobility, Elsevier, 2021.

[46] M. Madaio, O.L. Haimson, W. Zhang, X. Cheng, M. Hinds-Aldrich, B. Dilkina, D.H. Chau, Identifying and prioritizing fire inspections: a case study of predicting fire risk in Atlanta, in: Bloomberg Data for Good Exchange Conference, New York City, NY, vol 28, 2015.

[47] M. Madaio, S.-T. Chen, O.L. Haimson, W. Zhang, X. Cheng, M. Hinds-Aldrich, D. Horng Chau, B. Dilkina, Firebird: predicting fire risk and prioritizing fire inspections in atlanta, in: Proceedings of the 22nd ACM SIGKDD International Conference on Knowledge Discovery and Data Mining, ACM, 2016, pp. 185–194.

[48] B. Singh Walia, Q. Hu, J. Chen, F. Chen, J. Lee, N. Kuo, P. Narang, J. Batts, G. Arnold, M. Madaio, A dynamic pipeline for spatiotemporal fire risk prediction, in: Proceedings of the 24th ACM SIGKDD International Conference on Knowledge Discovery & Data Mining, ACM, 2018, pp. 764–773.

[49] A. Chojnacki, C. Dai, F. Arya, G. Shi, J. Webb, D.T. Zhang, J. Abernethy, E. Schwartz, A data science approach to understanding residential water contamination in flint, in: Proceedings of the 23rd ACM SIGKDD International Conference on Knowledge Discovery and Data Mining, ACM, 2017, pp. 1407–1416.

[50] M.A. Abdel-Aty, R. Pemmanaboina, Calibrating a real-time traffic crash-prediction model using archived weather and ITS traffic data, IEEE Transactions on Intelligent Transportation Systems 7 (2) (2006) 167—174.

[51] R. Yu, M.A. Abdel-Aty, M.M. Ahmed, X. Wang, Utilizing microscopic traffic and weather data to analyze real-time crash patterns in the context of active traffic management, IEEE Transactions on Intelligent Transportation Systems 15 (1) (2014) 205—213.

[52] Z. Chen, P. Li, Y. Jin, Y. Jin, J. Chen, W. Li, X. Song, R. Shibasaki, M. Chen, D. Yan, Using mobile phone big data to identify inequity of artificial light at night exposure: a case study in Tokyo, Cities (2022) 103803.

[53] B. Pan, Y. Zheng, D. Wilkie, C. Shahabi, Crowd sensing of traffic anomalies based on human mobility and social media, in: Proceedings of the 21st ACM SIGSPATIAL International Conference on Advances in Geographic Information Systems, ACM, 2013, pp. 344—353.

[54] F. Calabrese, G. Di Lorenzo, G. McArdle, F. Pinelli, E. Van Lierde, Real-time social event analytics, in: Netmob '15, 2015.

[55] X. Teng, Y.-R. Lin, X. Wen, Anomaly detection in dynamic networks using multi-view time-series hypersphere learning, in: Proceedings of the 2017 ACM on Conference on Information and Knowledge Management, ACM, 2017, pp. 827—836.

[56] X. Lin, K.A. Lachlan, P.R. Spence, Exploring extreme events on social media: a comparison of user reposting/retweeting behaviors on Twitter and Weibo, Computers in Human Behavior 65 (2016) 576—581.

[57] H. Zhang, J. Chen, Q. Chen, T. Xia, X. Wang, W. Li, X. Song, R. Shibasaki, A universal mobility-based indicator for regional health level, Cities (2022) 103452.

[58] A. Adam, E. Rivlin, I. Shimshoni, D. Reinitz, Robust realtime unusual event detection using multiple fixed-location monitors, IEEE Transactions on Pattern Analysis and Machine Intelligence 30 (3) (2008) 555.

[59] S. Oh, A. Hoogs, A. Perera, N. Cuntoor, C. Chih Chen, J. Taek Lee, S. Mukherjee, J.K. Aggarwal, H. Lee, L. Davis, A large-scale benchmark dataset for event recognition in surveillance video, in: IEEE International Conference on Advanced Video and Signal Based Surveillance, 2011, pp. 527—528.

[60] C. Lu, J. Shi, J. Jia, Abnormal event detection at 150 fps in matlab, in: IEEE International Conference on Computer Vision, 2014, pp. 2720—2727.

CHAPTER TWO

Quality assessment for big mobility data

Yuhao Yao[1], Haoran Zhang[2]
[1]Center for Spatial Information Science, The University of Tokyo, Kashiwa-shi, Chiba, Japan
[2]School of Urban Planning and Design, Peking University, Shenzhen, China

1. Introduction

Big mobility data provides sufficient information for urban planning [1], transportation management [2,3], ride-sharing systems [4], emergency management [5], and prevention of infectious diseases [6], which exerts an enormous impact on serving for Mobility-as-a-Service (MaaS) and improving urban mobility, accessibility, and reliability.

Big mobility data is usually represented by various mobility expressions. As Fig. 2.1 shows, at an individual level, a full-time trajectory is the most fundamental way to perfectly record an individual's mobility. Trajectory as spatial-temporal data records the position of the individual at different times and could be processed into nearly all other mobility metrics.

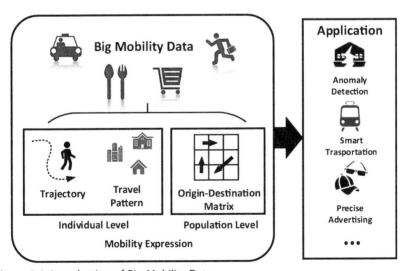

Figure 2.1 Introduction of Big Mobility Data.

Handbook of Mobility Data Mining, Volume 1
ISBN: 978-0-443-18428-4
https://doi.org/10.1016/B978-0-443-18428-4.00006-2

However, such a high-precision expression usually requires large storage space and lots of time to process. Therefore, individual trajectory data is usually processed into travel patterns such as most frequented locations and motifs, which is more proper in some circumstances. On the other hand, high precision is not necessary for many applications that just need aggregated statistics. Therefore, at a population level, some metrics are more widely used, such as Origin-Destination (OD) matrices.

No matter what kind of mobility expression is utilized, quality assessment plays a critical role in modeling dynamic human mobility. A variety of mobility observing datasets has been widely utilized to extract large-scale population flow information (including GPS [7], Bluetooth [8], GSM [9], automatic number plate recognition sensors [10,11] and smartphone Call Detailed Record (CDR) [12,13]). Due to the different observing mechanisms, gaps exist in the qualities of these data sources. Quality assessment is the step to measure how serious those errors will affect the mobility expression. To assess the data quality, mobility similarity comparison is the key point.

In this chapter, we will introduce methods of quality assessment or, to say, similarity comparison for different typical kinds of mobility expressions. Trajectory similarity at an individual level will be firstly introduced in Section 2. Then OD matrices similarity will be introduced in Section 3. In Section 4, we will introduce mobility patterns similarity.

2. Trajectory similarity

Trajectory refers to a set of points that describe the path one individual passes through in the target period, which includes both positions and corresponding timestamps. For example, a standard 2-dimensional trajectory T, contains a series of n timestamped points l_i, $i \in [1, n]$, will be $T = \{(t_1, l_1), (t_2, l_2), ..., (t_n, l_n)\}$ where t_i is the corresponding timestamp of l_i and $t_i < t_i + 1$.

A dense trajectory can highly describe the traveling of an individual and can be used to compute other metrics such as velocity and traveling direction. However, since the data collecting mechanisms are manifold, the time interval and positioning accuracy are not fixed. Fig. 2.2 demonstrates an example of the comparison between GPS trajectory and CDR trajectory of the same individual, while GPS records have shorter time intervals and higher accuracy.

The similarity between two trajectories is usually measured by a set of the distance between trajectories' points. Therefore, the point-to-point distance

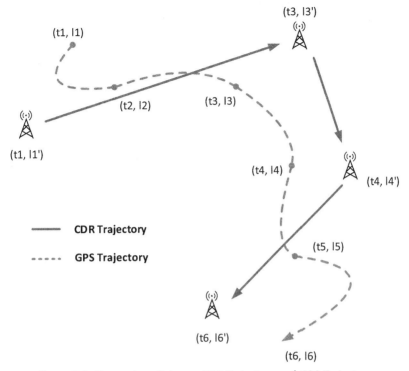

Figure 2.2 Comparison Between CDR Trajectory and GPS Trajectory.

metric is also one of the key points of trajectory similarity measurement. It is worth noting that some of the similarity functions were originally proposed for time series data. Since trajectory is a kind of particular time series in multidimensional space, these similarity functions are also suitable for trajectory data.

In this section, we will first introduce several point-to-point distance metrics in 2.1, then introduce the typical similarity functions for trajectory in 2.2, and finally, introduce the standard process of trajectory clustering and a specific algorithm, for example, in 2.3.

2.1 Point-to-point distance metric

2.1.1 Euclidean distance

Euclidean distance (also known as Euclidean Metric) is the most common definition of distance, which refers to the real distance between two points in n-dimensional space or the natural length of a vector, which is the distance between the point and the origin.

For two given points $A_1 = (x_1, y_1)$ and $A_2 = (x_2, y_2)$ in a two-dimensional space, we have:

$$D_{Euclidean}(A_1, A_2) = \sqrt[2]{(x_1 - x_2)^2 + (y_1 - y_2)^2} \# \qquad (2.1)$$

2.1.2 Manhattan distance

Manhattan distance (also known as Taxi Geometry) was proposed by Herman Minkowski in the 19th century. It is used in geometric space to indicate the sum of the absolute wheelbase of two points in the coordinate.

For two given points $A_1 = (x_1, y_1)$ and $A_2 = (x_2, y_2)$ in a two-dimensional space, we have:

$$D_{Manhattan}(A_1, A_2) = |x_1 - x_2| + |y_1 - y_2| \# \qquad (2.2)$$

Manhattan distance comes from the shortest driving path in a city where buildings are planned as square blocks, such as Manhattan, where most of the roadways there are in north–south or east–west directions, and there are just several inclined lanes. In this kind of city, the driving distance from one point to another equals the sum of the distance from the north–south direction and the distance from the east–west direction. Therefore, the Manhattan distance is also called Taxi Geometry. Obviously, Manhattan distance is not a distance invariant. When the coordinate axis changes, the distance between two points will be different. In the early computer graphics, coordinates of points were all integers. It was too hard to compute the Euclidean distance between two points to avoid a floating-point operation, which was expensive, slow, and inaccurate at that time. By using Manhattan distance, the computation just needs addition and subtraction, which avoids floating-point operation and can greatly improve the computation speed and accuracy.

2.1.3 Chebyshev distance

Chebyshev distance represents the maximum absolute wheelbase of two points in the coordinate system. For two given points $A_1 = (x_1, y_1)$ and $A_2 = (x_2, y_2)$ in a two-dimensional space, we have:

$$D_{Chebyshev}(A_1, A_2) = \max(|x_1 - x_2|, |y_1 - y_2|) \# \qquad (2.3)$$

If we place the chessboard in a two-dimensional coordinate system, in which the side length of the grid is defined as 1, the X and Y axes of the coordinate are parallel to the chessboard grid, then the number of steps required for the King to move from one position to another just equals to the Chebyshev distance between these two positions, so the Chebyshev distance is also called chessboard distance. In practice, Chebyshev distance is often used in warehouse logistics because the time for a crane to move objects just fits the rule of it.

2.1.4 Minkowski distance

Minkowski Distance is a group of distance definitions rather than a single kind of distance. For two given points in a two-dimensional space $A_1 = (x_1, y_1)$ and $A_2 = (x_2, y_2)$, we have:

$$D_{\text{Minkowski}}(A_1, A_2) = (|x_1 - x_2|^p + |y_1 - y_2|^p)^{\frac{1}{p}} \# \qquad (2.4)$$

where p is a constant.

It is not hard to see that Minkowski Distance includes all the above three distances. When $p = 1$, Minkowski Distance represents the Manhattan distance. When $p = 2$, Minkowski Distance represents the Euclidean distance. When $p = \infty$, Minkowski Distance represents the Chebyshev distance. It should be noticed that the Minkowski distance is related to the dimension of character parameters, so the Minkowski distance of character parameters with different dimensions is usually meaningless.

2.2 Similarity function of trajectory

Compared with the distance measurement between points or between points and trajectories, the similarity measurement between trajectories is more complex and needs to consider more factors, such as the sampling rate of trajectories, the timestamp of different points, and the noise. Basically, similarity functions of the trajectory can be divided into several types by what they lay particular emphasis on:

1. Point-based function measures the similarity by the distance between point pairs of two trajectories, such as Euclidean, DTW, LCSS, EDR, and ERP.
2. Shape-based function focuses on the shape similarity of two trajectories, such as Hausdorff distance and Frechet distance.
3. Segment-based function divides trajectories into different pieces and measures the similarity by distances between pieces, such as one-way distance and Locality in–Between Polylines (LIP) distance.

We will serially introduce these functions.

2.2.1 Euclidean distance

As a naïve similarity measure, Euclidean distance for trajectories is simple and clear, which is the mean value of the sum of distances between corresponding points of two trajectories. For two given trajectories $T_A = \{A_1, A_2, ..., A_n\}$ and $T_B = \{B_1, B_2, ..., B_n\}$ where A_i and B_i are the i-th points of T_A and T_B. We have:

$$D_{\text{Euclidean}}(T_A, T_B) = \frac{1}{n}\sum_{i=1}^{n} D_{\text{Euclidean}}(A_i, B_i)\#\qquad(2.5)$$

Similarly, there is another measure named Sum-of-Pairs Distance, which is the sum of distances between corresponding points of two trajectories. Although these two measures are simple and effective, which just have $O(n)$ computational complexity, they have obvious disadvantages. They struggle with different sampling rates and outliers and require trajectories of different lengths to be cut to equal size [14]. They are also sensitive to noises.

2.2.2 Dynamic time warping

As we see, the major limitation of Euclidean distance is that it requires two trajectories to have the same length, which is rare in practice. An ideal similarity measure should be flexible in the length of two trajectories. Dynamic Time arping (DTW) distance is the first method based on this motivation [15]. The basic idea of DTW is to allow some points to be repeated for the best alignment. By using DTW, the trajectories are "warped" in a nonlinear way to measure similarity while allowing for varying sampling rates [16]. For two given trajectories T_A and T_B with length m and n relatively, we have:

$$D_{DTW}(T_A, T_B) = \begin{cases} 0, & \text{if } m = 0 \text{ and } n = 0 \\ \infty, & \text{if } m = 0 \text{ or } n = 0 \\ D(Head(T_A), Head(T_B)) + \min \begin{cases} D_{DTW}(T_A, Rest(T_B)) \\ D_{DTW}(Rest(T_A), T_B) \\ D_{DTW}(Rest(T_A), Rest(T_B)) \end{cases}, & \text{otherwise} \end{cases} \#$$

$$(2.6)$$

where function D can be any point-to-point distance metric, *Head* refers to the first point of the trajectory, and *Rest* refers to the rest of the trajectory except the first point.

2.2.3 Longest common subsequence

Longest Common Subsequence (LCSS) comes from a classical algorithmic problem that is to find the LCSS of two sequences. Obviously, the similarity between two trajectories can just be represented by a kind of LCSS. LCSS distance [14] represents the number of points that can be regarded as the same one in two trajectories, that is, the number of point pairs that satisfy the minimum distance threshold in two trajectories. For two given trajectories T_A and T_B with length m and n relatively, we have:

$$D_{LCSS}(T_A, T_B) = \begin{cases} 0, \textit{if } m = 0 \textit{ or } n = 0 \\ 1 + D_{LCSS}(Rest(T_A), Rest(T_B)), \textit{if } D(Head(T_A), Head(T_B)) \leq \varepsilon \; \# \\ \max(D_{LCSS}(Rest(T_A), T_B), D_{LCSS}(T_A, Rest(T_B))), \textit{otherwise} \end{cases} \quad (2.7)$$

Same with DTW distance, function D can be any point-to-point distance metric, *Head*, and *Rest* functions refer to the first point of the trajectory and the rest of the trajectory except the first point relatively. ε is the set distance threshold.

Compared with Euclidean and DTW, LCSS is much more robust toward noise because the basic idea of LCSS is to allow points to be skipped instead of rearranged, so noise point that is far away from the real position will be ignored. However, it faces the problem that threshold ε is hard to determine for an inappropriate ε. There may be no similarity between two trajectories with high LCSS distance at all.

2.2.4 Edit distance on real sequence

Although LCSS can deal with trajectories with noise, it cannot distinguish trajectories with similar common subsequences. In order to cover it better, a new similarity function called Edit Distance on Real (EDR) sequence is proposed [17]. The fundamental idea of EDR is to count the minimum number of edits required to transfer one trajectory into the other. For two given trajectories T_A and T_B with length m and n relatively, we have:

$$D_{EDR}(T_A, T_B) = \begin{cases} n, & \text{if } m = 0 \\ m, & \text{if } n = 0 \\ \min \begin{cases} D_{EDR}(Rest(T_A), Rest(T_B)) + subcost(T_A, T_B) \\ D_{EDR}(Rest(T_A), T_B) + 1 \\ D_{EDR}(T_A, Rest(T_B)) + 1 \end{cases}, & \text{otherwise} \end{cases} \quad \# \quad (2.8)$$

where

$$subcost(T_1, T_2) = \begin{cases} 0, & \text{if } D(Head(T_1), Head(T_2)) \leq \varepsilon \\ 1, & \text{otherwise} \end{cases} \quad \# \quad (2.9)$$

Same with LCSS distance, function D can be any point-to-point distance metric, *Head*, and *Rest* functions refer to the first point of the trajectory and the rest of the trajectory except the first point relatively. ε is the set distance threshold.

Compared with LCSS, EDR punishes the result based on the gap length between two matching subtrajectories, which makes it more accurate. There is a basic transformation between LCSS and EDR as follows:

$$D_{EDR}(T_A, T_B) = num(T_A) + num(T_B) - 2*D_{LCSS}(T_A, T_B) \# \quad (2.10)$$

where function *num* refers to the number of points in the trajectory.

2.2.5 Edit distance with real penalty

Edit Distance with Real (EPR) Penalty is another edit distance-based measure. All the trajectory similarity functions discussed above cannot solve the problem of supporting time shifts and being metric together. To address this challenge, ERP is proposed [18].

By analyzing DTW distance, we may find that the reason why DTW is not a metric is that when the point in one trajectory is missed to match the other trajectory, it will repeat the previous point, so the distance between this point pair depends on the previous point. On the contrary, ERP uses a real penalty value for the distance between two matched points and a constant value for the distance between two mismatched points. Therefore, ERP can support time shift and is a metric. For two given trajectories $T_A = \{A_1, A_2, ..., A_m\}$ and $T_B = \{B_1, B_2, ..., B_n\}$ where A_i and B_i are the i-th points of T_A and T_B. We have:

$$D_{ERP}(T_A, T_B) = \begin{cases} \sum_{1}^{n} |B_i - R|, \text{if } m = 0 \\ \sum_{1}^{m} |A_i - R|, \text{if } n = 0 \\ \min \begin{cases} D_{ERP}(Rest(T_A), Rest(T_B)) + D(Head(T_A), Head(T_B)) \\ D_{ERP}(Rest(T_A), T_B) + D(Head(T_A), R) \quad , \text{otherwise} \\ D_{ERP}(T_A, Rest(T_B)) + D(Head(T_B), R) \end{cases} \end{cases} \text{\#}$$

(2.11)

where function D can be any point-to-point distance metric, *Head* refers to the first point of the trajectory, and *Rest* refers to the rest of the trajectory except the first point. R is a random point.

2.2.6 Hausdorff distance

Hausdorff Distance is a shape-based similarity measure, which refers to the maximum distance between the closest points of two trajectories. For two given trajectories T_A and T_B with length m and n relatively, we have:

$$D_{\text{Hausdorff}}(T_A, T_B) = \max(h(T_A, T_B), h(T_B, T_A)) \text{\#} \qquad (2.12)$$

where

$$h(T_1, T_2) = \max_{p \in T_1} \left(\min_{q \in T_2} (D(p, q)) \right) \text{\#} \qquad (2.13)$$

Function h is a unidirectional Hausdorff distance, and function D can be any point-to-point distance metric.

2.2.7 Frechet distance

The Frechet distance is among the most popular trajectory similarity measures [19]. It was first defined by Frechet [20] and can be applied to both continuous directed curves as well as discretized trajectories.

An intuitive interpretation for Frechet Distance is that a person is walking a dog with a dog leash. The dog will not always move on the person's trajectory. Both the dog and the person are able to change the moving speed and even stop, but obviously, at any time, the dog will not be more distant from the person than the length of the leash. The Frechet distance between the trajectories of the person and the dog is just the minimum length of the leash required to complete the traversal of both trajectories. For two given trajectories $T_A = \{A_1, A_2, ..., A_m\}$ and $T_B = \{B_1, B_2, ..., B_n\}$ where A_i and B_i are the i-th points of T_A and T_B. We have:

$$D_{\text{Frechet}}(T_A, T_B) = \begin{cases} \max_{1 \leq i \leq n} D(A_i, B_1), & \text{if } m = 1 \\ \max_{1 \leq i \leq m} D(A_1, B_i), & \text{if } n = 1 \\ \max \left\{ \min \begin{cases} D(A_m, B_n) \\ D_{\text{Frechet}}(Sub(T_A), T_B) \\ D_{\text{Frechet}}(T_A, Sub(T_B)) \\ D_{\text{Frechet}}(Sub(T_A), Sub(T_B)) \end{cases} \right\}, & \text{otherwise} \end{cases} \quad \# \quad (2.14)$$

where function D can be any point-to-point distance metric, and function *sub* represents the subtrajectory which removes the last point.

Frechet distance provides us with a simple and intuitive way to measure trajectory similarity, which can also achieve as good results as other methods. However, it cannot deal with noise points at all because every point of two trajectories is used in the calculation. If a point in one trajectory deviates a lot due to the noise, the Frechet distance will be much larger than it should be, which is far away from the ground truth.

2.2.8 One way distance

OWD [21] is a segment-based function. The basic idea of OWD distance is to measure the similarity between two trajectories based on the area enclosed by them. Obviously, when the area is large, the distance between trajectories is far, which means the similarity is low. On the contrary, if the enclosed area equals zero, two trajectories are exactly the same one, and the similarity is the highest. For two given trajectories T_A and T_B with length m and n relatively, we have:

$$D_{OWD}(T_A, T_B) = \frac{1}{2}(o(T_A, T_B), o(T_B, T_A)) \# \qquad (2.15)$$

where

$$o(T_1, T_2) = \frac{1}{|len(T_1)|} \int\limits_{p \in T_1} d(p, T_2) dp \# \qquad (2.16)$$

Here function o is a unidirectional OWD distance. Function *len* refers to the length of the trajectory, and function d of a point and a trajectory refers to the shortest distance between the point and the trajectory, which can be any distance metric.

2.2.9 Locality in-between polylines

LIP [22] method is also a segment-based function. It has a very similar basic idea to OWD, which is to measure the similarity between two trajectories based on the area enclosed by them. This time, it assigns different weights to enclosed regions by the proportion of their perimeters of the total length of two trajectories, which counteracts the interference of noise points to a certain extent. When the perimeter of a region accounts for a large proportion of the total length of two trajectories, the weight will be large. When the weight of the region is large, the gap between two trajectories is large, so the LIP distance is large. When the area of the region equals zero, obviously, there is no gap between two trajectories, so the LIP distance is 0. For two given trajectories T_A and T_B with length m and n relatively, R_i represents each region enclosed by the two trajectories, we have:

$$D_{LIP}(T_A, T_B) = \sum S(R_i) * w_i \# \qquad (2.17)$$

where

$$w_i = \frac{C(R_i)}{len(T_A) + len(T_B)} \# \qquad (2.18)$$

Here w_i is the weight function of R_i. S function is the area of the region, and C function is the perimeter of the region.

3. Travel pattern similarity

Travel pattern describes the individual's mobility regularity and general travel style in a target time period. Since it is a recapitulative mobility expression, different from trajectory or OD matrix, it does not have a fixed data structure. What it focuses on mainly depends on the research purpose. Some studies may also refer it in terms of "mobility pattern" [23–25], "activity pattern" [26] or "commute pattern" [27,28]. But the common thing is that all the research about it discusses how humans travel and conduct daily activities. Routine mobility between home and workplace is commonly discussed. Other places include tourist attractions [29], shopping [30], and catering [31] also be subdivided into some studies.

Extract travel pattern from an individual's mobility data is quite similar to semantic information-based trajectory segmentation, which shares some common steps such as stay point detection and moving mode detection, but there are still several differences: Travel patterns usually pay more attention to the moving mode, OD pair, travel purpose, instead of the trajectory itself. In addition, travel pattern usually describes several routes and assigns frequency to each route based on the individuals' mobility regularity, while semantic information-based trajectory segment is just a route.

Here we introduce a method [32] to use a support graph to express the travel pattern of different individuals, for example, and the way to convert support graphs of different individuals into a topology-attribute matrix (T-A matrix), then the similarity measurement of the matrix could be utilized for travel pattern.

Assume that we want to cluster the daily travel pattern of a group of people by their one-month mobility data, in which we just focus on where they are. For each user, we first build an individual graph that represents the location of each hour within one day. The nodes of the individual graph assume to begin from the top, and one layer of the individual graph represents one hour. Each node of the graph represents one significant place for a user within one hour. For users that stay at multiple significant places within one hour, we select the one with the longest duration. There is only one edge between the same source and target nodes. The direction of the edge is always from the node in the higher layer to the node in the lower layer.

Secondly, a support graph is constructed in the way that any of the individual graphs can always be found in the support graph to have the same topology. In the support graph, each edge is assigned a unique index in an ascending manner from top to bottom and from left to right. Then, the edges of the individual graph will be respectively assigned one index, which corresponds to the index of the edges with the same topology in the support graph by definition.

Then, we use the T-A matrix to represent the graphs. Let n denotes the number of edges in the support graph, a T-A matrix of one user one day will be generated with its row number being equal to the total index number of the support graph edges n. The first row of the T-A matrix corresponds to the first edge of the support graph, the second row to the second edge, and so forth. For an individual each day, the element in the i-th row is assigned the value one if the i-th edge of the support graph is also contained in the individual graph; otherwise, 0 is assigned to the element in the i-th row. Let $T_u = \left\{ T_{(u,1)}, T_{(u,2)}, \ldots, T_{(u,m)} \right\}$ corresponding to the T-A matrix of user u in day m, by computing the average value of T_u, we can obtain the average probability matrix $T_{\text{average } u}$ of user u with m days.

4. Origin-destination matrix similarity

OD matrix is an effective and the most widely used form to describe the high-dimensional information of human mobility, which describes the travel demand distributed between different origin and destination locations of a study site. OD matrix emphasizes the volume of population flow between different region pairs and exerts an enormous function in numerous fields.

In this section, we divide mobility tableau similarity comparison methods in literature into three types based on their key ideas: volume difference-focused measure, image-based measure, and transforming distance-based measure.

4.1 Volume difference focused measure

The key idea among volume difference-focused measures is to regard the population flow of different OD pairs as an independent statistic. Then traditional statistical metrics can be applied to measure the volume (dis)similarity of two mobility tableau.

Here several notable measures are listed: root mean square error (RMSE) [33—35]; normalized root mean square error (RMSN) [36]; mean square error (MSE) [37]; mean absolute error ratio (MAER) [38]; mean absolute percent error (MAPE) [39]; goodness of Theil's fit (GU) [40]; maximum possible absolute error (MPAE) [41]; relative error (RE) [42]; total demand deviation (TDD) [43]; R-squared (R^2) [44], and entropy measure (E) [45].

Eqs. (4.1)−(4.3) show formulations of three measures. Assume that X and Y are two mobility tableaus, $X_{i,j}$ and $Y_{i,j}$ represents population flows from region i to region j in X and Y, where $i, j \in K$, K is total number of regions.

$$RMSE(X, Y) = \sqrt{\frac{1}{K^2} \sum_{i,j \in K} \left(X_{i,j} - Y_{i,j} \right)^2} \# \tag{4.1}$$

$$GU(X, Y) = \frac{\sqrt{\frac{\sum_{i,j \in K} \left(X_{i,j} - Y_{i,j} \right)^2}{K^2}}}{\sqrt{\frac{\sum_{i,j \in K} X_{i,j}^2}{K^2}} + \sqrt{\frac{\sum_{i,j \in K} Y_{i,j}^2}{K^2}}} \# \tag{4.2}$$

$$E(X, Y) = \sum_{i,j \in K} \left(X_{i,j} \log\left(\frac{X_{i,j}}{Y_{i,j}}\right) - X_{i,j} + Y_{i,j} \right) \# \tag{4.3}$$

4.2 Image-based measure

4.2.1 Mean structural SIMilarity index (MSSIM)

SSIM [46] is the prototype to compare the structural degradation between two images by comparing pixels. Since cells of a matrix are similar to pixels in an image, Djukic et al. [47] applied MSSIM on OD matrices.

Three different components—luminance l, contrast c, and structure s are introduced in $SSIM$, which can be calculated by mean (μ_x and μ_y), standard deviation (σ_x and σ_y) and covariance (σ_{xy}). Here, x and y represent the group of OD pairs in the same $n \times n$ scale window in OD matrices X and Y.

$$SSIM(x, y) = \frac{\left(2\mu_x\mu_y + C_1 \right)\left(2\sigma_{xy} + C_2 \right)}{\left(\mu_x^2 + \mu_y^2 + C_1 \right)\left(\mu_x^2 + \mu_y^2 + C_2 \right)} \# \tag{4.4}$$

$$MSSIM(X, Y) = \frac{1}{\overline{W}} \sum\nolimits_{w \in \overline{W}} SSIM(x, y) \# \qquad (4.5)$$

Eq. (4.4) demonstrates the simplified form of $SSIM$. The constants C_1, C_2 are meant to stabilize the result when either mean or standard deviation is close to zero, which are respectively suggested to be 10^{-10} and 10^{-2} by Pollard et al. [48]. The average of all SSIM values (over $\overline{W}$ local windows) yields MSSIM as Eq. (4.5).

4.2.2 MSSIM's variants
Based on MSSIM, several improvements have been made in the literature:
- In 4D-MSSIM proposed by Van Vuren and Day-Pollard [49], neighborhood OD pairs are identified using spatial proximity between OD pairs by using Euclidian distance.
- In GSSI proposed by Behara et al. [50], geographical boundaries of higher-level zones are used to define the local windows;
- In SpSSIM proposed by Jin et al. [51], a series of spatial weight matrices are used to take the place of the original moving window.

4.3 Transforming distance-based measure
The main idea of distance-based measure is to measure mobility similarity by computing the least cost of transforming one mobility tableau into the other.

4.3.1 Wasserstein metric
One of the transforming distance-based measures utilizes Wasserstein distance (Ruiz de Villa et al. [52]), which used to be widely applied in mass transportation problems such as optimal cost required to transfer iron-ore from many mining locations to several factories etc. In the context of mobility tableaus, the Wasserstein distance between two mobility tableaus is defined as the minimum total travel time required to assign the trips between OD pairs of mobility tableau X and Y.

For example, for an OD pair $\tau = (\tau_o, \tau_d)$, if we want to transform mobility tableau X to Y, the difference of τ's population flow needs to be assigned into another OD pair $\gamma = (\gamma_o, \gamma_d)$, the cost of which can be computed by:

$$d(\tau, \gamma) = d(\tau_o, \gamma_o) + d(\tau_d, \gamma_d) \# \qquad (4.6)$$

Here $d(a, b)$ represents the average travel time cost of moving to a from b. By creating virtual population flow to a boundary, X and Y can have the same total population flows. Assume that v_γ^τ represents the population flow that needs to be assigned from τ to γ, of course, we have $v_\gamma^\tau > 0$. Then Wasserstein distance between X and Y can be computed by:

$$Wasserstein(X,\ Y) = min\left(\sum_{\tau,\gamma} v_\gamma^\tau d(\tau, \gamma)\right) \#\qquad(4.7)$$

Although this metric can measure the structural similarity by taking geographic correlation into account, it has two fatal limitations: First, as an optimization problem, when the number of regions is too large, it is computationally very expensive; second, when the total population flow number of two mobility tableau is different, there is no definite way to balance the difference, so the result is not unique.

4.3.2 Levenshtein metric

Another measure selects Levenstein distance (Behara et al. [53]), which used to be a measure of proximity between two strings. To be more specific, Levenstein distance calculates the least expensive set of insertions, deletions, or substitutions that are required to transform one string into another.

For a mobility tableau X, using $D_{X_i}^n$ and $A_{X_i}^n$ to, respectively, represent the i-th preferred destination and its corresponding demand value from n-th origin of X, the sorted set of destination IDs and corresponding demand from n th origin is expressed as $R_X^n = \left(D_X^n, A_X^n\right) = \left[\left(D_{x_1}^n, A_{x_1}^n\right), .. \left(D_{x_i}^n, A_{x_i}^n\right), .. \left(D_{x_m}^n, A_{x_m}^n\right)\right]$.

Let $S = (S_0, S_1, ..S_k, ... S_s)$ be the sequence of edit operations to transform R_Y into R_X, and the cost associated with each edit operation is $\beta = (\beta_0, \beta_1, ..\beta_k, ... \beta_s)$, respectively. While the LODn is an absolute comparison of nth rows, we can have a relative comparison by normalizing LODn with the trip productions (sum of origin flows) for nth row from both matrices. This normalized version of LODn is referred to as NLODn as Eq. (4.9):

$$LODn\left(R_Y^n, R_X^n\right) = \min_S \left(\sum_{k=0}^{k=s} \beta_k\right) \#\qquad(4.8)$$

$$NLODn\left(R_Y^n, R_X^n\right) = \frac{LODn\left(R_Y^n, R_X^n\right)}{\left(\sum_{j=1}^{j=M} A_{x_j}^n + \sum_{j=1}^{j=M} A_{Y_j}^n\right)} \# \tag{4.9}$$

$$LOD\left(R_Y^n, R_X^n\right) = \frac{\sum_{n=1}^{n=N} LODn\left(R_Y^n, R_X^n\right)}{N} \# \tag{4.10}$$

$$NLOD\left(R_Y^n, R_X^n\right) = \frac{\sum_{n=1}^{n=N} NLODn\left(R_Y^n, R_X^n\right)}{N} \# \tag{4.11}$$

The overall comparison between the mobility tableaus is obtained through the mean Levenshtein distance named LOD, which is the average of all LODn values, and the mean normalized Levenshtein distance named NLOD, which is the average of all NLODn as expressed in Eqs. (4.10) and (4.11), respectively.

5. Conclusion and future directions

In this chapter, we mainly introduce methods of quality assessment or, to say, similarity measurement for three typical kinds of mobility expressions: individual-level trajectory, individual-level travel pattern, and population-level OD matrices.

No matter in what kind of mobility expression, despite the dataset usually containing records of massive users, it just accounts for a very small part of the real population. This could bring a huge degree of bias and cause a significant impact on numerous applications. In the future, how to combine human mobility data with demographic information to get better estimation and analysis is a major challenge.

References

[1] T. He, et al., What is the human mobility in a new city: transfer mobility knowledge across cities, in: Proceedings of the Web Conference 2020, 2020.
[2] Q. Zhang, et al., Origin-destination-based travel time reliability under different rainfall intensities: an investigation using open-source data, Journal of Advanced Transportation 2020 (2020).
[3] J.-P. Wang, T.-L. Liu, H.-J. Huang, Tradable OD-based travel permits for bi-modal traffic management with heterogeneous users, Transportation Research Part E: Logistics and Transportation Review 118 (2018) 589–605.

[4] J. Ma, et al., Ridesharing user equilibrium problem under OD-based surge pricing strategy, Transportation Research Part B: Methodological 134 (2020) 1–24.

[5] Y. Wang, et al., Using mobile phone data for emergency management: a systematic literature review, Information Systems Frontiers (2020) 1–21.

[6] M.U. Kraemer, et al., The effect of human mobility and control measures on the COVID-19 epidemic in China, Science 368 (6490) (2020) 493–497.

[7] E. Huo, et al., Mining massive truck GPS data for freight OD estimation: case study of liaoning province in China, in: CICTP 2020, 2020, pp. 86–98.

[8] K. Behara, A. Bhaskar, E. Chung, A Methodological Framework to Explore Latent Travel Patterns and Estimate Typical OD Matrices: A Case Study Using Brisbane Bluetooth Multi-Density OD Database, 2020.

[9] M. Forghani, F. Karimipour, C. Claramunt, From cellular positioning data to trajectories: steps towards a more accurate mobility exploration, Transportation Research Part C: Emerging Technologies 117 (2020) 102666.

[10] M. Katranji, et al., Deep multi-task learning for individuals origin–destination matrices estimation from census data, Data Mining and Knowledge Discovery 34 (1) (2020) 201–230.

[11] S. Dey, S. Winter, M. Tomko, Origin–destination flow estimation from link count data only, Sensors 20 (18) (2020) 5226.

[12] M.S. Iqbal, et al., Development of origin–destination matrices using mobile phone call data, Transportation Research Part C: Emerging Technologies 40 (2014) 63–74.

[13] M. Mamei, et al., Evaluating origin–destination matrices obtained from CDR data, Sensors 19 (20) (2019) 4470.

[14] M. Vlachos, G. Kollios, D. Gunopulos, Discovering similar multidimensional trajectories, in: Proceedings 18th International Conference on Data Engineering, IEEE, 2002.

[15] D.J. Berndt, J. Clifford, Using dynamic time warping to find patterns in time series, in: KDD Workshop, 1994 (Seattle, WA).

[16] Y. Yuan, Image-based Gesture Recognition with Support Vector Machines, University of Delaware, 2008.

[17] L. Chen, M.T. Özsu, V. Oria, Robust and fast similarity search for moving object trajectories, in: Proceedings of the 2005 ACM SIGMOD International Conference on Management of Data, 2005.

[18] L. Chen, R. Ng, On the marriage of lp-norms and edit distance, in: Proceedings of the Thirtieth International Conference on Very Large Data Bases Vol 30, 2004.

[19] J. Gudmundsson, P. Laube, T. Wolle, Computational movement analysis, in: Springer Handbook of Geographic Information, Springer, 2011, pp. 423–438.

[20] M.M. Fréchet, Sur quelques points du calcul fonctionnel, Rendiconti del Circolo Matematico di Palermo (1884–1940) 22 (1) (1906) 1–72.

[21] B. Lin, J. Su, Shapes based trajectory queries for moving objects, in: Proceedings of the 13th Annual ACM International Workshop on Geographic Information Systems, 2005.

[22] N. Pelekis, et al., Similarity search in trajectory databases, in: 14th International Symposium on Temporal Representation and Reasoning (TIME'07), IEEE, 2007.

[23] S. Jiang, J. Ferreira, M.C. González, Activity-based human mobility patterns inferred from mobile phone data: a case study of Singapore, IEEE Transactions on Big Data 3 (2) (2017) 208–219.

[24] K. Liu, Y. Murayama, T. Ichinose, A multi-view of the daily urban rhythms of human mobility in the Tokyo metropolitan area, Journal of Transport Geography 91 (2021) 102985.

[25] W. Tu, et al., Uncovering online sharing vehicle mobility patterns from massive GPS trajectories, in: Spatial Synthesis, Springer, 2020, pp. 413–429.

[26] M.H. Hafezi, L. Liu, H. Millward, A time-use activity-pattern recognition model for activity-based travel demand modeling, Transportation 46 (4) (2019) 1369–1394.

[27] R.A. Acheampong, et al., Mobility-on-demand: an empirical study of internet-based ride-hailing adoption factors, travel characteristics and mode substitution effects, Transportation Research Part C: Emerging Technologies 115 (2020) 102638.

[28] H. Bai, et al., Measurement of the differential cross sections and angle-integrated cross sections of the 6Li (n,t) 4He reaction from 1.0 eV to 3.0 MeV at the CSNS Back-n white neutron source, Chinese Physics C 44 (1) (2020) 014003.

[29] S. Phithakkitnukoon, et al., Understanding tourist behavior using large-scale mobile sensing approach: a case study of mobile phone users in Japan, Pervasive and Mobile Computing 18 (2015) 18−39.

[30] T. Hu, et al., Mining shopping patterns for divergent urban regions by incorporating mobility data, in: Proceedings of the 25th ACM International on Conference on Information and Knowledge Management, 2016.

[31] F. Zhang, et al., Exploiting dining preference for restaurant recommendation, in: Proceedings of the 25th International Conference on World Wide Web, 2016.

[32] W. Li, et al., Effective Metagraph-Based Life Pattern Clustering with Big Human Mobility Data. arXiv Preprint arXiv:2104, 2021, p. 11968.

[33] K. Ashok, M.E. Ben-Akiva, Estimation and prediction of time-dependent origin-destination flows with a stochastic mapping to path flows and link flows, Transportation Science 36 (2) (2002) 184−198.

[34] J. Barceló Bugeda, et al., A Kalman-filter approach for dynamic OD estimation in corridors based on Bluetooth and Wi-Fi data collection, in: 12th World Conference on Transportation Research WCTR, 2010, 2010.

[35] O. Tamin, L. Willumsen, Transport demand model estimation from traffic counts, Transportation 16 (1) (1989) 3−26.

[36] C. Antoniou, M. Ben-Akiva, H.N. Koutsopoulos, Incorporating automated vehicle identification data into origin-destination estimation, Transportation Research Record 1882 (1) (2004) 37−44.

[37] E. Cascetta, Estimation of trip matrices from traffic counts and survey data: a generalized least squares estimator, Transportation Research Part B: Methodological 18 (4−5) (1984) 289−299.

[38] S.-J. Kim, W. Kim, L.R. Rilett, Calibration of microsimulation models using nonparametric statistical techniques, Transportation Research Record 1935 (1) (2005) 111−119.

[39] M. Cools, E. Moons, G. Wets, Assessing the quality of origin−destination matrices derived from activity travel surveys: results from a Monte Carlo experiment, Transportation Research Record 2183 (1) (2010) 49−59.

[40] J. Barceló, et al., Robustness and computational efficiency of kalman filter estimator of time-dependent origin−destination matrices: exploiting traffic measurements from information and communications technologies, Transportation Research Record 2344 (1) (2013) 31−39.

[41] H. Yang, Y. Iida, T. Sasaki, An analysis of the reliability of an origin-destination trip matrix estimated from traffic counts, Transportation Research Part B: Methodological 25 (5) (1991) 351−363.

[42] L. Gan, H. Yang, S.C. Wong, Traffic counting location and error bound in origin-destination matrix estimation problems, Journal of Transportation Engineering 131 (7) (2005) 524−534.

[43] S. Bera, K. Rao, Estimation of Origin-Destination Matrix from Traffic Counts: The State of the Art, 2011.

[44] A. Tavassoli, et al., How close the models are to the reality? Comparison of transit origin-destination estimates with automatic fare collection data, in: Proceedings 38th Australasian Transport Research Forum (ATRF), 2016.

[45] X. Ros-Roca, et al., Investigating the performance of SPSA in simulation-optimization approaches to transportation problems, Transportation Research Procedia 34 (2018) 83—90.

[46] Z. Wang, et al., Image quality assessment: from error visibility to structural similarity, IEEE Transactions on Image Processing 13 (4) (2004) 600—612.

[47] T. Djukic, S. Hoogendoorn, H. Van Lint, Reliability Assessment of Dynamic OD Estimation Methods Based on Structural Similarity Index, 2013.

[48] T. Pollard, et al., Comparing the quality of OD matrices in time and between data sources, in: Proceedings of the European Transport Conference, 2013 (AET Frankfurt, Germany).

[49] T. Day-Pollard, T. van Vuren, When are Origin-Destination Matrices Similar Enough?, 2015.

[50] K.N. Behara, A. Bhaskar, E. Chung, Geographical Window Based Structural Similarity Index for OD Matrices Comparison, 2020.

[51] C. Jin, et al., Similarity measurement on human mobility data with spatially weighted structural similarity index (SpSSIM), Transactions in GIS 24 (1) (2020) 104—122.

[52] A. Ruiz de Villa, J. Casas, M. Breen, OD Matrix Structural Similarity: Wasserstein Metric, 2014.

[53] K.N. Behara, A. Bhaskar, E. Chung, A novel approach for the structural comparison of origin-destination matrices: Levenshtein distance, Transportation Research Part C: Emerging Technologies 111 (2020) 513—530.

CHAPTER THREE

Noise filter method for mobile trajectory data

Defan Feng[1], Haoran Zhang[2], Xuan Song[1]

[1]SUSTech-UTokyo Joint Research Center on Super Smart City, Department of Computer Science and Engineering, Southern University of Science and Technology (SUSTech), Shenzhen, China
[2]School of Urban Planning and Design, Peking University, Shenzhen, China

1. Introduction

With the maturity of the application technology for big data, in the latest research, larger data size can bring better algorithmic results [1]. Nowadays, mobile trajectory data collected through cell phones are widely used in many fields such as destination determination [2], life pattern recognition [3], and many other areas [4—8] due to the advantages of large data volume and complete data variety.

Generally speaking, there are spatial errors [9—11] as well as temporal errors [12—14] in the trajectory data. The spatial errors are generally caused by the data noise or the lack of data collection system accuracy, which presents drastic fluctuations in the trajectory data. The temporal errors are usually reflected in the loss of records when the data sampling frequency is not high enough [15]. Traditional trajectory data sets, such as DiDi dataset [16,17], Uber dataset [18—20], and other dataset [21—24], have more complete data sampling and less deviation compared to the real data.

However, the sampling interval of mobile trajectory data is not well fixed, and there are often large segments of missing data. In addition, the accuracy of data acquisition by mobile devices cannot be compared with that of professional devices, and mobile device holders frequently enter poor signal areas, such as the interior of buildings, so the trajectory offset in space is more obvious [25,26]. Therefore, before using mobile trajectory data, the noise in the data should be filtered in order to better explore the mobile dataset. The content of this chapter focuses on the noise filter of the trajectory data, starting from multiple data denoising methods, and finally, the missing segments of the data are completed. In this way, the original low-

Handbook of Mobility Data Mining, Volume 1
ISBN: 978-0-443-18428-4
https://doi.org/10.1016/B978-0-443-18428-4.00003-7

quality data can be transformed into high-quality trajectory data with lower errors sampled in uniform time slices for the subsequent research.

In the process of obtaining human trajectory data through mobile GPS positioning, the obtained latitude and longitude will usually be offset to a certain extent, especially when indoors or through areas with poor signals. Fig. 3.1 shows a continuous track record formed by collecting the mobile GPS positioning information of the mobile phone, and the adjacent track points are directly connected by straight lines. Many of the trajectory recording points have obvious reentrant phenomena, as shown by the trajectory in the red circle in the figure, which is caused by the offset of the mobile trajectory positioning. Compared with traditional trajectory data whose data collection interval and data collection equipment are more stable, noise points in mobile trajectory data appear more frequently. These noise points will seriously interfere with the authenticity of the trajectory data, and easily lead to misjudgment of the travel mode, speed, and route area of the provider of the trajectory data in the follow-up research. Therefore, a noise filter algorithm that removes outlier noise points due to errors in the mobile positioning system is extremely important. It can make the trajectory smoother and more realistic and reduce the follow-up effects caused by system errors.

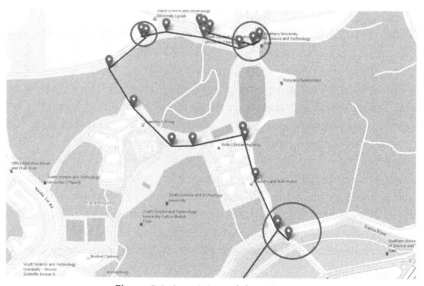

Figure 3.1 An origin mobile trajectory.

2. Simple data cleaning

A simple data cleaning of the original mobile trajectory dataset based on some prior knowledge can approach the requirements of the subsequent noise filter algorithm for trajectory accuracy to a certain extent [27—29]. Depending on the different datasets, the data cleaning rules can be established vary. For example, when the dataset is sampled with a clear range, the trajectory points beyond the specified range can be considered invalid data, and this part of the trajectory points can be deleted directly. When the way people move in the dataset is known, the trajectory points that move too fast will be considered error points, and most of the trajectories made up of error points will be deleted directly. Some trajectories usually show an extremely sharp angle for the localization error problem of moving trajectory data. Those points can be deleted based on the three trajectory points close to each other.

This simple way of cleaning the dataset based on prior knowledge has a good effect with less resource consumption. Therefore, it is recommended to perform simple cleaning on the dataset before using other data preprocessing methods.

3. Mean filter and median filter

Mean filter [30] and median filter [31] are two traditional noise filtering algorithms. They are used in many fields, including trajectory data noise, image noise, and so on [32—36]. The algorithm principles of mean filter and median filter are close, so they are discussed in this subsection together. These algorithms usually select a specific size time window as the reference trajectory for judging whether the next trajectory point is abnormal or not. Taking the last trajectory point as the n trajectory point and the size of the time window as k as an example, the algorithms will also consider the changes from $\left[\left(p_{i,n-k+1}, tr_{i,n-k+1}\right)\right]$ to $\left[\left(p_{i,n}, tr_{i,n}\right)\right]$ to judge the reasonableness of the $(n+1)^{th}$ trajectory point $\left[\left(p_{i,n+1}, tr_{i,n+1}\right)\right]$.

Usually, there are two main bases for judging the reasonableness of a trajectory: the distance between adjacent trajectory points or the speed at which a person moves between adjacent trajectory points. If the distance between adjacent trajectory points is used, the time interval between the sampled data should be standardized, which is easy to do in those dataset where the sampling frequency is dense and fixed. However, in the mobile trajectory data where the sampling interval is not fixed and there are often large missing data, it is difficult to judge the reasonableness of the trajectory based on the distance between two trajectory points. When judging the reasonableness of the next trajectory point based on the speed between adjacent trajectory points, the speed between trajectory points can be calculated by the distance between two adjacent trajectory points and the time difference of sampling, as shown in Eq. (3.1). As shown in Eq. (3.2), the distance between two coordinate points can be calculated based on the latitude and longitude, where Lat_1, Lon_1, Lat_2, Lon_2 represent the latitude and longitude of two different coordinate points, and R is the radius of the earth 6370 km [37].

$$\bar{v}_i = \frac{DIS(lat_i, lon_i, lat_{i+1}, lon_{i+1})}{begin\_time_{i+1} - end\_time_i} \tag{3.1}$$

$$DIS = (Rarccos(sin(Lat_1)sin(Lat_2)cos(Lon_2 - Lon_1) + cos(Lat_1)cos(Lat_2))\pi) \times /180 \tag{3.2}$$

Let's take the example of mean filter to determine the reasonableness of trajectory points based on velocity. Assuming that the size of the time window is k, the algorithm first considers the first k trajectory points as reasonable trajectory points and uses them as criteria for subsequent trajectory point reasonableness judgments. Let's take the example of mean filter to determine the reasonableness of trajectory points based on velocity. Assuming that the size of the time window is k, the algorithm first considers the first k trajectory points as reasonable trajectory points and uses them as criteria for subsequent trajectory point reasonableness judgments. When verifying a new trajectory point, it is assumed that there are already $n-1$ trajectory points considered to be correct, as shown in Eq. (3.3), and the mean value of $k-1$ average velocity between the total k reasonable trajectory points from the $(n - k)^{th}$ to $(n - 1)^{th}$ are used as the basis of judgment. Whether to add the new trajectory point to the set of corrected trajectory points is selected by comparing whether the average moving speed between the new trajectory point and the $(n - 1)^{th}$ trajectory point exceeds a certain threshold of the overall average moving speed, as shown in Eq. (3.4), where θ is the fluctuation range of the speed set in advance. Similarly, when using median filter, it can only modify the average velocity in Eq. (3.4) to the median of those velocities. While if other states are plan to use as the evaluation indicators in median/mean filter, modify the velocities in Eq.(3.3) and Eq.(3.4) to other states, for example, the distance between adjacent trajectory points.

$$\bar{v} = \frac{\sum_{i=n-k+1}^{n-1} \bar{v}_i}{k-1} \qquad (3.3)$$

$$\frac{\bar{v}_i - \bar{v}}{\bar{v}} \leq \theta \qquad (3.4)$$

These two algorithms have low time complexity and can handle the rare extreme error values during near-uniform motion very well, but is less effective in mobile trajectory data. People's travel trajectory is a mixture of different travel modes (e.g., walking, bicycle, bus, subway, etc.) [23,38,39], which leads to a large variation of speed between trajectory points at different times, and median filter and mean filter will misclassify large segments of trajectories with different motion patterns as noise, or increase the threshold θ so that the noise cannot be eliminated well, which leads to poorer final results. On the other hand, these two algorithms default the data at the beginning of the trajectory is correct, and use it to judge the reasonableness of the subsequent data. When the error exists at the beginning of a trajectory, the judgment of the whole trajectory data will be seriously affected, and at this time the median filter is relatively more robust than the mean filtering. In addition, these two algorithms consider a single state, for example, the deviation of the trajectory in the direction is not in the scope of filter.

4. Kalman filter

Kalman filter [40—43] is an optimal state estimator under the assumption of linearity and Gaussian noise [44]. Compared with the median and mean filters that only consider a single state of the historical trajectory, Kalman filter can view the movement and the velocity, acceleration, and uncertainty in the data [45—47]. And in the continuous iteration, Kalman filter can make the whole trajectory smoother. Kalman filtering algorithm considers that all data obtained from sensors have a certain error compared to the actual states. However, the prediction derived from the past observed state still has a certain reference value and can be used to the corrected real value in the future. Kalman filtering process is to continuously explore the changes of multiple unobserved states of the trajectory based on the observed states in the past. By comparing the next observed state and the predicted state based on the historical observed state, the predicted model can be iteratively modified and get better results.

Usually, the observations of mobile trajectory data contain only the latitude and longitude coordinates containing noise, as shown in Eq. (3.5). The area involved in a single trajectory is small, so the longitudinal and latitudinal spherical coordinates can be approximated as plane right-angle coordinates. In the process of one's movement, in addition to the change in position, there is also a change in magnitude and direction of velocity and acceleration. The direction of the vector can be obtained by splitting the vector, so usually the state of the trajectory point can be expressed by the current position x_i, y_i, the current velocity v_i^x, v_i^y and the current acceleration a_i^x, a_i^y, as shown in Eq. (3.6).

$$Z_i = \left(z_i^x, z_i^y \right)^T \tag{3.5}$$

$$X_i = \left(x_i, y_i, v_i^x, v_i^y, a_i^x, a_i^y \right)^T \tag{3.6}$$

The observations are generated by the actual states as well as the noise. The relationship between the observations and the actual states and noises is shown in Eq. (3.7). Where Z_i is the matrix of the observed states extracted from the total number of states, V_i represents the system's noise, and generally, the default noise is Gaussian distributed. Kalman filter can adaptively correct the noise expression when the noise distribution is unknown.

$$Z_i = HX_i + V_i, H = \begin{bmatrix} 1 & 0 & 0 & 0 & 0 & 0 \\ 0 & 0 & 0 & 1 & 0 & 0 \end{bmatrix}, V_i \sim N(0, R) \tag{3.7}$$

Kalman filter process can decompose into two steps, the prediction of the possible state situation at the next time based on the current state over time and the new state value determined based on Kalman gain combined with the observed values. As shown in Eq. (3.8), where $X_i^{(-)}$ represents the predicted value of the system for the state at i based on the real state $X_{i-1}^{(+)}$ at $i-1$, obtained after the state update based on the state transfer matrix Φ. To maintain the state changes, Kalman filter also maintains a covariance matrix for each state, thus aiding in the subsequent calculation of Kalman gain and thus determining the correlation between the predicted and observed values. The covariance matrix is updated as shown in (9). Due to the lack of prior knowledge, the initial covariance matrix p_0 and the noise matrix Q is a

6-dimensional unit matrix. The covariance prediction of the new state $P_i^{(-)}$ is obtained from the true value of the covariance of the previous state $P_{i-1}^{(+)}$ matrix transformation is obtained.

$$X_i^{(-)} = \Phi X_{i-1}^{(+)}, \Phi = \begin{bmatrix} 1 & \Delta t & \Delta t^2 & 0 & 0 & 0 \\ 0 & 1 & \Delta t & 0 & 0 & 0 \\ 0 & 0 & 1 & 0 & 0 & 0 \\ 0 & 0 & 0 & 1 & \Delta t & \Delta t^2 \\ 0 & 0 & 0 & 0 & 1 & \Delta t \\ 0 & 0 & 0 & 0 & 0 & 1 \end{bmatrix} \tag{3.8}$$

$$P_i^{(-)} = \Phi P_{i-1}^{(+)} \Phi^T + Q \tag{3.9}$$

Kalman gain coefficient, which weighs the relationship between the two, is updated as shown in Eq. (3.10) after obtaining the latest predicted values as well as the observed values. When Kalman gain K_i is smaller, the system will believe more in the predicted value found in Eq. (3.8) while when K_i is larger, the system will believe more in the observed value Z_i. And the actual value $X_i^{(+)}$ in the next stage will be based on Kalman gain to make the trade-off between the measured and actual values, as shown in Eq. (3.11). Similarly, the covariance matrix is determined based on the unit matrix and the difference of the current Kalman gain, as shown in Eq. (3.12).

$$K_i = P_i^{(-)} H^T \left(HP_i^{(-)} H^T + R \right)^{-1} \tag{3.10}$$

$$X_i^{(+)} = X_i^{(-)} + K_i \left(Z_i - HX_i^{(-)} \right) \tag{3.11}$$

$$P_i^{(+)} = (I - K_i H) P_i^{(-)} \tag{3.12}$$

Kalman filter is a process that continuously predicts the position state of new data and then iteratively updates Kalman gain and covariance matrix by combining the observed results. In its updating process, unlike mean filter and median filter, Kalman filter process takes into account the different states of the time, direction, and acceleration. It ensures a certain degree of uncertainty estimation by maintaining its covariance matrix.

The accuracy of Kalman filter is still primarily determined by the multiple trajectory points at the beginning of the trajectory. In case of significant errors at the beginning of the trajectory, the effect of Kalman filter will be affected. Kalman filter has better performance in trajectories without fixed lines, such as sailing [48,49] and flight [50–52] trajectories. But too smooth trajectories tend to deviate from the road network on urban roads. In the test, Kalman filter combined with road network matching can clear most of the noise points quickly, and then the generated trajectories can get better results with the help of road network matching.

5. Particle filter

In Kalman filter, the initial state and subsequent changes are assumed to be linear or Gaussian distributed. This assumption significantly reduces the computational effort in constructing the state transfer equation of the object and allows the Kalman filter algorithm to build an analytical motion equation quickly. However, many motion equations' initial state and subsequent changes differ significantly from this assumption. They may be nonlinear, so Kalman filter cannot achieve good results on this class of trajectories. Algorithms like Bayesian filter and Hidden Markov Localization can better represent this nonlinear or even irregular state transfer process. But compared to Kalman filter, the solution space of these algorithms rises exponentially with the state dimension. Particle filter [53–56] is proposed to solve this problem by constructing a large number of particles for Monte Carlo sampling [57]. This filter can quickly fit the state transfer process and the posterior probability of the current model in newly sampled data by counting the states of the particles [58].

Similar to Kalman filter, Particle filter is a filter algorithm that predicts the future state based on existing observations and corrects the current model. Particle filter differs in that it maintains the states of multiple particles and determines the filtered positions based on the different weights of the particles. The main processes can be divided into Particle Initialization, Prediction, Estimation, and Resampling.

In particle initialization, N particles with different state positions are generated randomly based on the preset number of particles and particle distribution. At first, each particle enjoys the same weight, $W_{i,0} = \frac{1}{N}$. Then the state and position of the particle at the next moment are predicted and updated based on the hidden state of the particle and the current position of the particle, as shown in Eq. (3.13), where the function f acts similarly to Eqs. (3.8 and 3.9), both of which update the current position of the particle after considering the upper noise.

$$P_k^i = f\left(X_{k-1}^i\right) \tag{3.13}$$

In the original Bayesian filter, the following model update is based on calculating the posterior probability of the model to the latest measurements. Particle filter translates the computation of posterior probabilities into sampling the data of multiple particles, updating weights based on the distance of particles from the latest measurements and normalization. Eq. (3.14) shows a method for updating the particle weights, Z^i is the latest observation, and R is the default system noise radius. The particle closer to the observation will have a higher weight. After all the particles' weights have been updated, the normalization process is performed on all the weights, as shown in Eq. (3.15).

$$W_k^{\prime i} = \frac{e^{-\frac{DIS\left(Z^i, P_k^i\right)}{2R}}}{\pi R^2} \tag{3.14}$$

$$W_k^i = \frac{W_k^{\prime i}}{\sum_j W_k^{\prime j}} \tag{3.15}$$

Since the particles are randomly generated in the initial stage, the filter effect is poor, and some particles need to be eliminated. After each round of estimation of all the particles, the system will resample N particles to determine the location of the trajectory points and the particle population for the next prediction. The particle's weight will be used as the probability of the particle being selected during resampling. Particles with lower weights have a lower probability of being resampled, and particles with higher weights will be sampled multiple times. After resampling, the weight of each particle in the new particle swarm is set to equal. And the average position of the newly selected particle swarm is output as the filter result of the particle filter for the last moment.

Particle filter can handle different types of motion models very well, especially nonlinear and Gaussian distribution models that cannot be handled well by Kalman filter. But compared to Kalman filter, maintaining the state of multiple particles makes the time complexity of particle filtering still high, so particle filter is not suitable for large-scale data processing in real time. In addition, particle filter has a certain probability of forgetting the optimal particles [59], which leads to a sudden decrease in the filtering effect.

6. Road network matching

Since the human trajectory is highly correlated with the road network, the error trajectory points can also be well filtered by road network matching [60–63]. Usually, road network matching can be divided into two steps: road points matching and road points connection. The road points, and the connections between road points, can be found in some open source urban road network datasets, such as the Open Street Map dataset [64]. Their data format is shown in Eq. (3.16). Each road point exists with an ID that uniquely identifies it and the latitude and longitude to which it corresponds. Each road is composed of a series of road points, the name of the road, and its label. A road point can participate in forming several different roads, and the road points in each road are connected according to the real route state. When the distance between road points is too large, it is easy to match the trajectory points to nearby other roads in road point matching. Therefore, before starting road point matching, further subdivision of farther road points in a road can significantly improve the final matching results.

$$RN_i = \{ID_i, LAT_i, LON_i\}, ROAD_j = \left\{ RN_{j1}, RN_{j2}, ..., RN_{jm}, tag_j \right\}$$

$$(3.16)$$

The matching problem of road points can be reduced to the problem of finding the nearest point of a point on a two-dimensional space, where the difficulty lies in a large number of record points of trajectories and existing waypoints. Hence, the matching of road points has a high requirement for time complexity. K-dimensional trees (KDTree) [65–67] or other better planar partitioning algorithms can improve the speed of waypoint matching. As an example, the KDTree algorithm, the product of expanding a binary search tree from a one-dimensional space to a multidimensional space, can complete a road point matching process with time complexity of $O(log_2(n))$. This algorithm first constructs the existing road points into a binary tree. As a new node is added to the tree, each pass through the odd layers will determine the next subtree of the node based on the latitude of the node. The longitude of the node is used for each pass through the even numbered layers. As a new node is added to the tree, each pass through the odd layers will determine the next subtree of the node based on the latitude of the node. The longitude of the node is used for each pass through the even numbered layers. Until the new node joining the KDTree becomes a new leaf node. This part of the construction process can be done in advance, thus not taking up the time for subsequent data preprocessing. New trajectory points will similarly enter the KDTree, and when a new trajectory point arrives at one of the tree's leaf nodes, the trajectory point matches the corresponding waypoint of the leaf node.

After the matching of road points is completed, two adjacent trajectory points are transformed into two road points on the road network. But two adjacent track points do not necessarily match two road points directly connected or on the same road segment. Suppose a straight line is directly used to connect the road points corresponding to two adjacent trajectory points. In that case, the final generated route will probably traverse part of the impassable area. The full source shortest path [68,69] between all road points is solved in advance, and the shortest road between two road points is used to replace the trajectory between two trajectory points to make the trajectory closer to the true value.

The road network matching algorithm can well correct minor scale trajectory errors. Still, it is not practical for more significant errors, so it is more suitable to use with other noise filtering methods. Moreover, in some areas without fixed roads, such as large open areas, road network matching is poor, but in the urban area, road network matching can restore the real state of the trajectory data very well.

7. An example of mobile trajectory data noise filter

Figure 3.1 shows a mobile trajectory. It has a more uneven sampling frequency, with a noticeable pause at the beginning of the trajectory and a lower sampling frequency in the subsequent. There is significant noise at the locations indicated by the red circles. The use of straight lines to connect adjacent trajectory points leads to crossing many building areas.

Based on the characteristics of this trajectory data, a simple noise filter algorithm combining data cleaning, Kalman filtering, and road network matching has good results, as shown in Fig. 3.2. The blue line represents the original trajectory data. In contrast, the red line is the trajectory data after data cleaning and Kalman filtering, and the green line is the result of matching the existing road network data based on the red line. The Kalman filter effectively filters the noise due to the fluctuation of the trajectory caused by the system's error, and all the error values that cause the trajectory have been removed in the displayed trajectory, and the whole trajectory looks smoother. However, in the case of the sharp road, the smooth trajectory deviates more from the entire route of the trajectory. The road network

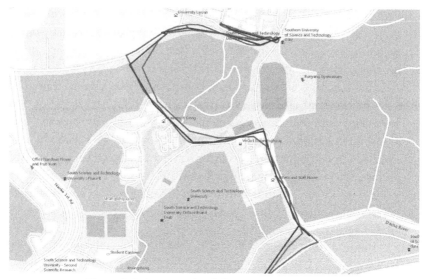

Figure 3.2 An example of the correction trajectory.

matching algorithm, which corrects the trajectory well, achieves excellent results on the filtered curve after the systematic deviation is removed. The green lines can be seen to fit the majority of the road network, thus correcting and completing a sparsely sampled section of the trajectory data that contains a large number of deviations.

References

[1] E. Junqué de Fortuny, D. Martens, F. Provost, Predictive modeling with big data: is bigger really better? Big Data 1 (4) (2013) 215–226.

[2] S. Park, Y. Xu, L. Jiang, Z. Chen, S. Huang, Spatial structures of tourism destinations: a trajectory data mining approach leveraging mobile big data, Annals of Tourism Research 84 (2020) 102973.

[3] H. Cao, F. Xu, J. Sankaranarayanan, Y. Li, H. Samet, Habit2vec: trajectory semantic embedding for living pattern recognition in population, IEEE Transactions on Mobile Computing 19 (5) (2019) 1096–1108.

[4] F. Giannotti, M. Nanni, D. Pedreschi, C. Renso, R. Trasarti, Mining mobility behavior from trajectory data, in: 2009 International Conference on Computational Science and Engineering, vol. 4, IEEE, 2009, pp. 948–951.

[5] D. Xia, S. Jiang, N. Yang, Y. Hu, Y. Li, H. Li, L. Wang, Discovering spatiotemporal characteristics of passenger travel with mobile trajectory big data, Physica A: Statistical Mechanics and Its Applications 578 (2021) 126056.

[6] K.-S. Lee, J.K. Eom, J. Lee, S. Ko, Analysis of the activity and travel patterns of the elderly using mobile phone-based hourly locational trajectory data: case study of gangnam, korea, Sustainability 13 (6) (2021) 3025.

[7] H. Wang, S. Zeng, Y. Li, P. Zhang, D. Jin, Human mobility prediction using sparse trajectory data, IEEE Transactions on Vehicular Technology 69 (9) (2020) 10155−10166.

[8] Q. Yu, H. Zhang, W. Li, Y. Sui, X. Song, D. Yang, R. Shibasaki, W. Jiang, Mobile phone data in urban bicycle-sharing: market-oriented sub-area division and spatial analysis on emission reduction potentials, Journal of Cleaner Production 254 (2020) 119974.

[9] S. Miura, L.-T. Hsu, F. Chen, S. Kamijo, Gps error correction with pseudorange evaluation using three-dimensional maps, IEEE Transactions on Intelligent Transportation Systems 16 (6) (2015) 3104−3115.

[10] C. Li, Y. Fu, F.R. Yu, T.H. Luan, Y. Zhang, Vehicle position correction: a vehicular blockchain networks-based gps error sharing framework, IEEE Transactions on Intelligent Transportation Systems 22 (2) (2020) 898−912.

[11] X. Liu, S. Nath, R. Govindan, Gnome: a practical approach to nlos mitigation for gps positioning in smartphones, in: Proceedings of the 16th Annual International Conference on Mobile Systems, Applications, and Services, 2018, pp. 163−177.

[12] Z. Fan, A. Arai, X. Song, A. Witayangkurn, H. Kanasugi, R. Shibasaki, A collaborative filtering approach to citywide human mobility completion from sparse call records, in: IJCAI, 2016, pp. 2500−2506.

[13] Y. Zhao, S. Shang, Y. Wang, B. Zheng, Q. Viet Hung Nguyen, K. Zheng, Rest: a reference-based framework for spatio-temporal trajectory compression, in: Proceedings of the 24th ACM SIGKDD International Conference on Knowledge Discovery & Data Mining, 2018, pp. 2797−2806.

[14] K. Zheng, Y. Zhao, D. Lian, B. Zheng, G. Liu, X. Zhou, Reference-based framework for spatio-temporal trajectory compression and query processing, IEEE Transactions on Knowledge and Data Engineering 32 (11) (2019) 2227−2240.

[15] Y. Yao, H. Zhang, D. Feng, J. Chen, W. Li, R. Shibasaki, X. Song, Modifiable Areal Unit Problem on Grided Mobile Crowd Sensing: Analysis and Restoration. IEEE Transactions on Mobile Computing, 2022.

[16] D.J. Sun, K. Zhang, S. Shen, Analyzing spatiotemporal traffic line source emissions based on massive didi online car-hailing service data, Transportation Research Part D: Transport and Environment 62 (2018) 699−714.

[17] S. Zhong, D.J. Sun, Assessing built environment and land use strategies from the perspective of urban traffic emissions: an empirical analysis based on massive didi online car-hailing data, in: Logic-Driven Traffic Big Data Analytics, Springer, 2022, pp. 255−280.

[18] X. Qian, D. Kumar, W. Zhang, S.V. Ukkusuri, Understanding the operational dynamics of mobility service providers: a case of uber, ACM Transactions on Spatial Algorithms and Systems (TSAS) 6 (2) (2020) 1−20.

[19] M.E. Gursoy, L. Liu, S. Truex, Y. Lei, Differentially private and utility preserving publication of trajectory data, IEEE Transactions on Mobile Computing 18 (10) (2018) 2315−2329.

[20] H. Yuan, G. Li, Distributed in-memory trajectory similarity search and join on road network, in: 2019 IEEE 35th International Conference on Data Engineering (ICDE), IEEE, 2019, pp. 1262−1273.

[21] Y. Sui, H. Zhang, X. Song, F. Shao, Y. Xiang, R. Shibasaki, R. Sun, Y. Meng, C. Wang, S. Li, et al., Gps data in urban online ride-hailing: a comparative analysis on fuel consumption and emissions, Journal of Cleaner Production 227 (2019) 495−505.

[22] W. Jiang, H. Zhang, L. Yin, J. Chen, Y. Sui, X. Song, R. Shibasaki, Q. Yu, Gps data in urban online ride-hailing: the technical potential analysis of demand prediction model, Journal of Cleaner Production 279 (2021) 123706.

[23] H. Zhang, X. Song, T. Xia, Y. Meng, Z. Fan, R. Shibasaki, Y. Liang, Battery electric vehicles in Japan: human mobile behavior based adoption potential analysis and policy target response, Applied Energy 220 (2018) 527−535.

[24] Y. Sui, H. Zhang, W. Shang, R. Sun, C. Wang, J. Ji, X. Song, F. Shao, Mining urban sustainable performance: spatio-temporal emission potential changes of urban transit buses in post-covid-19 future, Applied Energy 280 (2020) 115966.

[25] F. Meng, P. Chen, Signal offset optimization using vehicle trajectory data with different sampling frequencies, in: CICTP 2020, 2020, pp. 13−24.

[26] X. Fu, C. Xu, Y. Liu, C.-H. Chen, F.J. Hwang, J. Wang, Spatial heterogeneity and migration characteristics of traffic congestion—a quantitative identification method based on taxi trajectory data, Physica A: Statistical Mechanics and Its Applications 588 (2022) 126482.

[27] X. Yang, L. Tang, X. Zhang, Q. Li, A data cleaning method for big trace data using movement consistency, Sensors 18 (3) (2018) 824.

[28] N. Bahra, S. Pierre, A bidirectional trajectory prediction model for users in mobile networks, IEEE Access 10 (2021) 1921−1935.

[29] X. Cheng, L. Fang, L. Yang, S. Cui, Mobile Big Data, Springer, 2019.

[30] K. Adhinugraha, W. Rahayu, T. Hara, D. Taniar, Dealing with noise in crowdsourced gps human trajectory logging data, Concurrency and Computation: Practice and Experience 33 (19) (2021) e6139.

[31] M.R. Khokher, A. Bouzerdoum, S. Lam Phung, Crowd behavior recognition using dense trajectories, in: 2014 International Conference on Digital Image Computing: Techniques and Applications, Institute of Electrical and Electronics Engineers, 2014, pp. 1−7.

[32] J. Yang, J. Fan, D. Ai, X. Wang, Y. Zheng, S. Tang, Y. Wang, Local statistics and non-local mean filter for speckle noise reduction in medical ultrasound image, Neurocomputing 195 (2016) 88−95.

[33] C. Kandemir, C. Kalyoncu, Ö. Toygar, A weighted mean filter with spatial-bias elimination for impulse noise removal, Digital Signal Processing 46 (2015) 164−174.

[34] A. Roy, J. Singha, L. Manam, R.H. Laskar, Combination of adaptive vector median filter and weighted mean filter for removal of high-density impulse noise from colour images, IET Image Processing 11 (6) (2017) 352−361.

[35] S. Suman, F. Azmadi Hussin, A. Saeed Malik, N. Walter, K.L. Goh, I. Hilmi, et al., Image enhancement using geometric mean filter and gamma correction for wce images, in: International Conference on Neural Information Processing, Springer, 2014, pp. 276−283.

[36] Z.Y. Lv, W.Z. Shi, , Jón Atli Benediktsson, L.P. Gao, A modified mean filter for improving the classification performance of very high-resolution remote-sensing imagery, International Journal of Remote Sensing 39 (3) (2018) 770−785.

[37] X. Wu, X. Luo, S. KANG, L. GUO, The influence of the lower atmospheric refraction on measurements of down-looking radar, in: 2001 CIE International Conference on Radar Proceedings (Cat No. 01TH8559), IEEE, 2001, pp. 271−274.

[38] W. Yang, H. Chen, W. Wang, The path and time efficiency of residents' trips of different purposes with different travel modes: an empirical study in guangzhou, China, Journal of Transport Geography 88 (2020) 102829.

[39] E.-J. Kim, Y. Kim, S. Jang, D.-K. Kim, Tourists' preference on the combination of travel modes under mobility-as-a-service environment, Transportation Research Part A: Policy and Practice 150 (2021) 236−255.

[40] Q.I.A.O. Shao-jie, N. Han, Z.H.U. Xin-wen, S.H.U. Hong-ping, J.-ling ZHENG, C.-an YUAN, A dynamic trajectory prediction algorithm based on kalman filter, ACTA ELECTONICA SINICA 46 (2) (2018) 418.

[41]   Z. Ermayanti, E. Apriliani, H. Nurhadi, T. Herlambang, Estimate and control position autonomous underwater vehicle based on determined trajectory using fuzzy kalman filter method, in: 2015 International Conference on Advanced Mechatronics, Intelligent Manufacture, and Industrial Automation (ICAMIMIA), IEEE, 2015, pp. 156—161.

[42]   L.P. Perera, C. Guedes Soares, et al., Ocean vessel trajectory estimation and prediction based on extended kalman filter, in: The Second International Conference on Adaptive and Self-Adaptive Systems and Applications, Citeseer, 2010, pp. 14—20.

[43]   Y. Kim, H. Bang, Introduction to kalman filter and its applications, Introduction and Implementations of the Kalman Filter 1 (2018) 1—16.

[44]   J. Wang, N. Wu, X. Lu, W.X. Zhao, K. Feng, Deep trajectory recovery with fine-grained calibration using kalman filter, Institute of Electrical and Electronics Engineers Transactions on Knowledge and Data Engineering 33 (3) (2019) 921—934.

[45]   L. Xie, Y.C. Soh, Robust kalman filtering for uncertain systems, Systems & Control Letters 22 (2) (1994) 123—129.

[46]   J.R. Celaya, A. Saxena, K. Goebel, Uncertainty Representation and Interpretation in Model-Based Prognostics Algorithms Based on Kalman Filter Estimation. Technical Report, NATIONAL AERONAUTICS and SPACE ADMINISTRATION MOFFETT FIELD CA AMES RESEARCH ~ ..., 2012.

[47]   G.-H. Yang, J.L. Wang, Robust nonfragile kalman filtering for uncertain linear systems with estimator gain uncertainty, IEEE Transactions on Automatic Control 46 (2) (2001) 343—348.

[48]   Y. Wang, S. Chai, F. Khan, H. Duc Nguyen, Unscented kalman filter trained neural networks based rudder roll stabilization system for ship in waves, Applied Ocean Research 68 (2017) 26—38.

[49]   Y. Wang, S. Chai, H. Duc Nguyen, Unscented kalman filter trained neural network control design for ship autopilot with experimental and numerical approaches, Applied Ocean Research 85 (2019) 162—172.

[50]   C. Luo, S. I McClean, G. Parr, L. Teacy, R. De Nardi, Uav position estimation and collision avoidance using the extended kalman filter, IEEE Transactions on Vehicular Technology 62 (6) (2013) 2749—2762.

[51]   B.O.S. Teixeira, L.A.B. Tôrres, P. Iscold, L.A. Aguirre, Flight path reconstruction—a comparison of nonlinear kalman filter and smoother algorithms, Aerospace Science and Technology 15 (1) (2011) 60—71.

[52]   T. Wang, 4d flight trajectory prediction model based on improved kalman filter, Journal of Computer Applications 34 (6) (2014) 1812.

[53]   J. Carpenter, P. Clifford, F. Paul, Improved particle filter for nonlinear problems, IEE Proceedings—Radar, Sonar and Navigation 146 (1) (1999) 2—7.

[54]   A. Soto, Self adaptive particle filter, in: IJCAI, 2005, pp. 1398—1406.

[55]   F. Gustafsson, Particle filter theory and practice with positioning applications, IEEE Aerospace and Electronic Systems Magazine 25 (7) (2010) 53—82.

[56]   R. Wang, Y. Chen, L. Ye, P. Xu, P. Shen, High-precision initialization and acceleration of particle filter convergence to improve the accuracy and stability of terrain aided navigation, ISA Transactions 110 (2021) 172—197.

[57]   X. Xie, H. van Lint, V. Alexander, A generic data assimilation framework for vehicle trajectory reconstruction on signalized urban arterials using particle filters, Transportation Research Part C: Emerging Technologies 92 (2018) 364—391.

[58]   H. Xie, T. Gu, X. Tao, H. Ye, J. Lu, A reliability-augmented particle filter for magnetic fingerprinting based indoor localization on smartphone, IEEE Transactions on Mobile Computing 15 (8) (2015) 1877—1892.

[59] M. Jouin, R. Gouriveau, D. Hissel, M.-C. Péra, N. Zerhouni, Particle filter-based prognostics: review, discussion and perspectives, Mechanical Systems and Signal Processing 72 (2016) 2—31.

[60] Z. FU, Y. YANG, X. GAO, X. ZHAO, L. FAN, An optimization algorithm for multi-characteristics road network matching, Acta Geodaetica et Cartographica Sinica 45 (5) (2016) 608.

[61] M. Zhang, L. Meng, J. Bobrich, A road-network matching approach guided by 'structure', Annals of GIS 16 (3) (2010) 165—176.

[62] M. Schäfers, U.W. Lipeck, Simmatching: adaptable road network matching for efficient and scalable spatial data integration, in: Proceedings of the 1st ACM SIGSPA-TIAL PhD Workshop, 2014, pp. 1—5.

[63] Y. Diez, M.A. Lopez, J.A. Sellares, Noisy road network matching, in: International Conference on Geographic Information Science, Springer, 2008, pp. 38—54.

[64] S. Singh Sehra, J. Singh, H. Singh Rai, Assessment of Openstreetmap Data-A Review. arXiv Preprint arXiv:1309.6608, 2013.

[65] V. Ramasubramanian, K.P. Kuldip, Fast k-dimensional tree algorithms for nearest neighbor search with application to vector quantization encoding, Institute of Electrical and Electronics Engineers Transactions on Signal Processing 40 (3) (1992) 518—531.

[66] G. Zhang, F. Li, Application of the knn algorithm based on kd tree in intelligent transportation system, in: 2014 IEEE 5th International Conference on Software Engineering and Service Science, IEEE, 2014, pp. 832—835.

[67] A. Hackeloeer, K. Klasing, J. Matthias Krisp, L. Meng, Comparison of point matching techniques for road network matching, International Archives of the Photogrammetry Remote Sensing and Spatial Information Sciences, XL-2W1 (2013) 87—92.

[68] J.Y. Yen, An algorithm for finding shortest routes from all source nodes to a given destination in general networks, Quarterly of Applied Mathematics 27 (4) (1970) 526—530.

[69] A. Madkour, W.G. Aref, F. Ur Rehman, M. Abdur Rahman, S. Basalamah, A Survey of Shortest-Path Algorithms. arXiv Preprint arXiv:1705.02044, 2017.

CHAPTER FOUR

Modifiable areal unit problem in grided population density map

Yuhao Yao[1], Haoran Zhang[2]

[1]Center for Spatial Information Science, The University of Tokyo, Kashiwa-shi, Chiba, Japan
[2]School of Urban Planning and Design, Peking University, Shenzhen, China

1. Introduction

Extracting grid-based crowd density information from big human mobility datasets has become very popular because of its high precision and flexibility characteristics in representing the spatial-temporal feature of dynamic crowd distribution [1].

However, due to the different observing mechanisms, error of position estimation exists in the crowd density extraction, which leads to an inaccurate result. When gridded population estimation meets such a spatial-temporal deviation, the analyzable error becomes highly complex. Although spatial precision of population locations is critical, research that focuses on the error brought by mobility observing mechanisms and related restoration methods is still limited.

Research related to the relationship between the statistical error and areal unit division has been in-depth analyzed in spatial epidemiology, spatial statistics, or choropleth mapping, which is named modifiable areal unit problem (MAUP). MAUP affects results when point-based measures of spatial phenomena are aggregated into districts, for example, crowd density or illness rates. The resulting summary values (e.g., totals, rates, proportions, densities) are influenced by both the shape and scale of the aggregation unit.

In the early approaches, grid-based population estimation usually comes from other low-resolution population data, so reallocation of spatial data from source units into target units is required. Due to the low resolution of origin population data, areal interpolation, and statistical modeling are usually necessary.

The areal weighted interpolation is the simplest method that assumes populations are evenly distributed across grid cells within the input census unit [2−4]. Of course, this assumption is a gross simplification as population distributions are not uniform. Therefore, the allocation and representation

Handbook of Mobility Data Mining, Volume 1
ISBN: 978-0-443-18428-4
https://doi.org/10.1016/B978-0-443-18428-4.00008-6

of populations will always be subject to aggregation effects. These effects brought the MAUP [5], which refers to the analysis results varying with the definition of grid unit. According to MAUP, the census unit or administrative level and the shape of units will make the analysis challenging to predict.

Furthermore, population density maps based on this method indicate abrupt changes at the boundaries of units. Although smoothing functions are applied in some research to model population distribution as a continuous surface [6,7], the aggregation effect of the population distribution pattern indicates that populations in most areas are significantly disjunct and concentrated into smaller populations that are separated by larger areas of dispersed populations [8], which means smoothing functions are also unreliable. Even though the drawbacks of the areal method are apparent, the approach still has several advantages, such as the high computational efficiency and simplicity in creating spatially explicit and globally consistent population estimates [9]. Because of these vital points, products based on areal methods are well suited for informing policy-making efforts that do not require fine spatial resolution [10] or performing correlation analyses in which endogeneity issues are excluded [11].

Dasymetric methods utilize ancillary spatial data to inform the redistribution through areal interpolation from the source area to the target cell [3,12]. The ancillary variables include land cover, topography, land use zones, street networks, remote sensing data, and more [13]. Since ancillary spatial data are often produced and available in finer spatial detail than the input population data, they can develop weighting schemes for reallocating population from the source area to target units depending on existing or assumed relationships between the two. To be more specific, the dasymetric model assigns weights to density in two ways: representing the differences among different land use classes and representing the differences of the same class in different regions. Techniques that are used in the traditional dasymetric methods include binary dasymetric refinement, multi-dimensional adaption, and intelligent dasymetric mapping [3,14,15]. Many approaches begin to blur the line between statistical analysis and dasymetric mapping, in which the weights are statistically derived by regressing population counts or densities against various types of predictive variables [13]. More recently, an increasing number of hybrid approaches have started to rely on machine learning or ensemble prediction techniques to get more robust weight estimation [16–18].

Mobile big data as high-resolution spatial information can be used to estimate population after scaling up and used as ancillary data to support measuring unit weight [19]. Research related to using mobile big data to observe crowd information has been emerging in recent years. However, the MAUP theory is seldom involved in this topic, only occasionally mentioned in the discussion or future works parts of the related research. The characteristics of the error of raw mobile big data raise new challenges for MAUP theory, but few studies focus on this influence of the error of mobility observing mechanisms to estimate results.

To describe the problem more intuitively, we first define several concepts. The ground truth position of one position record from crowd U is described as $R_{u,\ t} = (lat, lon)$, where $u \in U$ represents the record owner, t refers to a specific timestamp, and the lon/lat are the longitude and latitude of the recorded position at time t.

Definition 1(Ground truth crowd density map): Given a mesh of the study site, namely a set of mesh grids $\{g_1,\ g_2,\ ...,\ g_k\}$, by counting the number of people in each grid, the crowd density map $D_t = \{P_{t,1}, P_{t,2}, ..., P_{t,k}\}$ at time t can be generated as:

$$P_{t,i} = \sum_{u \in U} F_i(u, t) \tag{4.1}$$

$$F_i(u, t) = \begin{cases} 0, \text{if } R_{u,t} \notin g_i \\ 1, \text{if } R_{u,t} \in g_i \end{cases} \tag{4.2}$$

where $P_{t,i}$ represents the number of people in g_i at time t.

The error of mobile data-based position estimation can be roughly divided into two types: spatial deviation and temporal deviation, as Fig. 4.1 shows.

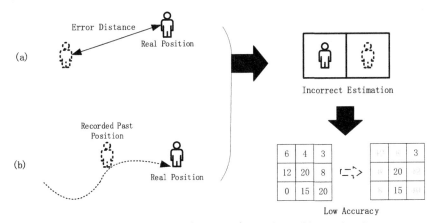

Figure 4.1 Spatial error and temporal error in position estimation.

Spatial deviation is usually caused by system error and noise. Because of the accuracy limitation, a recorded position usually has an error distance between its ground truth position, as shown in Fig. 4.1A. For example, GPS record, as one of the most common position data, suffers from the effect of multipath and nonline-of-sight propagation in urban canyons, and the error distance of it will achieve tens or even hundreds of meters [20].

Temporal deviation happens when the data sampling frequency is not high enough or some records are lost, so the position has not been correctly recorded, as Fig. 4.1B shows. Although position interpolation between two recent records is usually applied to get an estimated position [21], the error distance between the interpolated result and the ground truth is inevitable, and the problem is converted into spatial deviation again.

If there is no temporal deviation, the estimated position is the observed position from the mobility dataset. Otherwise, it is the interpolated position based on sensing data. It is described as an estimated position record $R'_{u,\,t} = (lat', lon')$ corresponding to ground truth position record $R_{u,\,t} = (lat, lon)$.

Definition 2 (Error distance): Because of spatial deviation and error of temporal interpolation, $R'_{u,\,t} \neq R_{u,\,t}$. Error distance d is defined as the Euclidean space distance between $R_{u,\,t}$ and $R'_{u,\,t}$.

Definition 3 (Error range): The error distance between an estimated position (x', y') and corresponding ground truth position (x, y) will be no more than a computable maximum value r. The error range is defined as the circle with r as the radius and the ground truth position (x, y) as the center. The area of the error range is represented by S_{ERR}.

Definition 4 (Distributing error rate): When $R_{u,\,t} \in g_i$ but $R'_{u,\,t} \notin g_i$, we call it distributing error. A distributing error rate E_{DISt} is defined to measure the overall degree of distributing error as:

$$E_{DISt} = \frac{\sum_{u \in U} \sum_{i \in [1,k]} G_i(u, t)}{NUM(U)} \tag{4.3}$$

$$G_i(u, t) = \begin{cases} 1, \text{if } R_{u,t} \in g_i \text{ and } R'_{u,\,t} \notin g_i \\ 0, \text{otherwise} \end{cases} \tag{4.4}$$

Definition 5 (Estimated crowd density map): Corresponding to the ground truth crowd density map, the estimated crowd density map $D'_t = \left\{ P'_{t,1}, P'_{t,2}, ..., P'_{t,k} \right\}$ at time t is generated by estimated position records.

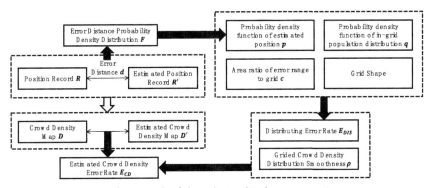

Figure 4.2 A framework of the relationship between main concepts.

Definition 6 (Estimated crowd density error rate): Estimated crowd density error rate E_{CD} is utilized to measure the error between the ground truth crowd density map and the estimated crowd density map, which is defined as :

$$E_{CD} = \frac{\sum_{i=1}^{n} |P_i - P_i'|}{\sum_{i=1}^{n} P_i} \tag{4.5}$$

In this section, based on the work of [22], we mainly discuss interfering factors that affect the error between the ground truth crowd density D_t and the observed crowd density $D\prime_t$. The relationship between major concepts is summarized in Fig. 4.2 and detailed analysis will be introduced in next section.

2. Error analysis

2.1 Distributing error rate

Assume that S_{GRI} represents the area of one grid, where $S_{GRI} = c^*$ S_{ERR}, the distributing error rate E_{DIS} is related to four factors: Error position probability density distribution, population probability density distribution inside grid, area ratio of error range to grid, and grid shape, as Fig. 4.3 demonstrates.

Definition 7 (Probability density function of estimated position): Error position probability density distribution is related to the probability density function $p_{(x,y)}(x', y')$, which is utilized to represent the probability for one position record at (x, y) to be estimated at (x', y'). Because (x', y') is always in the error range of (x, y), we have:

$$\int \int_{(x'-x)^2 + (y'-y)^2 \leq r^2} p_{(x,y)}(x', y') dx' dy' = 1 \tag{4.6}$$

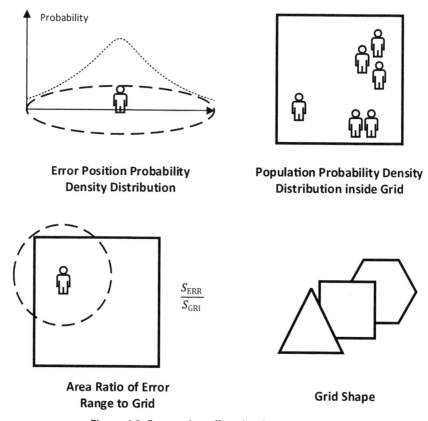

Error Position Probability   Population Probability Density
Density Distribution   Distribution inside Grid

Area Ratio of Error
Range to Grid   Grid Shape

Figure 4.3 Factors that affect distributing error rate.

When the error distance has a higher probability of being close to the maximum value, people have a higher probability of being incorrectly distributed into other grids.

Definition 8 (Probability density function of in-grid population distribution): Population probability density distribution inside the grid is directly affected by the probability density function $q_i(x, y)$, which is utilized to represent the probability for one position record in grid i being at (x, y), we have:

$$\int\int_{(x,y)\in g_i} q_i(x, y)dxdy = 1 \tag{4.7}$$

If people have a higher probability of gathering around the boundary of the grid, people have a higher probability of being incorrectly distributed into other grids.

The remaining two factors represent the scale effect and zoning effect of MAUP relatively. Scale effect means that when spatial data are aggregated to change their granularity or grid size, the analysis results also change; the Zoning effect means that when the polymerization scheme (such as the shape of the unit) changes at the same particle size or polymerization level, the analysis results also change.

To better discuss them, we assume that the probability density distribution of estimated position and the probability density function of in-grid population distribution are both uniforms. Then there is a strong symmetry inside the grid. Assume that the angle of the grid's corner is θ and the length of the side is l, where $l = \sqrt{2c(\pi - \theta)r^2\tan\frac{\pi-\theta}{2}}$, normally, the radius of the error range and the sides number of the grid is not large, we have $r \leq l \sin \theta$.

In this case, as Fig. 4.4 shows, for any side of the grid, draw a line perpendicular to it and keep the distance between them equal to r, denote the area bounded by this line and the grid side as S_{D1}. For any point $(x, y) \in S_{D1}$, denote the area bounded by the line where this side is and the circle at this point with radius r as $S_1(x, y)$. For any vertex of the grid, take the vertex as the center and r as the radius to draw a circle, draw two lines perpendicular to two neighbor sides and keep the distance between the line and side equal to r, denote the area bounded by part of the circle, two lines and grid sides as

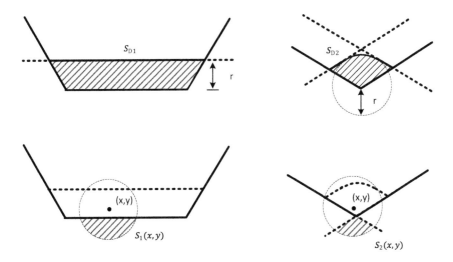

Figure 4.4 Region segmentation for distributing error rate integration.

S_{D2}. For any point $(x, y) \in S_{D2}$, denote the area bounded by lines where two sides are and the circle at this point with radius r as $S_2(x, y)$. We have:

$$E_{DIS} = \frac{N}{S_{GRI}} \iint\limits_{(x,y) \in S_{D1}} \frac{S_1(x, y)}{\pi r^2} dxdy - \frac{N}{S_{GRI}} \iint\limits_{(x,y) \in S_{D2}} \frac{S_2(x, y)}{\pi r^2} dxdy, r \leq l \sin\theta$$

(4.8)

where N is the number of edges of the grid shape, we have $N = \frac{2\pi}{\pi - \theta}$.

Once if $r \leq l \sin\theta$ does not hold, S_{D1} and S_{D2} will be incomplete, as Fig. 4.5 shows, and cannot be computed in the same way. In this case, it is nearly impossible to provide a general formula, we provide an approximate solution.

We first divide the grid into several same triangles by connecting the center of the grid and each vertex and making vertical lines from the center to each side. For any triangle, we establish a polar coordinate system with the center of the grid as the pole and the vertical line as the polar diameter. As Fig. 4.6 demonstrates, denote the area of the triangle as S_{D3}, the area of the error range beyond the grid as S_3, we have:

$$E_{DIS} = \frac{8}{l^2 \tan\dfrac{\theta}{2}} \int\!\!\!\int\limits_{(\rho,\alpha) \in S_{D3}} \frac{S_3(\rho, \alpha)}{\pi r^2} d\rho d\alpha, r > l \sin\theta$$

(4.9)

Draw a circle of the area S_{GRI} that shares the center with the grid, denote the area of the error range beyond the circle as S_3', we have $S_3' \approx S_3$. Therefore:

$$E_{DIS} \approx \frac{8}{l^2 \tan\dfrac{\theta}{2}} \int\!\!\!\int\limits_{(\rho,\alpha) \in S_{D3}} \frac{S_3'(\rho, \alpha)}{\pi r^2} d\rho d\alpha, r > l \sin\theta$$

(4.10)

When $\theta \in \left[\frac{\pi}{3}, \pi\right]$ and $c > 0$, $E_{DIS}\partial\theta$ and $E_{DIS}\partial c$ are both negative, which means the larger θ or c is, the lower the error rate is.

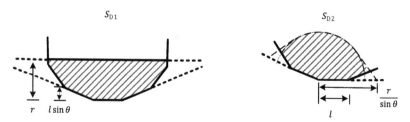

Figure 4.5 S_{D1} and S_{D1} when $r \leq l \sin\theta$.

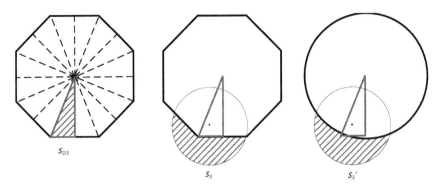

Figure 4.6 Approximate solution when $r \leq l \sin \theta$.

When c is large, the maximum error distance is relatively small compared with the distance of an individual to the boundary of the grid, so people have a lower probability of being incorrectly distributed into other grids. Fig. 4.7 demonstrates the error rate for three common grid shapes in different c.

θ is related to the grid shape. When θ is close to π, the shape of the grid is close to a circle, and the probability that people are correctly estimated in their grids is also large. Fig. 4.8 demonstrates the graph of distributing error rate versus the angle of grid shape for different c. For common grid shapes,

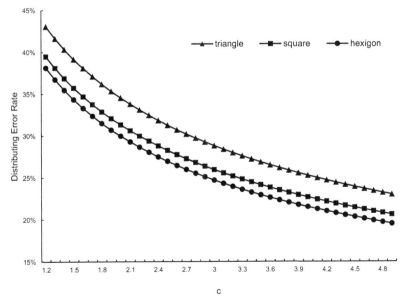

Figure 4.7 Graph of distributing error rate versus area ratio of error range to grid for different grid shapes.

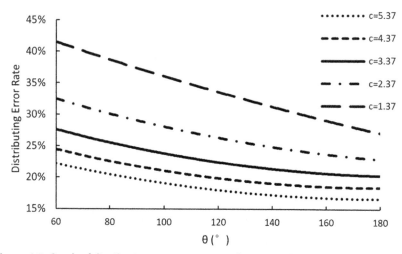

Figure 4.8 Graph of distributing error rate versus the angle of grid shape for different c (created by Monte Carlo simulation). When $r \leq l \sin \theta$, the computed result is consistent with the simulation result.

the hexagon grid has the best performance. This rule can also be extended to the irregular grid. For a region that needs higher precision, we could use a grid with more sides; for regions that do not have much population, we can simply use triangle grids.

2.2 Crowd density error rate

Although we have made clear the relationship between distributing error rate and various factors, the crowd density estimation error rate is not directly equivalent to distributing error rate.

For one grid i with population P_i and another grid j with population P_j where $g_j \in \mathrm{ADJ}(g_i)$, function $\mathrm{ADJ}(g_i)$ represents the set of all adjacent grids of grid i. Assume that $e_{i,j}$ and $e_{j,i}$ represents the distributing error rate from grid i to grid j and grid j to grid i relatively, a part of the population in i as $P_i e_{i,j}$ and j as $P_j e_{j,i}$ is incorrectly distributed into each other, so we have the estimated crowd density P_i' of i as:

$$P_i' = P_i - \sum_{g_j \in \mathrm{ADJ}(g_i)} P_i e_{i,j} + \sum_{g_j \in \mathrm{ADJ}(g_i)} P_j e_{j,i} \tag{4.11}$$

When $\sum_{j \in Adj(i)} P_i e_{i,j} = \sum_{j \in \mathrm{ADJ}(i)} P_j e_{j,i}$, no matter how high the error rates are, the estimated crowd density will not be affected. When $e_{i,j} \approx e_{j,i}$,

$\sum\limits_{j \in \mathrm{ADJ}(i)} P_j - P_i$ will determine whether the error is big or small. This phenomenon indicates that the smoothness of crowd density somehow reduces
the estimation error.

Definition 9 (Grided crowd density distribution smoothness): Grided
crowd density distribution smoothness ρ is utilized to measure the degree
of crowd density difference in any two grids. If the difference is very small,
then it is smooth; otherwise, it is rough.

Traditional graph smoothness is associated with global variance. However, two crowd density distributions with the same variance and distributing
error rate may have a totally different error. Fig. 4.9 demonstrates two examples of a one-dimensional area that consists of seven grids. In both cases
(a) and (b), variances of crowd density distributions are the same. Within a
20% distributing error rate to each neighbor grid, case (b) achieves 136 error
population, while case (a) just has 44 error population even if it has much
more boundary loss.

Therefore, we define the smoothness ρ based on a normalized mean
local standard deviation of crowd density distribution. For a n grids study
site, we have:

$$\rho = \frac{\sigma}{\sigma_{max}} \qquad (4.12)$$

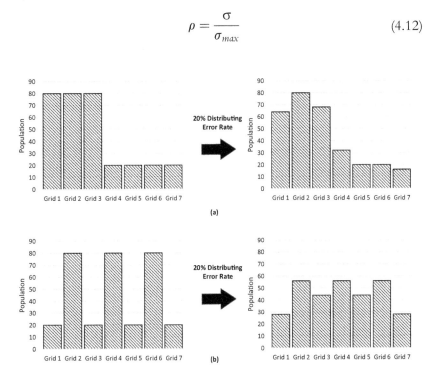

Figure 4.9 Examples of population distribution that have the same variance and
dividing error but different crowd density errors.

where

$$\sigma = \frac{1}{n} \sum_{i=1}^{n} \sqrt{\frac{\sum_{P_j \in \mathrm{ADJ}(P_i) \cup P_i} \left(P_j - \overline{P_j}\right)^2}{\mathrm{NUM}(\mathrm{ADJ}(P_i)) + 1}} \tag{4.13}$$

$$\overline{P_j} = \frac{\sum_{P_j \in \mathrm{ADJ}(P_i) \cup P_i} P_j}{\mathrm{NUM}(\mathrm{ADJ}(P_i)) + 1} \tag{4.14}$$

Specifically, when all the population gathers in one grid that has maximum neighbor grids, σ_{max} can be achieved where:

$$\sigma_{max} = \frac{1}{n} \sqrt{1 - \frac{1}{\max\limits_{i \in [1,n]} \mathrm{NUM}(Adj(P_i)) + 1}} \sum_{i=1}^{n} P_i \tag{4.15}$$

When ρ is close to 1, it means the crowd density distribution is smooth; when it is close to 0, it means the crowd density distribution is rough.

Although due to the complex interaction between adjacent grids, the same ρ may still correspond to a number of different situations, fortunately, human crowd density distribution is usually characterized by concentration in several points, so in practice, the varying range of crowd density error rate E for the same ρ will not be too large.

Fig. 4.10 demonstrates the result of an experiment about the changing tendency for E with ρ. In this experiment, we assume that the error position probability density distribution and the population probability density distribution inside grids are both uniforms, the area of the study site is set as 10×10 units, and the grid size of different shapes are all 1×1 unit. The radius of the error range is set as 0.5 units, so $c \approx 1.27$. We evenly pick about 20 different ρ to draw the curve. For each ρ, we do the simulation about 500 times to get a meaningful result. Because triangle grids and hexagon grids cannot exactly fill up the study site, in order to avoid the influence of irregular boundaries, we ignore the outermost ring of grids when we compute the error rate and smoothness for triangle and hexagon shapes.

From the result, we can see that the difference in error rate changing tendency with smoothness between different shapes is very small. Basically, the error rate decreases linearly with the increase in smoothness. Notice that when ρ is close to 1, there is a slight rebound, and even when $\rho = 1$, which means the distribution is perfectly smooth, there is still a low crowd density error rate. This part is caused by boundary loss. Since the boundary smoothness is out of the system, the population in boundary grids that are

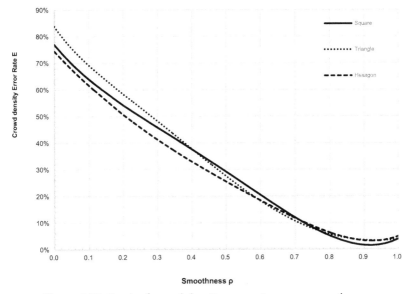

Figure 4.10 Graph of crowd density error rate versus smoothness.

incorrectly divided out of the study site leads to boundary loss. When ρ is close to 1, the population on the border will inevitably increase, which slightly makes the boundary loss larger. In practice, boundary loss is usually not serious because there will also be a population outside being incorrectly divided into the study site and cancel the loss. Normally, the larger the study site is, the smaller the boundary loss is.

3. Real case experiment

In this section, we demonstrate a real case experiment about CDR data-based crowd density estimation. Tokyo, Japan, is selected as the study site, which is approximately 40km × 40km. The used GPS and CDR data are all derived from an original dataset. The original dataset is a part of "Konzatsu-Tokei (R)" Data provided by Zenrin DataCom INC. "Konzatsu-Tokei (R)" Data refers to people flows data collected by individual location data sent from mobile phone under users' consent, through Applications provided by NTT DOCOMO, INC. Those data is processed collectively and statistically in order to conceal the private information. Original location data is GPS data (latitude, longitude) sent in about every a minimum period of 5 min and does not include the information to specify individual. *:Some applications such as "docomomap navi" service (map navi and local guide).

Table 4.1 Restoration effect of different grid shapes.

	Triangle	Square	Hexagon
MAE	234.17	231.52	216.43
RMSE	476.80	470.66	457.97
E	19.80%	19.33%	19.45%

To simulate an expanded dataset, we pick about 150 1000 individuals and select 6:00 p.m. as the target time slice every day from January 1st, 2011 to January 14th, 2011. Finally, the available, total population is about two million. The study site is divided into numerous 1km^2 grids in triangle, square, and hexagon shapes, respectively. Since the error range of GPS records compared with grid size is too small, we generate crowd density distribution D from GPS records as ground truth. Observed crowd density distribution D' is generated from CDR records. We construct a population density map based on different grid shape, compare the observed one and the ground truth and see will the result fit the analysis.

Table 4.1 demonstrates the comparison result. From the table, we can see that the real case generally fits the analysis we discussed before. Grid shape with more sides has higher accuracy.

4. Conclusion

In this chapter, by constructing a probability model, the error of MAUP in mobile crowd sensing is analyzed. A strong mathematical derivation is conducted to indicate the relationship between distributing error and the grid unit's size and shape, which could be extended to irregular mesh segmentation. The concept of smoothness is introduced to further analyze the deep relationship between the accuracy of the crowd distribution map and distributing error rate.

References

[1] K. Tsubouchi, R. Shibasaki, VLUC: An Empirical Benchmark for Video-like Urban Computing on Citywide Crowd and Tra ic Prediction, 2019.

[2] M.F. Goodchild, N.S.-N. Lam, Areal Interpolation: A Variant of the Traditional Spatial Problem, Department of Geography, University of Western Ontario London, ON, Canada, 1980.

[3] J. Mennis, T. Hultgren, Intelligent dasymetric mapping and its application to areal interpolation, Cartography and Geographic Information Science 33 (3) (2006) 179–194.

[4] B. Bhaduri, et al., LandScan USA: a high-resolution geospatial and temporal modeling approach for population distribution and dynamics, Geojournal 69 (1) (2007) 103–117.

[5] S. Openshaw, The modifiable areal unit problem, Quantitative Geography: A British View (1981) 60−69.

[6] D. Martin, Mapping Population Data from Zone Centroid Locations, Transactions of the Institute of British Geographers, 1989, pp. 90−97.

[7] W.R. Tobler, Cellular geography, in: Philosophy in Geography, Springer, 1979, pp. 379−386.

[8] A.W. Briggs, et al., Patterns of damage in genomic DNA sequences from a Neandertal, Proceedings of the National Academy of Sciences 104 (37) (2007) 14616−14621.

[9] M. Langford, Refining methods for dasymetric mapping using satellite remote sensing, Remotely Sensed Cities (2003) 137−156.

[10] E. Doxsey-Whitfield, et al., Taking advantage of the improved availability of census data: a first look at the gridded population of the world, version 4, Papers in Applied Geography 1 (3) (2015) 226−234.

[11] J.E. Cohen, C. Small, Hypsographic demography: the distribution of human population by altitude, Proceedings of the National Academy of Sciences 95 (24) (1998) 14009−14014.

[12] F.J. Goerlich, I. Cantarino, A population density grid for Spain, International Journal of Geographical Information Science 27 (12) (2013) 2247−2263.

[13] J. Mennis, D. Guo, Spatial data mining and geographic knowledge discovery—an introduction, Computers, Environment and Urban Systems 33 (6) (2009) 403−408.

[14] C.L. Eicher, C.A. Brewer, Dasymetric mapping and areal interpolation: implementation and evaluation, Cartography and Geographic Information Science 28 (2) (2001) 125−138.

[15] J. Mennis, Generating surface models of population using dasymetric mapping, The Professional Geographer 55 (1) (2003) 31−42.

[16] A.S. Nagle, et al., Recent developments in drug discovery for leishmaniasis and human African trypanosomiasis, Chemical Reviews 114 (22) (2014) 11305−11347.

[17] B.L. Stevens, F.L. Lewis, E.N. Johnson, Aircraft Control and Simulation: Dynamics, Controls Design, and Autonomous Systems, John Wiley & Sons, 2015.

[18] A. Sorichetta, et al., High-resolution gridded population datasets for Latin America and the Caribbean in 2010, 2015, and 2020, Scientific Data 2 (1) (2015) 1−12.

[19] B. Yu, et al., Integration of nighttime light remote sensing images and taxi GPS tracking data for population surface enhancement, International Journal of Geographical Information Science 33 (4) (2019) 687−706.

[20] S. Miura, et al., GPS error correction with pseudorange evaluation using three-dimensional maps, IEEE Transactions on Intelligent Transportation Systems 16 (6) (2015) 3104−3115.

[21] Z. Fan, et al., A collaborative filtering approach to citywide human mobility completion from sparse call records, in: IJCAI, 2016.

[22] Y. Yao, et al., Modifiable Areal Unit Problem on Grided Mobile Crowd Sensing: Analysis and Restoration, 2022.

CHAPTER FIVE

Few-shot count estimation of mobility dynamics by scaling GPS

Xiaodan Shi[1], Haoran Zhang[2], Quanjun Chen[1], Ryosuke Shibasaki[1]
[1]Center for Spatial Information Science, The University of Tokyo, Kashiwa-shi, Chiba, Japan
[2]School of Urban Planning and Design, Peking University, Shenzhen, China

1. Introduction

The understanding of people flow and vehicle flow in a city is critical for transportation engineering, urban planning, emergency management, and commercial activities, which has been further used for trip estimation, demand estimation, human behavior modeling, public area management, traffic management, etc. [1−5]. Some departments, such as government agencies and national departments, are beginning to take use of the massive mobility data to analyze people mobility patterns and further to facilitate their decision making [6−8]. However, real mobility data covering a whole city or a whole country is quite expensive to collect.

With the rapid development of telecommunication technology, a large amount of mobility log data, such as the global positioning system (GPS), has been verified as an effective information source that is able to provide a large amount of mobility data at a lower cost. Some studies pay attention to analyze the dynamics of people and vehicles using GPS data and has approved it as an effective way [9−11]. Although GPS can provide useful city-wide or country-wide mobility data, they only represent a sample of the overall mobility due to limited usage of GPS. Therefore, before informing any decisions based on mobility, it is critical to scale GPS trajectories to resemble the entire population of human movement or entire count of vehicle flow. By scaling GPS, we are able to have a glimpse of the total human flow in city block or traffic flow in city roads or high-way (Fig. 5.1).

Although GPS data can be easily obtained for a wide range, it is not easy to accurately scale GPS to match regional fine-grained population or traffic amount. Firstly, the usage of GPS changes over time and area. For example, urban users of GPS in the evening are more than that in other time period of

Handbook of Mobility Data Mining, Volume 1
ISBN: 978-0-443-18428-4
https://doi.org/10.1016/B978-0-443-18428-4.00004-9

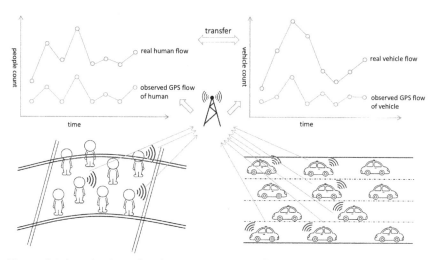

Figure 5.1 Introduction of real count estimation of people or vehicle dynamics by scaling GPS.

the day because people tend to utilize GPS for navigation to unfamiliar places for night entertainment. Meanwhile, people living in urban tend to use GPS more than people in rural area. Secondly, the real regional population of people flow or amount of vehicle flow in a road (ground truth) is not easy to obtain. Some research use population census data as ground truth to scale GPS data to match real mobility. However, census data are usually accumulated from larger, coarser areas, reflecting residential population, and have larger errors when used in fine-grained areas. In reality, few-shot real count of mobility data can be obtained in a certain area through survey. So it is critical for a model able to be trained with few data and still perform well over the current scenario. Moreover, it is also necessary for a model to generalize well to unseen scenarios without any ground truth. A straightforward approach to transfer a trained model to unseen scenarios is fine-tuning. But it still needs some samples, that is, both GPS data and the corresponding real count, from the new scenarios. It is not realistic to obtain time series real count everywhere due to a lot of manpower and expensive cost. So it is critical to transfer a trained model to total unseen scenario without any new samples.

We learn scaling factors, that are time series ratios between GPS data and real count of mobility dynamics, to scale partial GPS flow data to match the real count of mobility in fine-grained regional areas. Given the previous research discovering that the basic population pattern is homogeneous in the same functional area while is distinctive in the different functional areas, such as in business area and in residential area, we argue that scaling factors in the same functional scenario such as in a train station is quite stable and the connection between scaling factors of different scenarios is related to the relation between their GPS observations, that is more "similar" the time series GPS data from different areas are, the more similar the relation between GPS data and entire count of dynamics are. So we pay attention to both the discriminability and similarity of the extracted features of the time series GPS data. In this work, we use two Cross Attention Modules. Following [12], the first cross attention module is used to enhance the feature discriminability between different GPS flow observations by locating the most relevant timestep in the pair of GPS flow with and without ground truth. The second Cross Attention module measures the correlation between pairwise scaling factors by capturing the similarity between GPS flow observations. Moreover, it outputs coefficients to modify the existing scaling factors and further get the scaling factors of unseen data.

Experiments are conducted on multiple real-world datasets to compare the proposed method with existing approaches. Our method achieves best results on all datasets, which demonstrates the effectiveness of our method.

2. Related works

2.1 Population estimation

GPS data is ubiquitous and easy to get, which makes it a good data source for population estimation either as the main data or the auxiliary data. Fine-scale nonresident population of a certain area can be estimated according to GPS records, which provides solution in addressing critical social, health and environmental issues, such as natural disaster relief [13,14]. Hayano et al. estimate the total population moving into and out of the 20 km evacuation zone during Fukushima nuclear power plant accident based on "Auto-GPS" mobile phone data that are provided by NTT DOCOMO mobile phone service provider [15]. They divide the whole area into 250×250 m mesh grids and estimate the population by multiplying the observed handsets with the known ratio of Auto-GPS subscribers. The estimation accuracy ranges from 50% 80%. Klous et al. assess modes of transport including the duration people spent in motorized or nonmotorized transport and the distance from home for this movements based on GPS data for epidemiological studies [16]. They assign transport modes to GPS-tracks according to the speed patterns and realize that self-reported time spent walking and biking was strongly overestimated when compared to GPS measurements. Participants estimated their time spent in motorized transport accurately. Shimosaka et al. propose population prediction model named Spatiality Preservable Factorized Regression, to capture the population trends in a fine-grained point of interest (POI) densely distributed over large areas by extending their previous bilinear Poisson regression method with the idea of the factorized regression being actively explored in recommendation systems [17]. Besides applying GPS data for population estimation directly, many research use GPS data auxiliary data [18,19]. They mainly utilize nighttime light to predict residential population of fine-grids of a large city. GPS data are used to address the problem that nighttime light don't reflect the real residential population due to excessively high light radiance in specific types of areas such as commercial zones and transportation hubs by analyzing origin-destination of GPS-based people movements.

2.2 Vehicle flow estimation

Traffic prediction is important for many activities in daily life including path planning, tour decision making, intelligent traffic management etc. Surveys [20], automated vehicle identification (AVI) [21], probe vehicle [22], billing data [23] have been used to obtain traffic data. Recently years, GPS data are also utilized to predict traffic volume. Pogodzinska [24] estimates bicycle share by using the two-factor analysis of variance (ANOVA) and the Tukey post hoc test in the city of Poland. Experiments show that the examined share is not significantly different between individual days of the week but changes significantly between analyzed locations [24]. Miller et al. infer statewide traffic patterns by scaling massive GPS trajectory data in Utah by proposing a least absolute deviations model with controlled overfitting [25]. Experiments on 2.3 million trajectories show the model is able to scale GPS data to fit vehicle counts measured by 296 traffic sensors across the state. Yang et al. propose two methods SPP and PRA, to estimate the origin-destination patterns of probe vehicles using sampled positions of vehicles and link flow counts [26]. Experiments show that whether the distribution of probe vehicle data is homogeneous affects the estimation results. Besides the numerical or statistical methods, machine learning, and deep learning methods are also used to predict transportation. However, they mainly forecast the origin-destination patterns based on GPS observations not the real vehicle flow [27,28].

3. Methodology

The observed GPS data only represent a sample of real-world mobility, such as human flow or traffic flow. It can be scaled to closely match the actual number of people or vehicles However, real count of mobility dynamics used for scaling GPS flow data in real-world is difficult to obtain, especially in regional fine-grained areas, such as a city road or a train station. In this paper, we aim to scale unseen GPS data given very few ground truth. The whole architecture is shown in Fig. 5.2. Firstly, the classic Transformer encoder is used to extract features from time series GPS flow. Then, more discriminative representations of GPS flow without ground truth is learned by the first cross attention module. Based on the features, cross scaling factors module (the second cross attention module) is applied to learn the coefficients by measuring the similarity between GPS flow with ground truth and that without ground truth. Finally, real count is estimated by multiplying the estimated scaling factors with GPS flow.

3.1 Preliminary

Definition 1 (Block). A block is a steady closed area or check point that has a stream of people or traffic coming in and out, A block can be a train station, a road, or just a mesh grid.

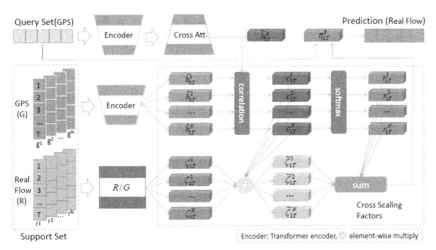

Figure 5.2 Overview of our model. Transformer encoder is used to extract features from time series GPS flow firstly. Then, more discriminative representations of GPS flow without ground truth is learned by the first cross attention module. Finally, cross scaling factors module (the second cross attention module) is applied to learn the coefficients used to modify the existing scaling factors by measuring the similarity between GPS flow with ground truth and that without ground truth.

Definition 2 (GPS Flow). GPS flow means daily traffic flow or human flow that can be defined as a time-ordered sequence $G = \{g_1 \rightarrow g_2 \cdots \rightarrow g_t \cdots \rightarrow g_T \}$, $1 \leq t \leq T$. gt is not a GPS record, but the total number of GPS records in a time period. The time period can be a hour or half an hour etc. and has a timestamp t. gt describes the amount of users coming in and out a block.

Definition 3 (Real Flow). Real flow means real traffic or human flow that comes in and out a block in a time period, is defined as $R = \{r_1 \rightarrow r_2 \rightarrow r_t \rightarrow r_T \}$, $1 \leq t \leq T$. rt is the real total number of people or vehicles in a time period, further paired with gt to label GPS flow.

Definition 4 (Scaling Factor). Scaling factor is defined as a daily set containing time-ordered ratios, and each ratio is denoted as rt/gt.

3.2 Problem define

We define the problem of scaling the number of total GPS records to match the real human or traffic flow is to estimate the scaling factor. We aim to predict "unlabeled" flow given few "labeled" GPS flow. Here, "labeled" means there are true human or traffic flow corresponding to GPS flow. So in fact, the problem is a few-shot regression problem. Following [12,29–31], we adopt the episode training mechanism. Episode training mechanism benefits the few-shot learning process by simulating the setting of test and has been verified as an effective approach. Each episode is constructed by one support set and one query set.

Given time series GPS trajectories count of all scenarios $= \{(G)^m \mid m = 1,M\}$, real count (ground truth) $P = \{(R)^m \mid m = 1,M\}$, M is the number of total scenarios. In the process of training, we define each episode is formed by randomly sampling N days labeled GPS flow data from C scenarios, $0 \leq C \leq M$, to construct support set $\Sigma = (G^{\Sigma}, R^{\Sigma}) = \{(G,R)^s \mid s = 1, 2, N\}$ and a fraction of the rest samples to construct the query set $\psi = (G^{\psi}, R^{\psi}) = \{(G,R)^q \mid q = 1, 2,B\}$, B is the number of query GPS flow data.

We estimate the scaling factors of query samples G^{ψ} by measuring the similarity between support samples G^{Σ} and query samples G^{ψ}. Further, given the scaling factors $\zeta^S = R^S/G^S = \{\zeta^s \mid s = 1, 2,N\}$ of support set S, we learn the coefficients to fix ζ^S and obtain scaling factors of query samples denoted as η^Q.

$$c = \Phi\left(G^s, G^Q; \theta^*\right), \tag{5.1}$$

$$\eta^Q = c \cdot \zeta^S, \tag{5.2}$$

$$R^Q = \eta^Q \cdot G^Q, \tag{5.3}$$

where, Φ ($\cdot$) with parameters θ^* is the function learned to estimate the scaling factors of query samples. Using the episode training mechanism to estimation scaling factors by measuring the similarity between two GPS flow, the model can also be applied to unseen scenarios naturally.

3.3 Feature extraction

The feature extraction module takes use of the embeddings h_1, h_2, , h_T of G from both support set and query set as input, and output a set of updated embeddings $\widehat{h}_1$,$\widehat{h}_2$, ,$\widehat{h}_T$ with temporal dependencies. h_1, h_2, , h_T are obtained by applying two fully connected layers with Sigmoid activation to each element g_t of G, considering each element of GPS flow at each time instance is independent.

Feature extraction module is shown as encoder in Fig. 5.2. A transformer encoder is used to extract features from GPS flow embeddings with temporal dependencies. Self-attention in transformer encoder firstly learns the query matrices Q_t, the key matrices K_t, and the value matrices V_t given h_1, h_2, , h_T. For t-th element, we have:

$$Q_t = f_{Q_t}(h_t), \quad K_t = f_{K_t}(h_t), \quad V_t = f_{V_t}(h_t) \tag{5.4}$$

where f_{Q_t}, f_{K_t} and f_{V_t} are the corresponding fully connected layers to obtain query, key, and value. Those layers are shared by GPS flow of any scenarios further. We compute the attention for each GPS count at any time instance. Similarly, we have the multihead attention (D heads) for the whole time series of GPS count as:

$$A(Q_t) = \sum_{\tau=1}^{T} \frac{exp(Q_t K_\tau)}{\sum_{j=1}^{T} exp(Q_t K_j)} V_\tau \tag{5.5}$$

$$\widehat{h}_t = \text{concat}(\text{head}_1, \text{head}_2, \cdots, \text{head}_D) \tag{5.6}$$

3.4 Cross attention

In this work, we resort to metric-learning to further calculate proper feature representations for GPS flow of query set. Since we assume the correlation of pairwise, scaling factors are relevant to the relationship of their daily GPS flows, we try to relate GPS flow of query set with that of support set. To achieve this goal, we use a Cross Attention Module (CAM) to further encode the GPS flow of query set. The CAM is similar with self-attention in encoder but with some differences. Query, key, value of self-attention is from the same data while query of CAM comes from the different data from the key and the value.

We denote features of support set $\widehat{h}^s_{1:T}$ as key and value of cross attention, features of query set $\widehat{h}^q_{1:T}$ as query. The cross attention will be applied over time horizon, i.e., from 1 to T, between query $\widehat{h}^q_{1:T}$ and each $\widehat{h}^s_{1:T}$ of support set respectively to fix $\widehat{h}^q_{1:T}$, which means the size of $\widehat{h}^q_{1:T}$ will change from $(1, T)$ to (N, T). The cross attention process is similar as Eqs. (5.5) and (5.6), but has different query, key and value settings. After cross attention, $\widehat{h}^q_{1:T}$ is fixed to be $\widetilde{h}^q_{1:T}$, H^Q is fixed as $\widetilde{H}^Q = \left\{ \widetilde{h}^q_{1:T} | q = 1, 2, \cdots, B \right\}$.

3.5 Cross scaling factors

We design a correlation layer between $\widetilde{H}^Q$ and H^S. The correlation layer has two effects: (1) to learn coefficients between scaling factors of support set and query set. By multiplying the coefficients and time series scaling factors of support set, we can get the initial scaling factors of query set, (2) to learn the weights of each sequence from support set on query data, which can make the model put more attention on support data more related to query data.

To obtain the coefficients, a fully connected layer is used on element-wise product of $\widetilde{H}^Q$ and H_S as follows:

$$c^s_{t,T} = \frac{f_c \left(\widehat{h}^s_{t,T} \cdot \widetilde{h}^q_{t,T} \right)}{\sqrt{d_{sq}}} \tag{5.7}$$

where, f_c is the fully connected layer, $d_{sk} = \sqrt{\left(\widehat{h}^s \right)^{\mathrm{T}} \widehat{h}^s} \cdot \sqrt{\left(\widehat{h}^q \right)^{\mathrm{T}} \widehat{h}^q}$, d_{sk} can normalize the calculation of correlation and help to stabilize the whole learning process. Based on the coefficients, the candidate set of scaling factors of query samples is obtained by an element-wise multiplication between it and scaling factors of support data. The length of scaling factor candidate set is the same as the number of support set, which is equal to N. Given the scaling factors set of support set $= \{\zeta_{1:T}^{s} | s = 1, 2, \cdots, N\}$, the scaling factor set $|_{q}' = \{\zeta_{1:T}^{s} | s = 1, 2, \cdots, N\}$, which is calculated as follows:

$$\widetilde{\zeta}_{tT}^{s} = \hat{c}_{tT}^{s} \bullet \zeta_{tT}^{s} \qquad (5.8)$$

where, coefficients $\hat{c}_{1:T}^{s}$ modify scaling factors of support set over time horizon, i.e., from 1 to T. Then, we combine the candidate scaling factor set of q query sample by applying a softmax function as follows:

$$r_{tT}^{s} = \frac{\exp\left(\hat{c}_{tT}^{s}\right)}{\sum\limits_{i=1}^{N} \exp\left(\hat{c}_{tT}^{i}\right)} \qquad (5.9)$$

$$\eta_{tT}^{q} = \sum_{s=1}^{N} r_{tT}^{s} \cdot \widetilde{\zeta}_{tT}^{s} \qquad (5.10)$$

where, η^{q}_{T} is the estimated scaling factors for query data q. By multiplying $\hat{q}._{T}$ and collected GPS data, we are able to get the real human flow or vehicle flow.

4. Experiments

In this section, we will demonstrate the effectiveness of our proposed method by conducting extensive experiments over multiple different scenarios and compare it with several baselines. We collect two large real-world datasets, considering scaling GPS flow to match real human flow and real traffic flow respectively.

4.1 Experimental setting

(1) *Datasets:* Two different real-world datasets describing human flow and vehicle flow are collected.

Human Flow Data: It is collected at 30 train stations in Tokyo, Japan. Each station have real-world GPS trajectories count and real number of human flow covering 19 h of a day for a whole month (30 days). The train stations locate at a famous line, Yamanote line. The details of human flow dataset are shown in Table 5.1. The human flow dataset not only have large train stations like Tokyo station, but also have small stations like Tabata station. To better illustrate the model performance on various train stations, we classify the train stations into five categories according to train stations' real

Table 5.1 Detailed information of human flow data and vehicle flow data.

Data	Num of scenes	Big	Small	up_ med.	Low med.	Med.	FPS	Days_per_ scene	Hours_per_ day	Avg.GPS	Std.GPS	Avg.real	Std.real	Avg.sf	Std.sf
Human	30	8	4	3	8	7	1h	30	19	157	113	5346	4789	0.04	0.07
Vechicle	32	7	6	4	7	9	1h	30	12	8	6	265	218	0.04	0.03

people flow per hour: big stations, up medium stations, medium, low medium stations, and small stations according to the thresholds 4500, 3500, 2700 and 1800 as shown in Fig. 5.3. To have the insight of the scaling factors more intuitively, we plot the detailed distributions of scaling factors in Fig. 5.5. All groups of this dataset have lots of outliers, especially group "mall," "medium," and "low medium." Meanwhile, scaling factors from group "small," "medium," and "low medium" are in a larger range than other two groups. If we don't consider outliers, we can see that scaling factors from different groups are in a similar range [0,0.25] and fluctuate over a day. Scaling factors in the morning peak and midnight are usually larger than those of other time.

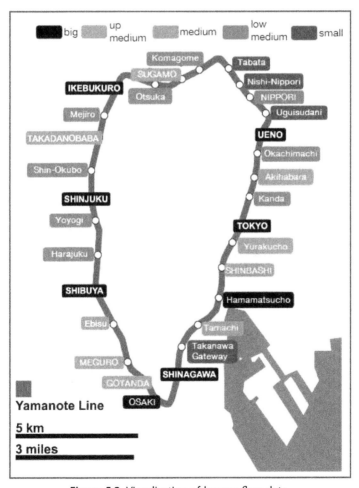

Figure 5.3 Visualization of human flow data.

Vehicle Flow Data: It is collected at 32 different check points on streets in Nagano Ken, Japan. At each check point, total GPS users for driving are recorded per hour. At the same time, staff standing at the check point of the street records the real count of vehicles as the ground truth. The real vehicle flow data of all the streets only cover from 7a.m. to 19p.m. for 1 day. To make the vehicle flow data useable for evaluating the proposed model's performance, we expand the data to 30 days by randomly adding Gaussian Noise. Similarly, we also classify the vehicle data into same five categories as shown in Fig. 5.4.

According to the thresholds 360, 290, 220 and 150. Detailed distributions of ratios of vehicle flow data are illustrated in Fig. 5.6. We can see that group "small" vehicle flow and group "medium" vehicle flow have

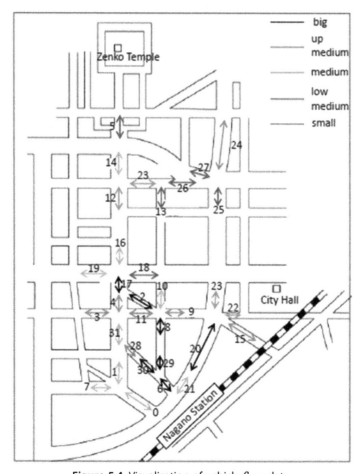

Figure 5.4 Visualization of vehicle flow data.

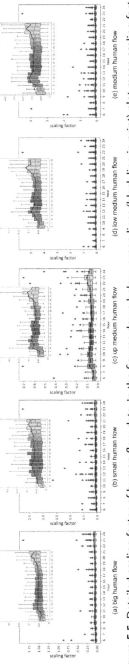

Figure 5.5 Detailed scaling factor of human flow data. In the figures down below, green lines (black lines in print) plot mean scaling factors versus time, black points are outliers, boxes plot distributions (quartiles) of the scaling factors. Boxes without outliers are shown in the figures up above.

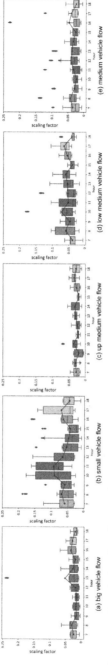

Figure 5.6 Detailed scaling factor of vehicle flow data. In all the figures, green lines (black line in print) plot mean ratio versus time, black points are outliers, boxes plot distributions (quartiles) of the ratio.

more outliers than the other groups. At the meantime, "small" vehicle flow shows more volatile scaling factors. Nevertheless, the standard deviation of scaling factors is not that large as human flow data (shown in Table 5.1), which means it is easier for the models to estimate for vehicle flow data. The vehicle flow data is collected at Nagano Ken that is much less crowded than Tokyo, especially one of the most crowded train line Yamanote. So we can see that the numbers of both the observed GPS and real vehicle flow are much smaller than that of human flow. Although we divide all data into five categories, basically the vehicle data is less crowded while the human data has large human flow.

(2) *Parameter Setting:* The experiments are implemented using Pytorch under Ubuntu 16.04 LTS with CPU. For all the models we implemented, the embedding layers are composed of a fully connected layer with size 32 and 64. For transformer encoder, the number of self-attention's heads is set to 4. For GRU, the hidden size is set to 64. Dropout with 0.05 and Sigmoid activation are also used for embedding layers. We clip the gradients of all the models with a maximum threshold of 10 to stabilize the training process. All the models are trained with Adam optimizer and learning rate 0.01 with weight decay 0.05. To test if the proposed model is able to learn from few training data and further benefit real-world data collection, we set C to 1 and N to 3.

(3) *Baselines:*

1. Poisson Regression. The method is from Ref. [17]. It uses one-hot encoding on time index of a day to infer the relationship between population and GPS observations on fine mesh grids of a city. For optimizing, we use quasi-Newton optimization to obtain parameters owing to the objective function that minimizes the regression errors between true population and predicted population.

2. Gaussian Process Regression. We denote the problem of scaling up GPS observations to match the real human flow or vehicle flow as a sequence regression problem and use White kernel for Gaussian process. The hyperparameters of kernel is updated through optimizing.

3. MLP. Multilayer perceptron takes time sequence GPS observations as input and directly output real human flow or vehicle flow. As for the representation of time factor, one-hot encoding is used.

4. RNN. Recurrent neural network models the time dependencies of GPS observations and output sequence of future directly. One-hot encoding is used to describe time factor.

(4) *Evaluation Metrics:* We use MAE, RMSE, MAPE to evaluate the how our method and baselines scale GPS count to match real people number or vehicle number.

4.2 Results

In this part, we compare the performance of our model and baselines by training and testing them over the same scenarios using only few labeled GPS flow for training. For each stations or each check point on streets, we train the model for both proposed method and baselines with 10% of the data and test models with the rest 90% of the data. 10% of the data covers 3 days of observation. Both the train and test data are exactly from the same stations or same check points. For example, there are 30 train stations, which means we have 30 trained models for baselines and the proposed model, respectively.

(1) *Human Flow Data*: The results are shown in Table 5.2. Our model gets better results than other baselines over all the evaluation metrics overall, especially for stations of big and medium. For all the stations, our method performs better than baseline MLP, RNN. Interestingly, GPR gets better results than our method over metric mae in stations of small, up medium, and low medium. Among all the stations, our model gets smaller mape over bigger stations, that is, big and up medium. Other baselines, GPR, RNN-, and MLP-based methods also follow this characteristic. For smaller stations, that is, small and low medium, RNN- and MLP- based method perform fairly with the proposed method over rmse and mae.

(2) *Vehicle Flow Data*: Results are shown in Table 5.3. Basically, all the models obtain acceptable results, especially GPR. Nevertheless, our model still does better to a large extent than all the other baselines.

4.3 Transfer learning

To better illustrate the generalization ability of the proposed method, we also test it on several transfer learning settings: (A) train with few data from one train station and test with other stations, (B) train with few data from one street check point and test with other check points, (C) train with few data from one station/check point and test with all check points/stations.

(1) *Human Flow Data:* We randomly select one station from the total 30 stations and then train the model using 10% of selected station data. Validation are done using the rest 29 different stations. The whole process is repeated 10 times, so that the overall performance can be largely evaluated. Transfer results are shown in Table 5.4. Our model largely outperforms the other baselines in the four types of train stations by using few training data. By evaluating performance using MAPE, we can see that all the models achieve better results on bigger stations than smaller stations, especially PR and RNN-based method. Overall, the transfer performance of the

Table 5.2 Testing results of human flow data. Train and test data are from the same station. The ratio of train and test is 0.1:0.9.

Stations	Methods														
	PR			GPR			MLP			RNN			Ours		
	Rmse	Mae	Mape	Rmse	Mae	Mape	Rmse	Mae	Mape	Rmse	Mae	Mape	Rmse	Mae	Mape
Big	5163.15	3811.88	1.15	4044.26	2797.63	0.65	5710.05	4060.13	0.94	5708.87	4059.88	0.95	**3136.12**	**2225.38**	**0.39**
Small	**923.35**	**667.75**	1.42	961.96	676.25	1.26	1001.40	715.75	1.27	1006.24	719.00	1.27	1003.04	713.75	**0.77**
Up medium	2748.97	2081.00	0.95	2112.51	**1548.50**	0.69	2961.41	2142.50	0.83	2961.76	2139.00	0.82	**2346.58**	1693.00	**0.44**
Low medium	1410.58	1048.22	1.38	**1278.96**	**920.22**	1.04	1518.17	1088.00	1.22	1515.59	1086.89	1.23	1460.67	1031.11	**0.65**
Medium	2104.13	1565.71	1.54	1988.01	1429.86	1.04	2390.53	1710.29	1.16	2391.87	1716.14	1.20	**1860.77**	**1327.43**	**0.78**
AVG	2597.36	1924.07	1.33	2195.12	1549.13	0.94	2866.87	2046.43	1.11	2866.76	2047.60	1.13	**1998.85**	**1420.53**	**0.60**

Table 5.3 Testing results of vehicle flow data. Train and test data are from the same street. The ratio of train and test is 0.1:0.9.

					Methods										
	PR			GPR			MLP			RNN			Ours		
Streets	Rmse	Mae	Mape	Rmse	Mae	Mape	Rmse	Mae	Mape	Rmse	Mae	Mape	Rmse	Mae	Mape
Big	260.27	184.29	0.49	121.82	96.86	0.22	260.64	185.57	0.51	260.79	188.00	0.52	22.64	15.86	0.04
Small	51.72	37.83	0.31	30.30	23.50	0.20	58.31	41.83	0.34	58.80	42.00	0.34	9.39	6.33	0.07
Up medium	147.13	105.00	0.31	78.44	61.25	0.22	141.85	103.00	0.33	142.61	103.25	0.32	18.43	11.50	0.04
Low medium	106.04	79.00	0.48	53.51	39.33	0.23	119.66	83.67	0.46	120.59	84.17	0.46	9.06	6.50	0.04
Medium	130.35	91.44	0.37	57.74	43.00	0.19	139.53	96.11	0.37	141.31	97.33	0.37	16.70	11.56	0.06
AVG	141.57	101.06	0.40	68.41	52.72	0.21	147.36	104.03	0.40	148.25	105.06	0.41	15.41	10.56	0.05

Table 5.4 Transfer results among human flow data.

Methods		Big	Small	Stations Up medium	Low medium	Medium	AVG
PR	Rmse	7506.14	1328.51	3307.27	1530.66	2282.52	3391.04
	Mae	5677.13	1166.40	2359.00	1209.22	1640.34	2572.20
	Mape	0.78	3.23	0.66	1.79	1.34	1.53
GPR	Rmse	6388.06	1079.42	3318.03	1684.60	2527.10	3163.64
	Mae	4481.25	715.25	2334.50	1161.67	1741.14	2200.77
	Mape	0.80	0.85	0.66	0.89	1.00	0.87
MLP	Rmse	5855.39	**947.37**	3119.48	1542.00	2321.17	2899.92
	Mae	4187.13	**671.00**	2258.50	1148.11	1713.14	2100.77
	Mape	1.02	1.29	0.80	1.40	1.52	1.27
RNN	Rmse	7570.94	1562.64	3296.95	1658.82	2325.03	3487.22
	Mae	5712.13	1403.70	2376.70	1351.22	1715.63	2674.52
	Mape	0.83	3.78	0.73	2.10	1.54	1.76
Ours	Rmse	**5093.56**	1025.23	**2809.23**	1536.63	**1920.11**	**2591.28**
	Mae	**3926.13**	735.00	**2033.00**	**1106.44**	**1357.71**	**1929.23**
	Mape	**0.54**	**0.69**	**0.53**	**0.61**	**0.64**	**0.60**

proposed method is slightly worse than original results shown in Table 5.2. Nevertheless, it achieves almost the same performance on Small stations, which also demonstrate the effectiveness of our model on unseen stations.

(2) *Vehicle Flow Data:* similar to transfer learning on human flow data, we also test our method and baselines on vehicle flow data and report results in Table 5.5. We can easily find that the proposed method achieves better results than the other baselines to a large extent, especially on data with small vehicle flow similar to the performance on human flow Data, RNN-based method get worst results on small vehicle flow data. It is interesting that GPR achieves good transfer performance. Although the transfer results of our method on vehicle flow data are worse than the original results shown in Table 5.3, the accuracy is still acceptable.

(3) *Cross Data:* To further demonstrate few-shot transfer performance of our model, we also validate it cross data, which is: (1) train with human flow data and test with vehicle flow data, (2) test with vehicle flow data and train with human flow data. Similar to Section 2 and Section 3, we randomly sample one scene and use 10% of it for training. The whole process is repeated 10 times to obtain results shown in Tables 5.6 and 5.7. In Table 5.6, MLP-based method and RNN-based method

Table 5.5 Transfer results among vehicle flow data.

				Stations			
Methods		Big	Small	Up medium	Low medium	Medium	AVG
PR	Rmse	354.40	224.20	207.68	205.98	205.02	241.81
	Mae	278.43	217.60	171.45	189.30	175.91	208.11
	Mape	0.69	2.76	0.63	1.55	0.94	1.30
GPR	Rmse	335.20	70.51	197.31	140.62	174.42	186.63
	Mae	244.43	53.50	150.25	97.00	123.78	135.28
	Mape	0.49	0.41	0.41	0.42	0.41	0.43
MLP	Rmse	278.39	49.25	136.52	127.71	150.83	149.49
	Mae	243.67	41.17	114.75	113.33	133.63	130.57
	Mape	0.64	0.51	0.48	0.99	0.79	0.70
RNN	Rmse	317.28	171.23	133.04	142.03	133.36	182.28
	Mae	234.29	164.17	100.75	127.67	110.78	149.72
	Mape	0.49	2.18	0.35	1.14	0.61	0.95
Ours	Rmse	**218.44**	**42.97**	**101.94**	**93.83**	**105.82**	**115.94**
	Mae	**166.57**	**33.17**	**78.25**	**71.00**	**80.11**	**88.28**
	Mape	**0.46**	**0.35**	**0.27**	**0.46**	**0.39**	**0.40**

perform almost the same on human flow data while PR performs the best in all the baselines. In Table 5.7, our method gets slightly better results than MLP- and RNN-based methods and largely outperforms PR and GPR. Interestingly, all baselines' performance is not stable when tested with different data. But our model consistently gets better results than others while maintaining stable performance, a key attribute of the model when used for real-world applications.

4.4 Predicting results on time horizon

To better demonstrate our model's performance, we further compare it and other baselines over time horizon and illustrate mape and standard deviation of mape when test and train with same scenes in Fig. 5.7. The hourly value of metrics here is obtained by aggregating all test data. For human flow data, errors of all methods are larger in the morning and evening peak than that in other time. All the baselines predicting human flow in the morning and evening don't match real human flow well. For vehicle flow data, larger errors of baselines appear in the morning peak and at noon. Our model performs stably and get best results in all time periods of a day.

We further depict detailed prediction results of shibuya station in human flow data as shown in Fig. 5.8. As we mentioned in Section 2, 90% of the total

Table 5.6 Cross-data transfer learning results. The model is trained with vehicle flow data and tested with human flow data.

Stations	PR			GPR			MLP			RNN			Ours		
	Rmse	Mae	Mape	Rmse	Mae	Mape	Rmse	Mae	Mape	Rmse	Mae	Mape	Rmse	Mae	Mape
Big	7425.85	5396.63	0.53	6287.50	4491.63	0.73	9564.24	8333.20	0.94	9557.08	8318.23	0.93	5116.72	4197.50	0.53
Small	1327.35	970.50	0.94	1066.72	748.75	1.17	1300.08	996.15	0.76	1297.95	993.75	0.77	1054.88	793.25	0.72
Up medium	3890.57	2902.50	0.53	3279.57	2394.50	0.72	4861.37	4162.80	0.89	4855.01	4150.20	0.89	2470.46	1963.50	0.48
Low medium	2108.16	1541.33	0.81	1726.74	1226.56	1.00	2330.03	1881.76	0.80	2325.14	1871.53	0.80	1538.62	1166.00	0.62
Medium	3129.88	2347.29	0.92	2555.05	1826.00	1.14	3551.45	2874.26	0.84	3546.22	2862.89	0.84	1934.82	1470.00	0.61
AVG	3779.33	2772.10	0.76	3151.73	2251.27	0.96	4575.58	3867.71	0.85	4570.27	3856.84	0.85	2582.85	2048.80	0.60

Methods

Table 5.7 Cross-data transfer learning results. The model is trained with human flow data and tested with vehicle flow data.

Streets	PR			GPR			MLP			RNN			Ours		
	Rmse	Mae	Mape	Rmse	Mae	Mape	Rmse	Mae	Mape	Rmse	Mae	Mape	Rmse	Mae	Mape
Big	650.03	600.33	1.60	611.75	497.67	1.17	252.23	**181.17**	0.36	269.87	185.17	0.34	**251.72**	186.67	0.38
Small	84.85	71.00	0.84	169.07	138.83	1.39	52.35	39.17	0.35	55.09	39.50	0.34	**50.63**	**37.67**	0.34
Up medium	253.83	226.25	1.03	411.59	342.50	1.19	140.93	103.75	0.33	152.72	108.25	0.31	**129.14**	**94.25**	0.29
Low medium	217.17	191.83	1.73	234.21	190.17	1.26	112.93	86.17	0.54	117.10	84.17	0.47	**93.98**	**67.00**	0.39
Medium	299.52	272.00	1.64	278.52	228.13	1.07	135.85	100.50	0.43	143.14	100.00	0.38	**134.32**	**95.75**	0.39
AVG	304.13	275.33	1.41	332.16	271.83	1.21	138.52	101.93	0.41	146.95	102.87	0.37	**132.31**	**96.37**	0.36

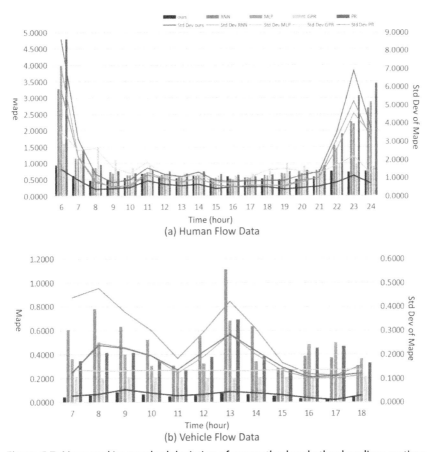

Figure 5.7 Mape and its standard deviation of our method and other baselines on time horizon. No matter over mape or standard deviation, our model consistently outperforms other baselines.

data are used for testing, which are actually 27days' data. The monthly real people flow counts from 6a.m. in the morning to 24p.m. in the midnight show periodic to some extent. But the periodicity is not stable. Our model's prediction result match the real people count the best even on day 14 to day 17, when temporal real counts are very different from the other days.

4.5 Ablation study

(1) *Amount of Training Days (variable N):* We try to figure out the amount of training days needed to obtain a fair performance in transfer learning. For cross transfer learning, we only take use of 1, 2, 3, 4, 5 days data of

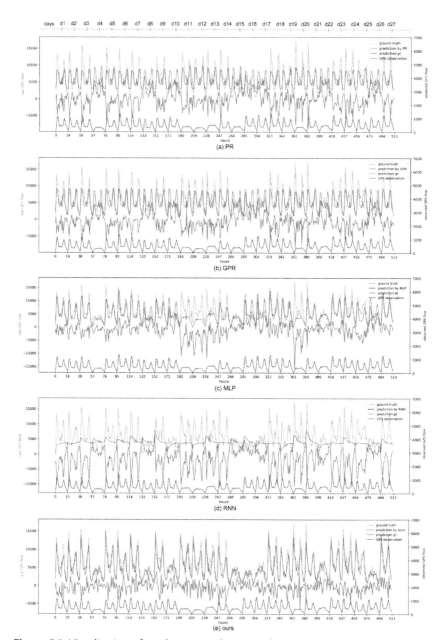

Figure 5.8 Visualization of prediction results on 27 days in station. For each day, real people counts from 6a.m. in the morning to 24p.m. in the midnight are estimated. Train and test data are both from the station and their ratio is 0.1:0.9. Blue lines use y-axis in the right and the other lines use the lines in the left.

one check point' data from vehicle flow data as training data and test the models' performance on all the human flow data. For internal transfer learning, similarly, we take use of one station data as training data and test the models' performance on all the rest human flow data. Here, internal transfer refers to section C (A) and (B). The results are shown in Fig. 5.9. It is interesting that there is big leap in performance when 3 days data are used as training even for cross transfer. The performance of 3, 4, and 5 days training is almost the same, inferring that our model does not require more training data to achieve good performance, which further demonstrates the effectiveness of our model in practical applications.

(2) *Amount of Training Scenarios (variable C)*: We also test how the number of training scenarios effects the model performance as shown in Fig. 5.10. We set N as 5 and randomly select it from scenarios from 1 to 5. There is

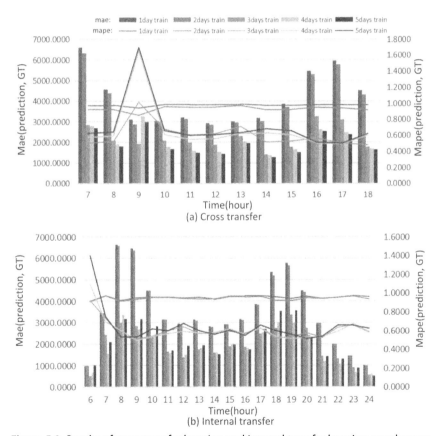

Figure 5.9 Results of cross transfer learning and internal transfer learning over human flow data trained by 1day, 2days, 3days, 4days, 5days data. There is a big leap in accuracy when training model with 3days data.

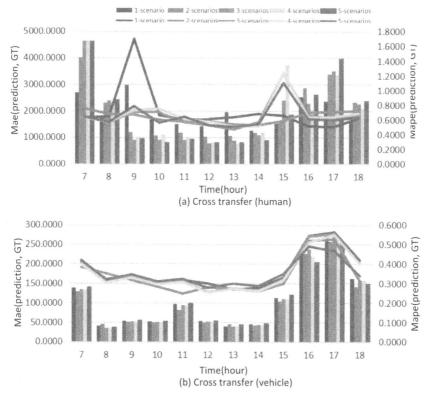

Figure 5.10 Results of cross transfer learning over human flow data and vehicle flow data trained by randomly sampling 5 days from 1 scene, 2 scenes, 3 scenes, 4 scenes, 5 scenes data. There is a small leap in accuracy when training model with few data from 2 scenes.

a slight performance leap when 2 scenes are used for training. Interestingly, there isn't big performance difference among models trained with different number of scenarios, indicating that few data collected from a single scene is sufficient for real-world transfer applications, which can further alleviate the difficulties of real-world training data collection.

Sensitivities of Different Parts of Model: To better illustrate the capability of our model, an ablation study is implemented by setting:1. rnn encoder: Transformer encoder is replaced by rnn encoder, 2. w/o cross attention: the first cross attention module is not used, 3. w/o softmax: instead of using softmax function in Eqs. (5.9) and (5.10), we use mean function to get the final scaling factors, 4. w/o cross scaling factor: a fully connected layer is directly used to the features from cross attention module instead of using cross scaling factors. The results on cross data transfer learning in details are shown in Table 5.8. The entire model obtains best performance overall.

Table 5.8 Ablation study.

Ablation settings	w/o			Cross att.			W/o softmax			W/o cross sf			Entire		
	Rmse	Mae	Mape	Rmse	Mae	Mape	Rmse	Mae	Mape	Rmse	Mae	Mape	Rmse	Mae	Mape
Human	3697.13	2980.57	0.69	4125.78	3478.53	0.80	2791.55	2201.53	0.60	2821.76	2413.63	1.51	2591.28	1929.23	0.60
Vehicle	270.96	240.37	0.90	218.89	191.77	0.68	262.41	215.43	0.75	188.47	139.17	0.46	115.94	88.28	0.40

Our model gains most from the two cross attention modules, which verify the efficiency of our model. By replacing the Transformer encoder with RNN encoder, we can easily tell Transformer encoder also benefits the entire model.

5. Conclusion

In this paper, we investigate to scale partial GPS flow data to match the real count of mobility dynamics including people and vehicles in regionally fine-grained areas. Two cross attention modules are proposed to solve the problems of transferring to unseen scenarios and learning from few labeled data. The first one helps the model to learn discriminative features from GPS flow while the second one measures the similarity between scaling factors of unseen data and that of labeled data. Extensive experiments over two large real-world datasets demonstrate that the proposed method is rational, robust, and able to learn from few training data while maintaining fairly stable performance when transferred to other scenarios.

References

[1] J.L. Toole, S. Colak, S. Bradley, L.P. Alexander, A. Evsukoff, M.C. Gonzalez, The path most traveled: travel demand estimation using big data resources, Transportation Research Part C: Emerging Technologies 58 (2015) 162−177.
[2] T.M. Brennan Jr., S.M. Remias, L. Manili, Performance measures to characterize corridor travel time delay based on probe vehicle data, Transportation Research Record 2526 (1) (2015) 39−50.
[3] N. Andrienko, G. Andrienko, G. Fuchs, P. Jankowski, Scalable and privacy-respectful interactive discovery of place semantics from human mobility traces, Information Visualization 15 (2) (2016) 117−153.
[4] Y. Xu, M.C. Gonzalez, Collective benefits in traffic during mega events via the use of information technologies, Journal of the Royal Society Interface 14 (129) (2017) 20161041.
[5] F. Pinelli, R. Nair, F. Calabrese, M. Berlingerio, G. Di Lorenzo, M. Luca Sbodio, Data-driven transit network design from mobile phone trajectories, IEEE Transactions on Intelligent Transportation Systems 17 (6) (2016) 1724−1733.
[6] N. Markovic, P. Sekula, Z. Vander Laan, G. Andrienko, N. Andrienko, Applications of trajectory data from the perspective of a road transportation agency: literature review and Maryland case study, IEEE Transactions on Intelligent Transportation Systems 20 (5) (2018) 1858−1869.
[7] P. Sekula, N. Markovic, Z. Vander Laan, K. Farokhi Sadabadi, Estimating historical hourly traffic volumes via machine learning and vehicle probe data: a Maryland case study, Transportation Research Part C: Emerging Technologies 97 (2018) 147−158.
[8] S. Dabiri, N. Markovic, K. Heaslip, C.K. Reddy, A deep convolutional neural network based approach for vehicle classification using large-scale gps trajectory data, Transportation Research Part C: Emerging Technologies 116 (2020) 102644.

[9]   Z. Fan, X. Song, R. Shibasaki, Cityspectrum: a non- negative tensor factorization approach, in: Proceedings of the 2014 ACM International Joint Conference on Pervasive and Ubiquitous Computing, 2014, pp. 213—223.

[10] T. Konishi, M. Maruyama, K. Tsubouchi, M. Shimosaka, Cityprophet: city-scale irregularity prediction using transit app logs, in: Proceedings of the 2016 ACM International Joint Conference on Pervasive and Ubiquitous Computing, 2016, pp. 752—757.

[11] R. Jiang, X. Song, Z. Fan, T. Xia, Q. Chen, Q. Chen, R. Shibasaki, Deep roi-based modeling for urban human mobility prediction, Proceedings of the ACM on Interactive, Mobile, Wearable and Ubiquitous Technologies 2 (1) (2018) 1—29.

[12] S.-sheng Wu, X. Qiu, Le Wang, Population estimation methods in gis and remote sensing: a review, GIScience and Remote Sensing 42 (1) (2005) 80—96.

[13] B. Yu, T. Lian, Y. Huang, S. Yao, X. Ye, Z. Chen, C. Yang, J. wu, Integration of nighttime light remote sensing images and taxi gps tracking data for population surface enhancement, International Journal of Geographical Information Science 33 (4) (2019) 687—706.

[14] F. Qiu, H. Sridharan, Y. Chun, Spatial autoregressive model for population estimation at the census block level using lidar- derived building volume information, Cartography and Geographic Information Science 37 (3) (2010) 239—257.

[15] H. Hara, Y. Fujita, K. Tsuda, Population estimation by random forest analysis using social sensors, Procedia Computer Science 176 (2020) 1893—1902.

[16] S. Miller, Z. Vander Laan, N. Markovic, Scaling gps trajectories to match point traffic counts: a convex programming approach and Utah case study, Transportation Research Part E: Logistics and Transportation Review 143 (2020) 102105.

[17] R. Hou, H. Chang, B. Ma, S. Shan, X. Chen, Cross attention network for few-shot classification, Advances in Neural Information Processing Systems 32 (2019).

[18] E.M. Weber, V.Y. Seaman, R.N. Stewart, T.J. Bird, A.J. Tatem, J.J. McKee, B.L. Bhaduri, J.J. Moehl, A.E. Reith, Census-independent population mapping in northern Nigeria, Remote Sensing of Environment 204 (2018) 786—798.

[19] Y. Zhou, M. Ma, K. Shi, Z. Peng, Estimating and interpreting fine-scale gridded population using random forest regression and multisource data, ISPRS International Journal of Geo-Information 9 (6) (2020) 369.

[20] R.S. Hayano, R. Adachi, Estimation of the total population moving into and out of the 20 km evacuation zone during the fukushima npp accident as calculated using "auto-gps" mobile phone data, Proceedings of the Japan Academy, Series B 89 (5) (2013) 196—199.

[21] G. Klous, A.M.S. Lidwien, F. Borlee, R.A. Coutinho, M.-jam EE Kretzschmar, D.J.J. Heederik, A. Huss, Mobility assessment of a rural population in The Netherlands using gps measurements, International Journal of Health Geographics 16 (1) (2017) 1—13.

[22] M. Shimosaka, Y. Hayakawa, K. Tsubouchi, Spatiality preservable factored Poisson regression for large-scale fine-grained gps- based population analysis, in: Proceedings of the AAAI Conference on Artificial Intelligence, vol. 33, 2019, pp. 1142—1149.

[23] H. Chen, B. Wu, B. Yu, Z. Chen, Q. Wu, T. Lian, C. Wang, Q. Li, J. Wu, A new method for building-level population estimation by integrating lidar, nighttime light, and poi data, Journal of Remote Sensing (2021) 2021.

[24] Y. Sekimoto, R. Shibasaki, H. Kanasugi, T. Usui, Y. Shimazaki, Pflow: reconstructing people flow recycling large-scale social survey data, IEEE Pervasive Computing 10 (4) (2011) 27—35.

[25] X. Zhou, H.S. Mahmassani, Dynamic origin-destination demand estimation using automatic vehicle identification data, IEEE Transactions on Intelligent Transportation Systems 7 (1) (2006) 105—114.

[26] P. Cao, T. Miwa, T. Yamamoto, T. Morikawa, Bilevel generalized least squares estimation of dynamic origin- destination matrix for urban network with probe vehicle data, Transportation Research Record 2333 (1) (2013) 66−73.

[27] J. White, I. Wells, Extracting Origin Destination Information from Mobile Phone Data, 2002.

[28] S.M. Eisenman, F. Xiang, X. Zhou, H.S. Mahmassani, Number and location of sensors for real-time network traffic estimation and prediction: sensitivity analysis, Transportation Research Record 1964 (1) (2006) 253−259.

[29] S. Pogodzinska, M. Kiec, C. D'Agostino, Bicycle traffic volume estimation based on gps data, Transportation Research Procedia 45 (2020) 874−881.

[30] X. Yang, Y. Lu, H. Wei, Origin-destination estimation using probe vehicle trajectory and link counts, Journal of Advanced Transportation (2017) 18, 2017 Article ID 4341532.

[31] T. Huang, Y. Ma, Z.T. Qin, J. Zheng, H.X. Liu, H. Zhu, J. Ye, Origin-destination flow prediction with vehicle trajectory data and semi-supervised recurrent neural network, in: 2019 IEEE International Conference on Big Data (Big Data), IEEE, 2019, pp. 1450−1459.

Further reading

[1] S. Miyazawa, X. Song, T. Xia, R. Shibasaki, H. Kaneda, Integrating gps trajectory and topics from twitter stream for human mobility estimation, Frontiers of Computer Science 13 (3) (2019) 460−470.

[2] Jake Snell, S. Kevin, R. Zemel, Prototypical networks for few-shot learning, Advances in Neural Information Processing Systems 30 (2017).

[3] S. Adam, S. Bartunov, M. Botvinick, D. Wierstra, T. Lillicrap, Meta-learning with memory-augmented neural networks, in: International Conference on Machine Learning, PMLR, 2016, p. 18421850.

[4] Oriol Vinyals, C. Blundell, T. Lillicrap, D. Wierstra, et al., Matching networks for one shot learning, Advances in Neural Information Processing Systems 29 (2016).

CHAPTER SIX

Trip segmentation and mode detection for human mobility data

Yuhao Yao[1], Haoran Zhang[3], Qi Chen[2]
[1]Center for Spatial Information Science, The University of Tokyo, Kashiwa-shi, Chiba, Japan
[2]School of Geography and Information Engineering, China University of Geosciences (Wuhan), Wuhan, Hubei, China
[3]School of Urban Planning and Design, Peking University, Shenzhen, China

1. Introduction

Trip segmentation is the process of cutting a long trajectory into several trip slices based on semantic information (usually the travel mode), which is usually the most basic step in complex human mobility data processing. Mode detection is the process of detecting the travel mode of a sequence of trajectory records, which is usually the most important step for trip segmentation.

Numerous studies have been conducted on Machine Learning approaches in travel mode detection either using various types of neural networks [1−6] or through the application of other machine learning techniques, such as Adaptive Boosting (AdaBoost) [7−10], Random Forest (RF) [11−16], Support Vector Machine (SVM) [17−20], etc.

Basically, the moving mode could be divided into four types: *Stay, Non-motorized, Motor,* and *Metro. Stay* type means the device holder stops moving and stays in a small region. *Non-motorized* type means the device holder moves without a motor vehicle, usually by foot or bicycle. *Motor* type means the device holder moves by motor vehicle, usually by own car or bus. *Metro* means the device holder moves by metro, including underground and ground. We correspondingly utilize $\{1, 2, 3, 4\}$ to code them.

For mobility records set of an individual u in date d as $R(u, d) = \{r_0, r_1, ..., r_n\}$, where r is one mobility record that contains timestamp t and the position p, we could have the moving mode sequence $S(u, d) = \{s_1, s_2, ..., s_n\}$, $s_i \in \{1, 2, 3, 4\}$, where m_i is the moving mode between r_{i-1} and r_i. Since the moving mode sequence could not be observed directly, we need to estimate $S(u, d)$ based on $R(u, d)$.

Handbook of Mobility Data Mining, Volume 1
ISBN: 978-0-443-18428-4
https://doi.org/10.1016/B978-0-443-18428-4.00011-6

For example, as Fig. 6.1 shows, if one mobile terminator device holder walks for at first 10 min to go back home, stays at home for 15 min then takes a taxi for 10 min, finally takes the metro for 10 min, a 5 min interval moving mode sequence should be {2, 2, 1, 1, 1, 3, 3, 4, 4}.

Based on the moving mode sequence, we could divide the whole day trajectory into different segments by moving mode changing.

2. Hidden Markov Model

If we describe moving mode changing as a Markov process, the moving mode sequence could be regarded as a hidden state sequence, and we need to estimate it based on observable information. We apply a Hidden Markov Model to solve it.

Hidden Markov Model (HMM) is a statistical model that describes a Markov process with unknown parameters. Its states cannot be observed directly but could be indirectly observed through the observation vector sequence. Each observation vector is expressed as various states through some probability density distribution, and each observation vector is generated by a state sequence with corresponding probability density distribution. Therefore, HMM is a dual stochastic process, i.e., a set of hidden Markov chains with a certain number of states and a set of dominant random functions. As an important direction of signal processing, it has been successfully utilized in speech recognition, behavior recognition, character recognition, fault diagnosis, and other fields.

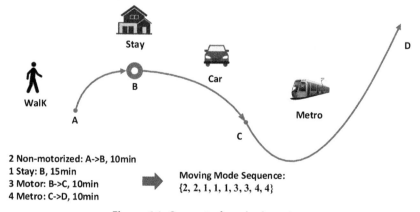

Figure 6.1 Concept of mode detection.

An HMM could be described as five elements: hidden states S, observable states O, initial state probability matrix π, state transfer probability matrix A and emission probability matrix B. In our model, we create two layers v and t, for observable states. Therefore we have two observable states O_v and O_t to form O and two emission probability matrices B_v and B_t to form B.

Hidden states S in our model represent the moving mode of device holders, i.e., *Stay, Non-motorized, Motor,* and *Metro.*

2.1 Transferring speed state

Observable states O_v relates to the position transferring speed. We divide transferring speed into four types: *Stop, Low Speed, Medium Speed,* and *High Speed,* and correspondingly utilize {0, 1, 2, 3} to code them. Here we take CDR data, for example, and create a transferring speed distribution boxplot of different moving modes from the field research, as Fig. 6.2 shows.

From the graph, we can see that the transferring speed of moving by foot is usually lower than 6 km/h, sometimes equal to 0 or more than 6 km/h, but never more than 15 km/h. The transferring speed of moving by motor vehicle is usually more than 15 km/h, sometimes between 6 and 15 km/h. Metro is similar to motor type, but with higher average speed and could achieve lower than 6 km/h due to unstable signal. Although the sampling

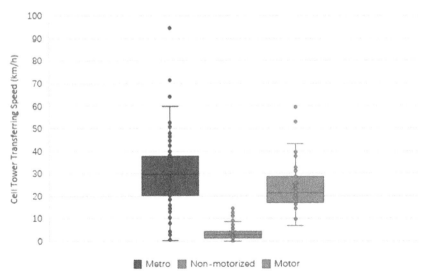

Figure 6.2 Boxplot of connected cell tower transferring speed distribution in different moving modes.

conditions may affect the speed distribution, the influence is very small, so we just based on this boxplot to build the observable state. For the connected cell tower transferring speed mode sequence of an individual u in date d as $V(u, d) = \{v_1, v_2, \ldots, v_n\}$, $v_i \in \{0, 1, 2, 3\}$, where v_i is the connected cell tower transferring speed mode between r_{i-1} and r_i, we have:

$$
v_i = \begin{cases}
0, & \dfrac{\text{distance}\left(p_{r_{i-1}}, p_{r_i}\right)}{t_{r_i} - t_{r_{i-1}}} = 0 \\[2ex]
1, & 0 < \dfrac{\text{distance}\left(p_{r_{i-1}}, p_{r_i}\right)}{t_{r_i} - t_{r_{i-1}}} \leq 6 \\[2ex]
2, & 6 < \dfrac{\text{distance}\left(p_{r_{i-1}}, p_{r_i}\right)}{t_{r_i} - t_{r_{i-1}}} \leq 15 \\[2ex]
3, & \dfrac{\text{distance}\left(p_{r_{i-1}}, p_{r_i}\right)}{t_{r_i} - t_{r_{i-1}}} > 15
\end{cases} \quad , 1 \leq i \leq n \qquad (6.1)
$$

2.2 Position state

Observable states O_t depend on where is the observed position. We roughly divide the type of observed position into five types: *Outdoor, Indoor, Uncertain, Tunnel,* and *Station,* and correspondingly utilize $\{0, 1, 2, 3, 4\}$ to code them.

- *Outdoor* means the position is in some open area.
- *Indoor* means the position is inside some tall buildings.
- *Uncertain* means the position could be both outdoor and indoor.
- *Tunnel* means the position is in a tunnel.
- *Station* means the position is in a subway station.

3. Model training

Basically, the model training method could be divided into supervised learning and unsupervised learning two ways.

3.1 Supervised learning

When field research is conducted and the ground truth data is sufficient, we could apply the supervised learning method *Maximum Likelihood Estimation* to train initial state probability, state transfer probability, and emission probability matrices.

Assume the total number of mobility records set of each mobile termi-nate device holder on different days is N.

For initial state probability matrix π, set a function $K_i(j)$, when the first hidden state of mobility records set j equals to i, function $K_i(j)$ equals to 1, else equals to 0. We could have:

$$\pi_i = \frac{\sum_{j=1}^{N} K_i(j)}{N}, i \in \{0, 1, 2, 3\} \tag{6.2}$$

For state transfer probability matrix A, for $i, j \in \{0, 1, 2, 3\}$, we gather the statistics of the frequency of each hidden state transfer pair (i, j) from all the moving mode sequences as $C_{i,j}$. Then we have:

$$A_{i,j} = \frac{C_{i,j}}{\sum_{m=0}^{3} C_{i,m}}, i, j \in \{0, 1, 2, 3\} \tag{6.3}$$

For emission probability matrix B, for $i, j_v \in \{0, 1, 2, 3\}, j_t \in \{0, 1, 2, 3, 4\}$, we gather the statistics of frequency of each hidden state equals to i and observable state v and t equals to j_v and j_t as D_{i,j_v,j_t}. Then we have:

$$B_{i,j_v,j_t} = \frac{D_{i,j_v,j_t}}{\sum_{m=0}^{3}\sum_{n=0}^{4} B_{i,m,n}}, i, j_v \in \{0, 1, 2, 3\}, j_t \in \{0, 1, 2, 3, 4\} \tag{6.4}$$

3.2 Unsupervised learning

When the ground truth data is not sufficient to calculate the accurate param-eters, we need to utilize an unsupervised method.

Usually, *Baum-Welch Algorithm* is utilized for training HMM parameters as an unsupervised learning method. Because the parameter estimation of the hidden Markov model is a maximum likelihood estimation of hidden vari-ables, *Baum-Welch Algorithm* utilizes *Expectation-Maximization (EM) algorithm* to solve the above-mentioned parameter estimation problem. From the *EM algorithm*, it gets the Q function, from which the partial derivative of the Q function and the extreme value of the maximum likelihood function could be calculated. The properties of the node graph help to calculate the joint probabilities to reduce the complexity of node calculation with intermediate variables.

However, due to the loss of information, the result of the *Baum-Welch Algorithm* is not good enough. For our case, its max estimation accuracy is no more than 60%. Meanwhile, indeed we have sufficient prior knowledge about the relationship between two observable states and hidden states. Therefore, we generate several rules based on prior knowledge and manually construct each probability matrix based on those rules.

For example:

1. It tends to maintain its hidden state rather than change it
2. It tends to start with "Stay"
3. "Stay" state only act as "Stop"
4. "Non-motorized" state can also act as "Stop" but no more than 10 min
5. "Low Speed" tends to be "Non-motorized", but sometimes "Car" or "Metro"
6. "SS" records must be "Metro"

After constructing the probability matrices, we manually make some simple adjustments to correct them based on ground truth.

4. Decoding

We utilize *Viterbi Algorithm* to decode the hidden states sequence. The *Viterbi algorithm* was proposed by *Andrew Viterbi* in 1967 for deconvolution in digital communication links to eliminate noise. It is a dynamic programming algorithm utilized to find the most likely hidden states sequence that may generate the observable states sequence, especially in the context of the Markov information source and Hidden Markov Model. Nowadays, it is widely utilized in speech recognition, keyword recognition, computational linguistics, and bioinformatics.

For a given Hidden Markov Model S, assume that the probability of initial state i is π_i, the probability of state i transferring into j is $a_{i,j}$, *and the* emission probability of hidden state i to observable state j is $b_{i,j}$. If the observable sequence is $[y_1, y_2, ..., y_T]$, and the corresponding most likely hidden states sequence is $[x_1, x_2, ..., x_T]$, based on the *Viterbi algorithm*, we could have:

$$V_{1,k} = b_{k,y_1} {}^* \pi_k \tag{6.5}$$

$$V_{t,k} = B_{k,y_t} {}^* max_{x \in S} \left(a_{x,k} {}^* V_{t-1,x} \right) \tag{6.6}$$

Where $V_{t,k}$ is the probability of the first t events' most likely hidden states sequence of which the final state is k. We could save the states x in formula (6.6) to get the Viterbi path. Define a function $Path(k, t)$: when $t = 1$, it returns k; else it returns x, which is utilized in calculating $V_{t,k}$. Then we can get the hidden states sequence by:

$$x_T = argmax_{x \in S}\left(V_{T,x}\right) \tag{6.7}$$

$$x_{t-1} = Path(x_t, t) \tag{6.8}$$

5. Application

In this section, based on the mode detection and trip segmentation result, we perform the correlation analysis and spatial lag regression to investigate the relationship between walkability and pedestrian activities.

We choose Tokyo and Osaka, the most populous prefectures in eastern and western Japan, as the study areas for this research (see Fig. 6.3A). Tokyo, the capital of Japan, has a population of over 13 million as of 2010 and covers a total area of 2200 km^2. As shown in Fig. 6.3B, the eastern 23 municipalities make up the core and the most populous part of Tokyo, originally known as "Tokyo City". Osaka Prefecture covers a total area of about 1900 km^2 and has a population of nearly 9 million as of 2010. As shown in Fig. 6.3C, Osaka City is the capital of this prefecture. It is also the center of the Osaka-Kobe-Kyoto area, a major economic hub in western Japan. In this study, for ease of presentation, we use "Tokyo" and "Osaka" to refer to the two prefectures and the term "main city" to refer to Tokyo City or Osaka City of the corresponding prefecture.

We use a mobile phone dataset to extract short-range movements from the users. The dataset contains GPS location records generated by about 1.6 million users in the entire Japan for a year (from August 1st, 2010 to July 31st, 2011). With the users' agreement, the records were collected from mobile phones with enabled AUTO-GPS function through the "docomo map navi" service by one of the leading mobile operators (NTT Docomo, Inc.). The collected data is completely anonymized for privacy protection. According to the operator's design, the mobile phones are set to upload the GPS record (not including any personal information, such as gender or age) approximately every 5 min. Each record contains information on user ID, latitude, longitude, altitude, timestamp, and positioning accuracy level (there are three levels due to different satellite's signal strength correspondingly the positioning error would be within 100 m, 200 m, or 300 m). However, the recording interval exceeds 5 min occasionally due to loss of signal or battery power. Besides, the positioning function would

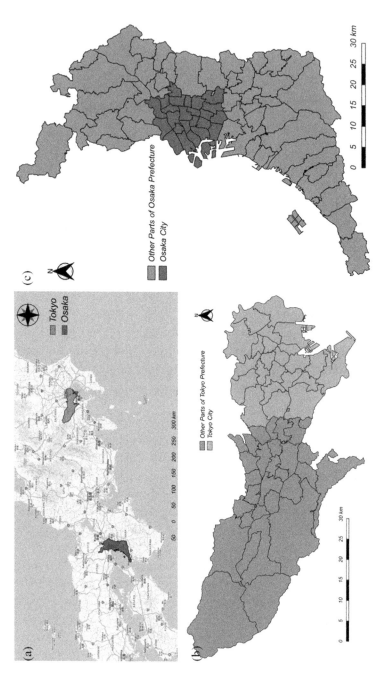

Figure 6.3 The two study areas, Tokyo and Osaka Prefecture, of this work. (A) shows the locations of the two prefectures in Japan; (B) and (C) show their administrative divisions. (Tokyo Prefecture also administers two island chains in Pacific Ocean. These islands are not displayed in this Figure. Our research will focus on the mainland portion of the prefecture).

be suspended when no motion is detected. In this case, no records will be uploaded. After filtering the records outside of Tokyo and Osaka, the two prefectures have about 1.2 billion and 650 million records for 680,365 and 394,980 unique users, respectively.

Meanwhile, we use other four built environment datasets to measure walkability in Tokyo and Osaka under a fine spatial granularity:

(a) *Geolocations of residential properties.* This dataset was collected by Zenrin Co. Ltd. in Japan in 2009. It contains detailed residential building information, including the geographic coordinates, number of floors, and so on. We use this data to estimate the residential density for the study areas.

(b) *Road network data.* We have the digital road maps of Tokyo and Osaka in 2013, which can be used to measure the intersection density of the road network. This dataset is obtained from the company of Sumitomo Electric Industries.

(c) *Point of interest (POI) data.* POI data was obtained from the Yellow Pages of Japan in 2010. We use this dataset to measure the facility accessibility of the study areas.

(d) *Geolocations of parks.* This data is obtained from the National Land Numerical Information of Japan in 2010, it provides detailed information, including the geographic coordinates, and space sizes of the parks or green spaces within the study areas.

5.1 Spatial distributions of the short trips

The days of the year covered by the mobile phone dataset are grouped into 241 weekdays and 114 holidays. In Tokyo, over 145 million and 55 million short trips are extracted on weekdays and holidays, respectively. In Osaka, due to a smaller population, over 72 million and 31 million short trips are extracted on weekdays and holidays, respectively.

We generate the grid maps of the daily average short-trip density to approximate the spatial distributions of pedestrian movements in the two prefectures. Fig. 6.4 illustrates the distributions on weekdays and holidays. From every grid map, we extract several representative grids called "hot spots" that have the highest density among the whole study area and annotate their actual locations on the map. In general, the four study cases have similar density distributions, which include most short trips within the main cities (i.e., Tokyo City and Osaka City) as well as a few hot spots scattered across other areas. However, we can still observe the difference between the short-trip distribution patterns on weekdays and holidays.

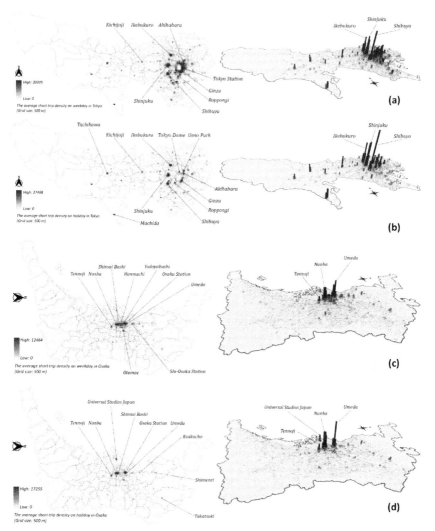

Figure 6.4 Spatial distribution patterns of average short-trip density on (A) weekdays in Tokyo; (B) holidays in Tokyo; (C) weekdays in Osaka; and (D) holidays in Osaka.

On weekdays, as shown in Fig. 6.4A and C, a large number of short trips occur at big railway stations (e.g., Tokyo Station and Osaka Station) and central commercial areas (e.g., Ikebukuro, Shinjuku, Shibuya, Ginza in Tokyo, and Umeda, Shinsai Bashi, Yodoyabashi, Nanba in Osaka). These hot spots, most located within the main cities, also promote the short-trip density of their surrounding areas.

On holidays, the short movements of people appear to be much more concentrated in the above commercial areas (see Fig. 6.4B and D). Meanwhile, some popular tourist destinations (e.g., Ueno Park in Tokyo and Universal Studios Japan in Osaka) and event places (e.g., Tokyo Dome) have also become hot spots due to people's recreational activities. Another observation is that some places far away from the main cities (e.g., Tachikawa, Machida in Tokyo, and Shinsenri, Takatsuki in Osaka) have higher density and become hot spots. The likely explanation is that some commuters no longer have to enter the main cities from outside, which leads to more short movements around their living places.

5.2 Spatial patterns of walkability and its components

Fig. 6.5 shows the spatial patterns of the walkability index (W) as well as the four subindices. As illustrated in Fig. 6.5A,B,F,G, the residential density index ($W_{residential}$) and road intersection density index (W_{road}) have similar distribution patterns in the two prefectures, where large areas (mostly in the main cities and their surrounding areas) have high $W_{residential}$ and W_{road}. The areas that have lower $W_{residential}$ and W_{road} mainly include the mountainous areas (e.g., the western part of Tokyo, the northern, southern parts, and the eastern border area of Osaka), the industrial areas (e.g., the southeastern border areas of Tokyo and the west coastal areas of Osaka), the airports (e.g., Tokyo International Airport located in the southeastern corner of Tokyo and Kansai International Airport located in the southwestern island of Osaka), and the rivers or forests within the prefectures. The areas that have high $W_{residential}$ and W_{road} are generally strong in facility accessibility index ($W_{facility}$) (see Fig. 6.5C and H), but it can be observed that the gaps between dense and sparse areas are widened. Meanwhile, as illustrated in Fig. 6.5D and I, the park accessibility index (W_{park}) varies a lot in local areas because of the relatively sparse distributions of the green spaces and parks. In general, the spatial distribution patterns of W (see Fig. 6.5E and J) are mainly constructed by $W_{residential}$ and W_{road}, while the $W_{facility}$ and W_{park} further strengthen the local differences.

Fig. 6.6 illustrates the histograms of the five indices for all grids in the study areas. The two areas both have large numbers of grids with $W_{residential}$ and W_{road} close to 0. Due to the different methods of calculation, the $W_{facility}$ and W_{park} appear to be smoother than the other two subindices. The distributions of $W_{facility}$ in the two prefectures, both show two obvious peaks at the low and high range of the index, respectively. The distributions

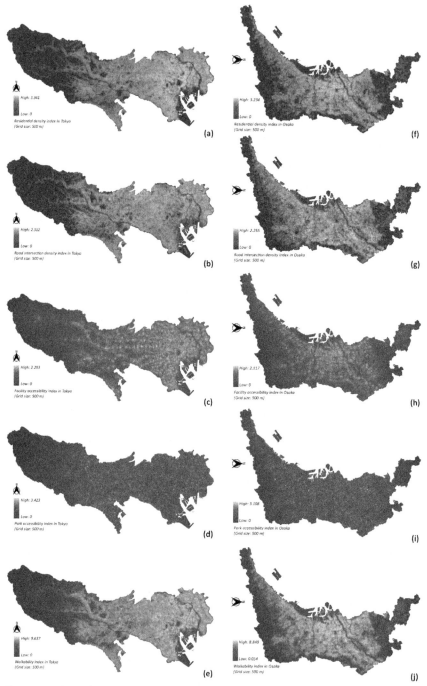

Figure 6.5 Spatial patterns of indices of residential density, road intersection density, facility accessibility, park accessibility, and walkability in: (A)—(E) Tokyo; and (F)—(J) Osaka.

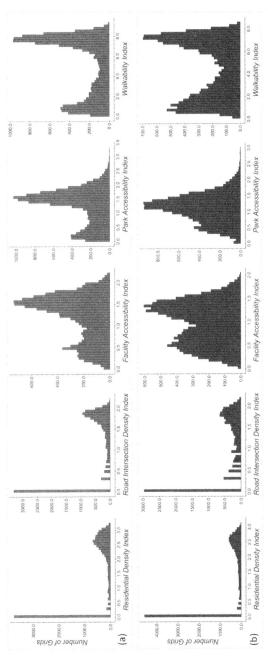

Figure 6.6 Histograms of indices of residential density, road intersection density, facility accessibility, park accessibility, and walkability for all grids in: (A) Tokyo; and (B) Osaka.

of W_{park} in Tokyo and Osaka have a distinct difference, which is mainly caused by the unbalanced distribution of the green spaces and parks in Tokyo compared with Osaka. The W, which is obtained by accumulating the subindices, tends to be polarized and distributed in the two prefectures, where Tokyo is more differentiated than Osaka.

5.3 Correlation between walkability and short-trip density

5.3.1 Linear regression results between the subindices of walkability and short-trip density index

Fig. 6.7 shows the fitting results of the linear regression between the four subindices of walkability and short-trip density index (I_{trip}). It can be observed that the R^2 values of the subindices have identical rankings in the four study cases. Specifically, $W_{facility}$ is the most correlated index with I_{trip} (with R^2 ranging from 0.803 to 0.832), which reflects that compared with the other three components, the accessibility to common facilities plays a more important role in promoting people's walking activities. Higher residential density and a more developed road network will naturally attract more pedestrians; thus, the $W_{residential}$ and W_{road} also show considerable correlations with I_{trip}. However, the W_{park} has a significantly weaker correlation with I_{trip} other subindices. This can be explained by two reasons: first, the low density of crowd in green spaces and parks lead to few pedestrian activities; second, the access to parks has little impact on people's daily routines like commuting, eating or shopping, in which much more time is spent for an average person. In general, the regression results of the two prefectures both show that the R^2 values of all the indices become slightly higher on holidays than those on weekdays. A possible explanation is that in people's own time, their activities decrease in low-walkability areas and become concentrated in areas with higher walkability.

5.3.2 Spatial lag regression results between walkability index and short-trip density index

Table 6.1 shows the spatial lag regression results between walkability index (W) and short-trip density index (I_{trip}) solved by GeoDa software [21]. The β values of the four cases demonstrate the positive correlation between W and I_{trip}. The values λ are high, which shows that the spatial autocorrelation of I_{trip} is significant in the study areas. The high R^2 values indicate that the input indices are well fitted by the spatial lag regression model.

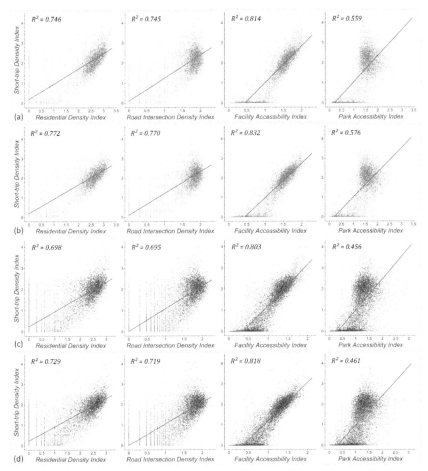

Figure 6.7 Scatter plots of subindices of walkability versus short-trip density index on: (A) Weekdays in Tokyo; (B) holidays in Tokyo; (C) weekdays in Osaka; and (D) holidays in Osaka. The solid line in each plot denotes the regression line, and the R^2 value in each plot denotes the goodness of fit of the linear regression between the two indices.

Table 6.1 The spatial lag regression results between walkability index and short-trip density index.

Area	α	β	λ	R^2
Tokyo (weekday)	−0.198	0.127	0.663	0.881
Tokyo (holiday)	−0.198	0.141	0.600	0.884
Osaka (weekday)	−0.205	0.126	0.691	0.875
Osaka (holiday)	−0.215	0.140	0.635	0.877

Fig. 6.8 shows the geographic distributions of the matching index (i.e., e) calculated by Eq. (6.8). The red and blue cells refer to areas where short-trip densities and walkability are somewhat incomparable. In particular, red grids refer to the places where short trips are notable higher (than expected) while the blue cells refer to areas with a lower level of pedestrian activities.

Note that we identify several statistically significant areas with the high or low matching index for further analysis. We refer to the two kinds of grids as "walkability-deficit spots" and "walkability-surplus spots" and annotate them with red and blue dashed lines in Fig. 6.8.

The walkability-deficit spots can be classified into two types. The first type is mostly a result of extremely high I_{trip} rather than low W. These areas are mainly central commercial districts on holidays (e.g., Ikebukuro, Shinjuku, Shibuya in Tokyo, and Umeda in Osaka), where the W values are all at high levels. However, since the I_{trip} values are much higher than others (see Fig. 6.5), these areas are still identified as walkability-deficit spots.

The second type does reflect the imbalance between low W and relatively higher I_{trip}. On weekdays, these spots are primarily some universities outside the main cities (e.g., Soka University, Chuo University in Tokyo, Osaka University of Health and Sports Sciences, and Osaka Kyoiku University) and some industrial factories. These places are both relatively far away from busy streets, the $W_{residential}$ and $W_{facility}$ There do not seem to meet the large walking requirements of the students and workers. On holidays, the walkability deficit mainly occurs in some sports areas (e.g., Maishima Sports Island in Osaka) and tourism or entertainment places (e.g., Odaiba, Tokyo Racecourse, Universal Studios Japan, and Kansai Cycle Sports Center). This is large because they are both relatively isolated from their surroundings and have low $W_{residential}$ and W_{road}, these two factors apparently do not affect people's intention of walking when they are engaged in sports and recreational activities. Some other places, such as exhibition centers (e.g., Tokyo Big Sight and Izumiotsu Phoenix in Osaka) and airports, are designed and built for particular purposes. For these spots, the walkability deficit is understandable to some extent because more efforts have been made to improve productivity or transport efficiency.

The identified walkability-surplus spots are all far away from the main cities. After excluding the grids located at mountains, rivers, and lakes, we divide these spots into three groups: temples, parks or forests, and residential areas. The temples are mostly identified together with small neighborhoods; thus, their walkability is generally low but not insignificant. However, since

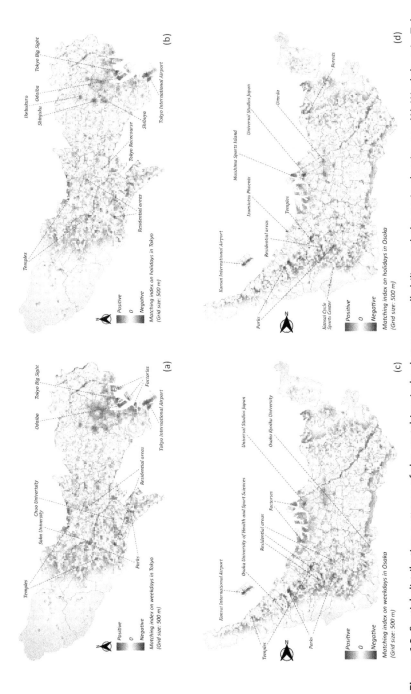

Figure 6.8 Spatial distribution patterns of the matching index between walkability and short-trip density on: (A) Weekdays in Tokyo; (B) holidays in Tokyo; (C) weekdays in Osaka; and (D) holidays in Osaka.

these temples are almost unknown spots for lots of people, quite a few short trips can be detected there, which leads to an obvious walkability surplus. The walkability of parks or forests is mostly contributed by their high W_{park}, but apparently, few walking activities are observed from the mobility dataset. What surprises us is that quite a few residential areas with dense neighborhoods appear to have excessive W for I_{trip}. After further investigation, we find that although the $W_{residential}$, W_{road}, and even W_{park} are high in these places, the $W_{facility}$ values are relatively low. Particularly, the distances from these neighborhoods to the nearest tram or subway station (where many living facilities exist) are greater than half a mile, which means that people living there are very likely to reach the common facilities by bike or car.

References

[1] S. Dabiri, Inferring transportation modes from GPS trajectories using a convolutional neural network, Transportation Research Part C: Emerging Technologies 86 (2018) 360−371.

[2] Y. Song, J. Preston, D. Ogilvie, New walking and cycling infrastructure and modal shift in the UK: a quasi-experimental panel study, Transportation Research Part A: Policy and Practice 95 (2017) 320−333.

[3] R. Tambi, P. Li, J. Yang, An efficient CNN model for transportation mode sensing, in: Proceedings of the 16th ACM Conference on Embedded Networked Sensor Systems, 2018, pp. 315−316.

[4] X. Liang, G. Wang, A convolutional neural network for transportation mode detection based on smartphone platform, in: 2017 IEEE 14th International Conference on Mobile Ad Hoc and Sensor Systems (MASS), IEEE, 2017, pp. 338−342.

[5] Y. Endo, H. Toda, K. Nishida, A. Kawanobe, Deep feature extraction from trajectories for transportation mode estimation, in: Pacific-Asia Conference on Knowledge Discovery and Data Mining, Springer, 2016, pp. 54−66.

[6] Y. Xu, R.D. Clemente, M.C. González, Understanding Vehicular Routing Behavior with Location-Based Service Data, EPJ Data Science 10 (1) (2021) 1−17.

[7] Y. Qin, H. Luo, F. Zhao, Z. Zhao, M. Jiang, A traffic pattern detection algorithm based on multimodal sensing, International Journal of Distributed Sensor Networks 14 (10) (2018), 1550147718807832.

[8] M. Etemad, A.S. Junior, S.J. Matwin, On feature selection and evaluation of transportation mode prediction strategies, arxiv (2018).

[9] S.-H. Fang, Y.-X. Fei, Z. Xu, Y. Tsao, Learning transportation modes from smartphone sensors based on deep neural network, IEEE Sensors Journal 17 (18) (2017) 6111−6118.

[10] H. Wang, H. Luo, F. Zhao, Y. Qin, Z. Zhao, Y. Chen, Detecting transportation modes with low-power-consumption sensors using recurrent neural network, in: 2018 IEEE SmartWorld, Ubiquitous Intelligence & Computing, Advanced & Trusted Computing, Scalable Computing & Communications, Cloud & Big Data Computing, Internet of People and Smart City Innovation (SmartWorld/SCALCOM/UIC/ATC/CBDCom/IOP/SCI), IEEE, 2018, pp. 1098−1105.

[11] B. Wang, L. Gao, Z. Juan, Travel mode detection using GPS data and socioeconomic attributes based on a random forest classifier, IEEE ITSS 19 (5) (2017) 1547−1558.

[12] M. Elhenawy, H. Rakha, Random forest-hidden Markov transportation mode recognition model using smartphone sensor data, in: TRB 96th Annual Meeting Compendium of Papers: Transportation Research Board 96th Annual Meeting, Transportation Research Board, 2017.

[13] Z.A. Lari, A. Golroo, Automated transportation mode detection using smart phone applications via machine learning: case study mega city of Tehran, in: Proceedings of the Transportation Research Board 94th Annual Meeting, Washington, DC, USA, 2015, pp. 11–15.

[14] Y. Ji, L. Gao, D. Chen, Y. Zhou, Y. Zhang, Functional Analysis of Public Transport Network in Trip Mode Detection from Personal Smartphone Trajectory Data, 2017.

[15] R. Chapleau, P. Gaudette, T. Spurr, Application of machine learning to two large-sample household travel surveys: a characterization of travel modes, Transportation Research Record Journal of the Transportation Research Board 2673 (4) (2019) 173–183.

[16] A. Efthymiou, E.N. Barmpounakis, D. Efthymiou, E.I. Vlahogianni, Identifying Transportation Mode of Unimodal Trips Using Smartphone Data and Machine Learning Algorithms, 2018.

[17] G. Xiao, Z. Juan, C. Zhang, Travel mode detection based on GPS track data and Bayesian networks, Computers, Environment and Urban Systems 54 (2015) 14–22.

[18] W. Xu, X. Feng, J. Wang, C. Luo, J. Li, Z. Ming, Energy harvesting-based smart transportation mode detection system via attention-based LSTM, Special Section on Intelligent Data Sensing, Collection and Dissemination in Mobile Computing 7 (2019) 66423–66434.

[19] C.A.M. De Quintella, L.C. Andrade, C.A.V. Campos, Detecting the transportation mode for context-aware systems using smartphones, in: 2016 IEEE 19th International Conference on Intelligent Transportation Systems (ITSC), IEEE, 2016, pp. 2261–2266.

[20] J. Hagenauer, M. Helbich, A comparative study of machine learning classifiers for modeling travel mode choice, Expert Systems with Applications 78 (2017) 273–282.

[21] L. Anselin, I. Syabri, Y. Kho. GeoDa: an introduction to spatial data analysis[M]// Handbook of applied spatial analysis, Springer, Berlin, Heidelberg, 2010, pp. 73–89.

CHAPTER SEVEN

Benchmark of travel mode detection with smartphone GPS trajectories

Jinyu Chen[1], Wenjing Li[1], Qing Yu[2], Ryosuke Shibasaki[1], Haoran Zhang[3]

[1]Center for Spatial Information Science, The University of Tokyo, Kashiwa-shi, Chiba, Japan
[2]The Key Laboratory of Road and Traffic Engineering, Ministry of Education, Tongji University, College of Transportation Engineering, Shanghai, China
[3]School of Urban Planning and Design, Peking University, Shenzhen, China

1. Introduction

Travel mode detection in GPS trajectory is a long-term hot topic [1,2] because there are a lot of existing works that used the information of travel mode in big GPS trajectory dataset as the base of research [3−6]. Stenneth et al. [7] developed a hybrid Bayes network merged with a decision tree to distinguish the travel mode. Widhalm et al. [8] created a decision tree followed by a Discrete Hidden Markov Model and proposed 77 features for distinguishment. Zong et al. [9] used the nested logit model and its variances. There are also many examples that have developed enormous methodologies to detect travel mode [10−13]. Successful detection of travel mode requires not only a reliable method [14,15] but also a comprehensive dataset that covers the various situation to serve as the benchmark. In some comparative studies [16−18], In most previous works [19−21], authors operated their own custom dataset collection and trained the model. In this work, we provide and introduce a complete travel mode detection process, including a GPS trajectory dataset marked with travel mode as the training dataset and model selection and training. The dataset is collected by seven independent volunteers and covers the time period of a complete month. The travel mode ranges from walking to the railway. We also provide a case study of distinguishing trip walking and bicycle with our collected training dataset. The two kinds of trips are hard to distinguish as they are nonmotorized trips and their trajectory are similar to the GPS dataset. The whole process consists of ground truth data collection, velocity analysis, and training of the detection model.

Handbook of Mobility Data Mining, Volume 1
ISBN: 978-0-443-18428-4
https://doi.org/10.1016/B978-0-443-18428-4.00009-8

117

2. Ground truth data collection

A considerable part of works in travel mode detection employed the collection of GPS data of different travel modes by using different kinds of devices like smartphones [22,23], and GPS loggers [1,24,25]. Therefore, we also operated the ground truth collection of GPS data considering both bikes traveling and walking by using an Android smartphone. The accuracy of GPS records is 10^{-7} m in open areas. This refers to about 2—3 m on the surface of the earth, which is enough for study. The time interval of the GPS record is set to be 1s.

The data collection covers the whole month of October 2020, collected by seven volunteers. There are total of 212 walking trips, 138 bicycle trips, 56 bus trips, and 69 railway trips. The least durance of each trip is required to be 10 min.

Firstly, we introduce the bike trips. The bike trips are mainly located in a classical urban and rural fringe. There are both downtowns, which contain a high density of buildings and high traffic volume, as well as remote rural areas where there are residential houses, industrial factories, and campuses. The distribution of bike trips is shown in Fig. 7.1 A part of roads is repeatedly traveled at various times at different time slots to experience different road conditions.

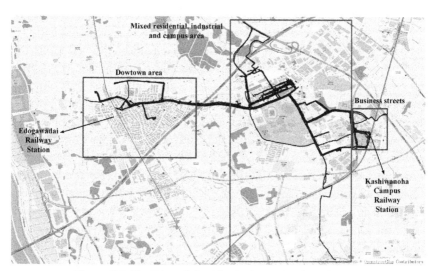

Figure 7.1 The Trips of the Bike in the Ground Truth Data.

The walking trips are scattered and distributed in places that are away from each other. Therefore, we choose to mainly show the representative samples of trips in urban and rural fringe and urban areas in Fig. 7.2.

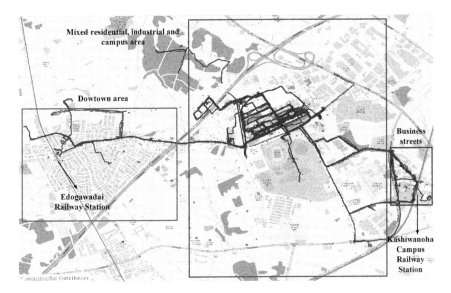

(a) Samples of walking trips in urban and rural fringe

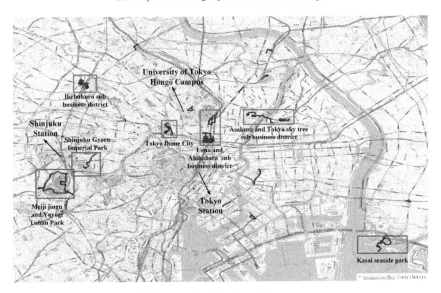

(b) Samples of walking trips in Urban area

Figure 7.2 Samples of Walking Trips (A) Urban and Rural Fringe (B) Urban Area.

The part of urban and rural fringe is similar to bike trips. In urban areas, the walking trips cover a majority part of places of interest in the greater Tokyo area. The places marked with purple are the main parks, which residents and tourists usually visit for leisure and tourism; The orange ones are the major subbusiness district areas. Because of great traffic volumes and high accessibility, walking is also a very common travel behavior in these areas. Other walking trips are located in some corners, like the Hongo Campus of the University of Tokyo.

Railway trips are also distributed both in rural and crowded areas. The spatial distribution of railway trips is shown in Fig. 7.3. Trips with the shape of a blue line are on the railways that connect different urban centers or subcenters. For example, Joban Line connects the city center of Kashiwa and the subcenter of Tokyo; Tobu Urban Park Line and Keiyo Line connect the city center of Kashiwa and the center. Trips with the shape of green lines are one of the railways that are all in the crowded urban area. The difference

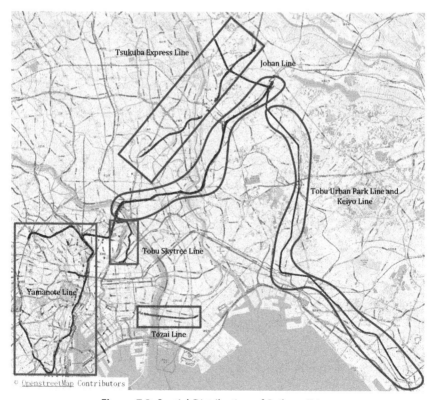

Figure 7.3 Spatial Distribution of Railway Trips.

is that the distance among stations on center—center lines is larger so that the travel time among lines is shorter. The train usually needs to go through rural areas where there is no station. However, the distance on urban lines is the opposite. Therefore, the features of traveling on two lines, including average distance and travel time, are different. In the ground-truth dataset, we include trips on both kinds of lines. Some lines are repeatedly traveled in different time slots.

Finally, we introduce the trajectory dataset of bus trips. The trajectories mainly cover Tokyo, a metropolis, and Kashiwa city, a normal and average-level city in Chiba prefecture, Japan. The trajectories with blue line rectangles are on the bus lines that connect downtown and suburbs. The ones with green line rectangles are on the bus lines that operate fully in downtown and crowded commercial areas. Like railway, the travel pattern is also different between the two kinds of bus lines (Fig. 7.4).

In summary, the ground truth trips cover various kinds of urban districts with different traffic volumes. They range from crowded subbusiness districts in the city center to remote industrial and residential areas. The collection is suitable for the analysis of real travel behaviors.

3. Method for travel mode detection

Then, we will introduce how to detect the travel mode of a segment of travel. Travel mode detection is currently a hot topic for a long time [2,26,27]. Former studies have shown numerous methods. Xiao et al. developed a Bayesian network consisting of a K2 algorithm and conditional probability tables [28]. The model can distinguish walk, bike, bus, and car travel with an accuracy of 86%. Nguyen et al. [29] adopted a random forest model for travel mode detection. The accuracy can reach 89.1% on the classification of Bus, motorcycle, car, walk, and bike. Zhou et al. [22] utilized random forests but different features to accomplish the same goal. In their case, the accuracy reaches 94.1%. Besides, there are also other algorithms or methods like deep learning [30], Support Vector Machine [31], or a hybrid combination of deep learning and optimization [32]. Whatever kind of method, the common thing is that they all need ground truth trajectory data labeled with real travel mode as the basis. Generally, ground-truth data is not open source. The author probably needs to collect data by employing volunteers. The ground-truth data should follow the principle of (1) collection from as many people as possible to eliminate the difference in travel behavior among people. (2) covering various functional areas like

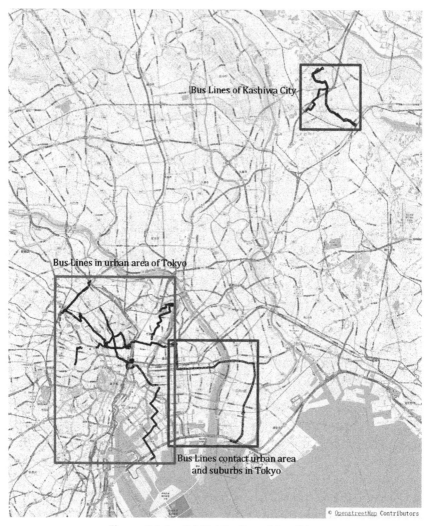

Figure 7.4 Spatial Distribution of Bus Trips.

commercial, residential and rural areas. (3) covering a long time period to ensure the variety of road conditions and weather. (4) covering all of the travel modes that want to be detected. The GPS device can either be a smartphone [33] or professional GPS data logger [34].

As introduced before, former studies have developed enormous methodologies to detect travel mode. In addition to the method itself, the input feature is also an essential factor. Despite the features found by former studies, it is encouraged that the author uses the regression model to find more novel features and methodologies. A good feature should show a high correlation with the variable of travel mode. In Table 7.1, we provide a partial selection of typical studies considering the problem of travel mode detection.

Table 7.1 Table of studies.

Study	Feature	Methodology
Stenneth et al. [7]	1. Distance to all buses 2. Distance to selected buses 3. Distance to the nearest railway line 4. Number of GPS records that are closer to the bus station than a threshold 5. Accuracy of GPS records 6. Average speed 7. Average change rate of direction 8. Average acceleration	(1) Naive bayes (2) Bayesian network (3) Decision trees (4) Random forest
Widhalm et al. [8]	Totally 77 features regarding: 1. Velocity 2. Acceleration 3. Deceleration 4. Direction change 5. Signal 6. Power spectrum of device	Decision trees followed by a discrete hidden Markov model
Xiao et al. [35]	1. Average speed 2. Speed of 95th percentile 3. Average absolute acceleration 4. Travel distance 5. Proportion of records of low speed 6. Average change rate of direction	Continuous hidden Markov model

(Continued)

Table 7.1 Table of studies.—cont'd

Study	Feature	Methodology
Zong et al. [36]	1. Average speed 2. Maximal speed 3. Speed of 75th percentile 4. Acceleration 5. Acceleration of 75th percentile 6. Travel time 7. Travel distance 8. Standard deviation of speed	Nested logit model and its variance
Rezaie et al. [37]	1. Travel time 2. Average speed 3. Travel distance 4. Distance between transit station and origin as well as destination 77 features including:	Random forest model and label propagation
Nitsche et al. [38]	1. Speed 2. Accelerations 3. decelerations 4. direction change per time 5. high-frequency accelerometer magnitude 6. power spectrum of the accelerometer	An ensemble of probabilistic classifiers combined with a discrete hidden M

From Table 7.1, it can be informed that there are a large variety of candidate methods. Each method has its own character and significance. Here, we will give a simple introduction to classical technologies.

Random Forest: The group of random forests is an ensemble learning method for classification, regression, and other tasks that operates by constructing a multitude of decision trees at training time and outputting the class that is the mode of the classes or classification or mean/average prediction or regression of the individual trees. Generally, it is an assembly of decision trees. Each single decision tree is trained to decide the classification of the target, so random forest employees many trees to vote for the output. To avoid the same output produced by all the trees, each decision tree only learns a part of the features of the total dataset. In the long-term application, it has been proved to outperform the decision tree. Random forest is a supervised learning method. Therefore, it relies on the quality of data. The works that adopted random forest include Chapleau et al. [39], Ji et al. [40], efthymiou et al. [41], Guvensan et al. [42].

Bayesian Network: It is a probabilistic graphical model that represents a set of variables and their conditional dependencies via a directed acyclic graph. A Bayesian network is ideal for taking an event that occurred and predicting the likelihood that any one of several possible known causes was the contributing factor. For example, a Bayesian network could represent the probabilistic relationships between diseases and symptoms. Given symptoms, the network can be used to compute the probabilities of the presence of various diseases. An effective and widely used algorithm to solve the Bayesian network is the Markov chain Monte Carlo algorithm. The strength of the Bayesian network is that it can model cause and effect with uncertainty. Hence, it is powerful in solving uncertain problems. What's more, the Bayesian network can integrate and absorb various inputs and information effectively. The works that used the Bayesian network include Bedogni et al. [43], DE Quintella et al. [44], Balli et al. [45], Feng et al. [46], Xu et al. [47].

Hidden Markov Model: Hidden Markov Model is a statistical Markov model in which the system being modeled is assumed to be a Markov process with unobservable states. Different from the normal Markov Model, the state of the hidden Markov model is directly unobservable. The state should be inferred by the observable parameters affected by the state. The states are usually expressed by the probability distribution. The model is usually used to deal with serial data or problems like natural language processing and trajectory computing. Currently, there are three kinds of algorithms to solve the Hidden Markov Model: forward propagation, Viterbi algorithm, and Baum-Welch algorithm. The works that used the Hidden Markov Model include Liao et al. [48], Waga et al. [49], Reddy et al. [50], Muller et al. [51], Krumm et al. [52].

Artificial Neural Network: Artificial neural network is assembled by a large number of units or nodes called neurons. Each of them represents a specific number in the computation process. An artificial neuron receives signals then processes them and can signal neurons connected to it. The whole neural network uses thousands or millions of neurons as parameters to imitate the thinking process of the human brain. Normally, the neurons are embedded into layers. The layers use a transition matrix to export the result to their next neighbors. The parameters in the transition matrix are fitted by the training data with the method of gradient descent. The works that used the Artificial Neural Network include Song et al. [53], Endo et al. [54], Liang et al. [55], Tambi et al. [56], Dabiri et al. [57].

There is no obvious advantage or disadvantage. On the other hand, the selections of features in all of the studies are very similar. Almost all of them are time, distance, and velocity-related. In addition, we can also see that in addition to the information extracted from trajectory data, much GIS information is also integrated with the feature, which is very helpful in judging the trip on public transportation. Trajectories of public transportation are especially important in the analysis of MaaS-related research as the relationship between traditional public transportation, and MaaS is one of the essential topics [58–60].

An important topic in the studies that are related to the usage of trajectory with travel mode is political analysis. In the work of [61], Lewis tried to use the CHTS and NHTS to collect the GPS data from participants. The dataset contains the private auto modes, public auto modes, and nonauto modes for analysis. In the result, they found that in the five levels of urbanization of rural, exurban, suburb, dense suburb, and urban core, the urban core has the highest miles of travel per person per day in the mode of nonauto trips and the lowest in the mode of auto trips. Also, bikes and walks are traveled most in the urban core area. The difference between the two travel modes is that the mile of walking monotonically increases with the growth of urbanization while the bicycle is traveled both greatly in the rural and urban core areas. To attract more trips to the transit, speed is the key because efficiency is an essential factor to attract more ridership from private autos. The findings provided some basic and general conclusions about traffic and urban planning. Nguyen et al. [62] focused on another problem. They combined the GPS data and surveyed to introduce the promotion of elderly's mobility. In the processing of GPS data, they firstly detect the start and the end of the trip and then categorize the segment of trips by nonmotorized (walking and cycling), personal mobility (Electricity-assisted bicycle and motorbike), public transport, and motorbike. Then, they built the regression model in different forms by choice of travel mode as the regression target and socioeconomic, demographic, and topographical factors as the regression variables. The regression result shows that with the growth of age, personal nonmotorized mobility is less preferred. If one owns a car, He or she will prefer to travel by car more. In topography aspects, the change in altitude makes people prefer to travel more with assisted bicycles and motorbikes than vehicles. Therefore, to help improve the mobility of the elderly in hilly residential areas, the author suggests policy should promote more electricity-assisted transportation tools. Huang et al. [63] studied the mobility pattern in Shanghai at the level of the trip chain, which means the combination of different travel segmentations in one time of out-going to the final destination. They analyze the usage of travel modes of vehicle, public transit, bicycle, and walk in the GPS trajectory of residents. They found that vehicle is used more often as the only travel mode in the complex trip chain while public transit, bicycle, and walking are mostly used as a single way to the internal stop or destination. This is mainly because the vehicle is more accessible and utilized to a greater degree in the context of complex trip chain patterns. The demographic factors have a great effect on the travel mode choice. Travelers who are middle-aged or leave work after 9 p.m. are unwilling to choose a complicated trip chain. However, travelers who have children under six are the opposite. Married travelers are more likely to drive cars. Low-income travelers adopt public transit and nonmotorized modes due to economic limitations. The number of private cars is positively correlated to car mode and negatively correlated to others. The number of bicycles is positively correlated to bicycle mode only. The closer distance to public transit stations is, the more possible it is for travelers to adjust public transit. Higher bicycle ownership can promote more bicycle adoption in daily life travel. This also leads to competition between the bicycle and public transportation systems. The significance of this work is that it can provide suggestions for policy decisions. Transit-oriented development is suggested as it can increase the convenience of public transportation. Travelers consider the adoption of different travel modes mainly based on the travel time rather than money cost. Therefore, future travel planning should pay more attention to the accessibility of public transportation even if the travel cost of the public could rise.

4. Case study

In this study, we use our dataset to train a model for travel mode detection and try to distinguish the bike and walking trips in the massive GPS trajectory dataset.

4.1 Velocity analysis

The raw ground truth data collection always needs a preprocess. Because of the bad signal of the GPS device in the smartphone, sometimes the error of recorded position could be too enormous. In the raw data, the estimated error of each recorded position is also recorded by the application in the smartphone as an independent column. We operated statistics on the recorded errors shown in Fig. 7.5.

Under normal circumstances, the error isn't too large. The Q3 value is lesser than 50 m. On the other hand, the upper bound of error is computed to be 93.1 m. Values higher than 93.1 probably refer to the ones with abnormal errors in position. Therefore, in the preprocess, we removed these records.

Then, to fit the ground truth trip collection to the DOCOMO trajectory dataset, we subsample the ground truth trajectory by the interval of multiple of 1 min until 5 min. The logic of subsampling is:

1. Set the time interval of subsampling
2. Set the first GPS record as the initiation of sampled trajectory and reference point
3. Sample the point with a time interval or point closest to it if it does not exist in the original trajectory for sampling.
4. Set the sampled point as the new reference point.

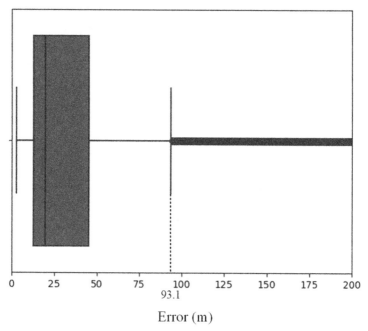

Error (m)

Figure 7.5 Boxplot of Recorded Errors.

Then, in the subsampled trajectory, we compute the shortest distance between the neighboring points and divide it by their time interval as the average velocity from the previous one to the latter one. Here, we show to illustrate the change of distribution of velocity in walking and bike trips due to the increase in a time interval (Fig. 7.6).

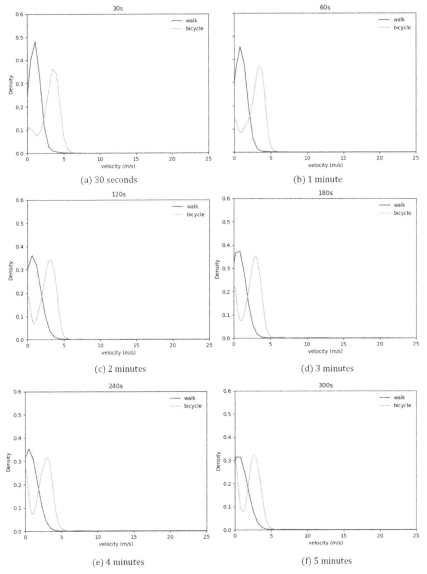

Figure 7.6 Distribution of Velocity Under Different Time Intervals.

It is easy to obvious from the figure that with the increase in the time interval, the distribution of the velocity of walking and bike trips is getting closer. The KS test statistic value of both distributions decreases from 0.732 to 0.597 as the time interval increases from 1 min to 5 min. So, there is an obvious approach to two distributions. What's more, we found a growing peak near the 0 value. This is caused by the lack of trajectory information due to the growing time interval (Fig. 7.7).

As shown in Fig. 7.7, suppose the traveler started from the position at the top, passed by the position of two transparent and blurred icons, and finally went back to the origin or the position nearby. This is originally a round trip. However, the subsampling may only capture the origin and destination in this round trip so that the computed shortest distance between two sampled positions is near 0, and the computed velocity is also nearly 0.

Consequently, in the trajectory with long time intervals, it's very hard to distinguish the walking and bike travels by pure velocity. Therefore, in the training of the detection model, we carefully choose the features to finish the job.

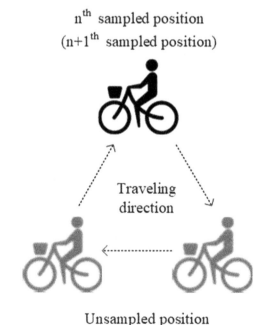

Figure 7.7 Zero Velocity is Caused by a Long Time Interval.

4.2 Training of the detection model

In reference to the results of the comparison and former studies that focus on travel mode detection [21,29,64], we adopted the random forest method for the detection of bike travels in the study area. An important key step in the construction of features. In [21], the author stated that velocity-related features could mostly help extract the walking trip and bike trip. In [22], besides velocity-related features, some global features like total travel distance and travel time can account for as large as the contribution of distinguishment of travel mode. Therefore, considering the special case that the time interval in our dataset is at least 5 min, we added some new features and finally adopted the ones listed in Table 7.2.

Then, we will explain how these features are computed.

Since the GPS records are a series of tuple of position and time, the series can be implemented as:

$$GPS = [(P_1, t_1), (P_2, t_2), \ldots\ldots, (P_n, t_n)] \tag{7.1}$$

Thus, the distance between the neighboring records should also be a series, the element of which is

$$D_i = Dis(P_i, P_{i+1}), i = 1, 2, \ldots\ldots, n-1 \tag{7.2}$$

Where the function $Dis()$ is used to compute the shortest distance.

The feature 1 Distance equals the summary of D_i:

$$Distance = sum(\{D_i | i = 1, 2, \ldots\ldots, n-1\}) \tag{7.3}$$

Feature 2 Time equals to:

$$Time = t_n - t_1 \tag{7.4}$$

Table 7.2 The features of the random forest model in our study.

Feature Name	Physical significance
1. Distance	The total traveled distance in the moving segment
2. Time	The time span of moving segment
3. Points	The number of GPS records in the moving segment
4. VCR	The average change rate of velocity
5. MVCR	The maximal change rate of velocity
6. MaxAcceleration	Maximal acceleration
7. Avgspeed_1	The timely average velocity
8. Minspeed	Minimal velocity
9. Maxspeed	Maximal velocity
10. Avgspeed_2	The quantitively average velocity

The velocity can be computed by:

$$V_i = \frac{D_i}{t_{i+1} - t_i} \qquad (7.5)$$

Feature 8 Minspeed and feature 9 Maxspeed are separately the minimum and maximum of a group of V_i.

In this study, we define the change rate of velocity as:

$$vcr_i = \frac{|V_{i+1} - V_i|}{V_i}, \ i = 1, 2, \ldots\ldots, n - 2 \qquad (7.6)$$

Therefore, feature 4 VCR, and feature 5 MVCR refers to the average and maximum of a group of vcr_i in one moving segment. Also, the acceleration is computed by:

$$acc_i = \frac{|V_{i+1} - V_i|}{t_{i+1} - t_i}, i = 1, 2, \ldots\ldots, n - 2 \qquad (7.7)$$

Feature 6 MaxAcceleration is the maximum of a group of acc_i; feature 7 Avgspeed_1 is:

$$Avgspeed\_1 = \frac{Distance}{Time} \qquad (7.8)$$

Feature 10 Avgspeed_2 is:

$$Avgspeed\_2 = \frac{sum(\{V_i | i = 1, 2, \ldots\ldots, n - 2\})}{Points} \qquad (7.9)$$

The ground truth trips will be preprocessed by the above equations and fed into the random forest model for training.

We computed the features in the subsampled trajectory set by using Eqs. (7.1)–(7.9). Then, the subsampled trajectory set will be converted and aggregated as the dataset for training. The whole dataset is randomly divided into a training set and test set by 80% and 20% to prevent overfitting. To furtherly test the reliability of the model, we operated 10-fold cross-validation on the model. The accuracy ranges from 89.29% to 100%. We adopted the model with a test score of 100% to detect the bike and walking travels in the GPS dataset for big picture analysis [65,66]. Similarly, there are also other studies that are based on the information of the travel model [67,68].

5. Conclusion

In this chapter, we introduce a standard process of travel mode detection for GPS trajectory. The process includes ground-truth GPS dataset collection and detection model training. A dataset that contains a month of GPS trajectory marked by travel mode is collected. The data is collected by seven volunteers and contains 212 walking trips, 138 bicycle trips, 56 bus trips, and 69 railway trips. Also, the least durance of each trip is 10 min. The trips cover various urban functional areas of uncrowded industrial, campus, and residential areas and crowded downtown and business streets. Some roads and streets are traveled at different times of day to cover the various traffic conditions. Then, we provide a case study of distinguishing bike and walking trips in the GPS dataset of a long sampling time interval. We analyze the velocity under different sampling time intervals and fit it to the dataset for detection to construct the input feature of the detection model. At last, we provide a review of several advanced models for travel mode detection and choose the traditional random forest model to complete the detection task in our case study. In 10-fold cross-validation, the accuracy ranges from 89.29% to 100%.

References

[1] H. Gong, C. Chen, E. Bialostozky, C.T. Lawson, A GPS/GIS method for travel mode detection in New York City, Computers, Environment and Urban Systems 36 (2012) 131−139.

[2] L. Wu, B. Yang, P. Jing, Travel mode detection based on GPS raw data collected by smartphones: a systematic review of the existing methodologies, Information 7 (2016) 67.

[3] Q. Yu, H. Zhang, W. Li, Y. Sui, X. Song, D. Yang, et al., Mobile phone data in urban bicycle-sharing: market-oriented sub-area division and spatial analysis on emission reduction potentials, Journal of Cleaner Production 254 (2020) 119974.

[4] H. Zhang, J. Chen, J. Yan, X. Song, R. Shibasaki, J. Yan, Urban power load profiles under ageing transition integrated with future EVs charging, Advances in Applied Energy 1 (2021) 100007.

[5] H. Zhang, J. Chen, Q. Chen, T. Xia, X. Wang, W. Li, et al., A universal mobility-based indicator for regional health level, Cities 120 (2022) 103452.

[6] J. Chen, Q. Zhang, N. Xu, W. Li, Y. Yao, P. Li, et al., Roadmap to hydrogen society of Tokyo: locating priority of hydrogen facilities based on multiple big data fusion, Applied Energy 313 (2022) 118688.

[7] L. Stenneth, O. Wolfson, P.S. Yu, B. Xu, Transportation mode detection using mobile phones and GIS information, in: Proceedings of the 19th ACM SIGSPATIAL International Conference on Advances in Geographic Information Systems, 2011, pp. 54−63.

[8] P. Widhalm, P. Nitsche, N. Brändie, Transport mode detection with realistic smartphone sensor data, in: Proceedings of the 21st International Conference on Pattern Recognition (ICPR2012), IEEE, 2012, pp. 573−576.

[9] F. Zong, Y. Yuan, J. Liu, Y. Bai, Y. He, Identifying travel mode with GPS data, Transportation Planning and Technology 40 (2017) 242−255.

[10] F. Namdarpour, M. Mesbah, A.H. Gandomi, B. Assemi, Using genetic programming on GPS trajectories for travel mode detection, IET Intelligent Transport Systems 16 (2022) 99−113.

[11]   V. Patil, S.B. Parikh, P.K. Atrey, Geosecure-O: a method for secure distance calcula-
       tion for travel mode detection using outsourced gps trajectory data, in: 2019 IEEE Fifth
       International Conference on Multimedia Big Data (BigMM), IEEE, 2019, pp. 348–356.
[12]   Y. Zhu, Y. Liu, J. James, X. Yuan, Semi-supervised federated learning for travel mode
       identification from GPS trajectories, IEEE Transactions on Intelligent Transportation
       Systems 23 (2021) 2380–2391.
[13]   J. James, Travel mode identification with GPS trajectories using wavelet transform and
       deep learning, IEEE Transactions on Intelligent Transportation Systems 22 (2020)
       1093–1103.
[14]   P. Sadeghian, J. Håkansson, X. Zhao, Review and evaluation of methods in transport
       mode detection based on GPS tracking data, Journal of Traffic and Transportation En-
       gineering 8 (2021) 467–482.
[15]   D. Yang, C. Xiong, L. Tang, L. Zhang, Travel Mode Detection Using Smartphone GPS
       Data: A Comparison between Random Forest and Wide-and-Deep Learning, 2019.
[16]   S. Zhu, H. Sun, Y. Duan, X. Dai, S. Saha, Travel mode recognition from GPS data
       based on LSTM, Computing and Informatics 39 (2020) 298–317.
[17]   J. Broach, J. Dill, N.W. McNeil, Travel mode imputation using GPS and accelerom-
       eter data from a multi-day travel survey, Journal of Transport Geography 78 (2019)
       194–204.
[18]   G. Xiao, Q. Cheng, C. Zhang, Detecting travel modes using rule-based classification
       system and Gaussian process classifier, IEEE Access 7 (2019) 116741–116752.
[19]   G. Xiao, Z. Juan, C. Zhang, Travel mode detection based on GPS track data and
       Bayesian networks, Computers, Environment and Urban Systems 54 (2015) 14–22.
[20]   M.A. Shafique, E. Hato, Travel mode detection with varying smartphone data collec-
       tion frequencies, Sensors 16 (2016) 716.
[21]   B. Wang, L. Gao, Z. Juan, Travel mode detection using GPS data and socioeconomic
       attributes based on a random forest classifier, IEEE Transactions on Intelligent Trans-
       portation Systems 19 (2017) 1547–1558.
[22]   C. Zhou, H. Jia, J. Gao, L. Yang, Y. Feng, G. Tian, Travel mode detection method
       based on big smartphone global positioning system tracking data, Advances in Me-
       chanical Engineering 9 (2017), 1687814017708134.
[23]   E.F.S. Soares, K. Revoredo, F. Baião, C.A. de MS Quintella, C.A.V. Campos,
       A combined solution for real-time travel mode detection and trip purpose
       prediction, IEEE Transactions on Intelligent Transportation Systems 20 (2019)
       4655–4664.
[24]   J. Zhao, C. Xiong, D. Yang, Y. Ji, L. Tang, L. Zhang. A Wide-and-Deep Learning
       Model of Travel Mode Detection.
[25]   S. Kraft, T. Květoň, V. Blažek, L. Pojsl, J. Rypl, Travel diaries, GPS loggers and Smart-
       phone applications in mapping the daily mobility patterns of students in an urban
       environment, Moravian Geographical Reports 28 (2020) 259–268.
[26]   H. Gong, C. Chen, E. Bialostozky, C. Lawson, Environment, Systems U. A GPS/GIS
       Method for Travel Mode Detection in New York City, vol. 36, 2012, pp. 131–139.
[27]   Y. Zhu, S. Zhang, Y. Liu, D. Niyato, J. James, Robust federated learning approach for
       travel mode identification from non-IID GPS trajectories, in: 2020 IEEE 26th Inter-
       national Conference on Parallel and Distributed Systems (ICPADS), IEEE, 2020,
       pp. 585–592.
[28]   G. Xiao, Z. Juan, C. Zhang, Travel mode detection based on GPS track data and
       Bayesian networks, Computers, Environment and Urban Systems 54 (2015) 14–22.
[29]   M.H. Nguyen, J. Armoogum, Hierarchical process of travel mode imputation from
       GPS data in a motorcycle-dependent area, Travel Behaviour and Society 21 (2020)
       109–120.

[30] L. Li, J. Zhu, H. Zhang, H. Tan, B. Du, B. Ran, et al., Coupled application of gener-
      ative adversarial networks and conventional neural networks for travel mode detection
      using GPS data, Transportation Research Part A: Policy and Practice 136 (2020)
      282−292.
[31] A. Jahangiri, H. Rakha, Developing a support vector machine (SVM) classifier for
      transportation mode identification by using mobile phone sensor data, in: Transporta-
      tion Research Board 93rd Annual Meeting 14, 2014, p. 1442.
[32] G. Xiao, Z. Juan, J. Gao, Travel mode detection based on neural networks and particle
      swarm optimization, Information vol. 6 (2015) 522−535.
[33] X. Zhou, W. Yu, W.C. Sullivan, Making pervasive sensing possible: effective travel
      mode sensing based on smartphones, Computers, Environment and Urban Systems
      58 (2016) 52−59.
[34] Y.-J. Byon, B. Abdulhai, A. Shalaby, Real-time transportation mode detection via
      tracking global positioning system mobile devices, Journal of Intelligent Transportation
      Systems 13 (2009) 161−170.
[35] G. Xiao, Q. Cheng, C. Zhang, Detecting travel modes from smartphone-based travel
      surveys with continuous hidden Markov models, International Journal of Distributed
      Sensor Networks 15 (2019).
[36] F. Zong, Y. Yuan, J. Liu, Y. Bai, Y. He, Identifying travel mode with GPS data, Trans-
      portation Planning and Technology 40 (2017) 242−255.
[37] M. Rezaie, Z. Patterson, J.Y. Yu, A. Yazdizadeh, Semi-supervised travel mode detec-
      tion from smartphone data, in: 2017 International Smart Cities Conference (ISC2),
      IEEE, 2017, pp. 1−8.
[38] P. Nitsche, P. Widhalm, S. Breuss, N. Brändle, P. Maurer, Supporting large-scale
      travel surveys with smartphones—A practical approach, Transportation Research Part
      C: Emerging Technologies 43 (2014) 212−221.
[39] R. Chapleau, P. Gaudette, T. Spurr, Application of machine learning to two large-
      sample household travel surveys: a characterization of travel modes, Transportation
      Research Record 2673 (2019) 173−183.
[40] Y. Ji, L. Gao, D. Chen, Y. Zhou, Y. Zhang, Functional Analysis of Public Transport
      Network in Trip Mode Detection from Personal Smartphone Trajectory Data, 2017.
[41] A. Efthymiou, E.N. Barmpounakis, D. Efthymiou, E.I. Vlahogianni, Identifying
      Transportation Mode of Unimodal Trips Using Smartphone Data and Machine
      Learning Algorithms, 2018.
[42] M.A. Guvensan, B. Dusun, B. Can, H.I. Turkmen, A novel segment-based approach
      for improving classification performance of transport mode detection, Sensors 18
      (2017) 87.
[43] L. Bedogni, M. Di Felice, L. Bononi, Context-aware Android applications through
      transportation mode detection techniques, Wireless Communications and Mobile
      Computing 16 (2016) 2523−2541.
[44] C.A.M. De Quintella, L.C. Andrade, C.A.V. Campos, Detecting the transportation
      mode for context-aware systems using smartphones, in: 2016 IEEE 19th International
      Conference on Intelligent Transportation Systems (ITSC), IEEE, 2016,
      pp. 2261−2266.
[45] S. Ballı, E.A. Sağbaş, Diagnosis of transportation modes on mobile phone using logistic
      regression classification, IET Software 12 (2018) 142−151.
[46] T. Feng, H.J. Timmermans, Comparison of advanced imputation algorithms for detec-
      tion of transportation mode and activity episode using GPS data, Transportation Plan-
      ning and Technology 39 (2016) 180−194.
[47] Y. Xu, R.D. Clemente, M.C. González, Understanding vehicular routing behavior
      with location-based service data, European Physical Journal Data Science 10 (2021)
      1−17.

[48] L. Liao, D.J. Patterson, D. Fox, H. Kautz, Learning and inferring transportation routines, Artificial Intelligence 171 (2007) 311−331.

[49] K. Waga, A. Tabarcea, M. Chen, P. Fränti, Detecting movement type by route segmentation and classification, in: 8th International Conference on Collaborative Computing: Networking, Applications and Worksharing (CollaborateCom), IEEE, 2012, pp. 508−513.

[50] S. Reddy, M. Mun, J. Burke, D. Estrin, M. Hansen, M. Srivastava, Using mobile phones to determine transportation modes, ACM Transactions on Sensor Networks 6 (2010) 1−27.

[51] I.A.H. Muller, Practical activity recognition using GSM data, in: Proceedings of the 5th International Semantic Web Conference (ISWC) Athens: Citeseer, 2006.

[52] J. Krumm, E. Horvitz, LOCADIO: inferring motion and location from Wi-Fi signal strengths, Mobiquitous (2004) 4−13.

[53] Y. Song, J. Preston, D. Ogilvie, I. Consortium, New walking and cycling infrastructure and modal shift in the UK: a quasi-experimental panel study, Transportation Research Part A: Policy and Practice 95 (2017) 320−333.

[54] Y. Endo, H. Toda, K. Nishida, A. Kawanobe, Deep feature extraction from trajectories for transportation mode estimation, in: Pacific-Asia Conference on Knowledge Discovery and Data Mining, Springer, 2016, pp. 54−66.

[55] X. Liang, G. Wang, A convolutional neural network for transportation mode detection based on smartphone platform, in: 2017 IEEE 14th International Conference on Mobile Ad Hoc and Sensor Systems (MASS), IEEE, 2017, pp. 338−342.

[56] R. Tambi, P. Li, J. Yang, An efficient cnn model for transportation mode sensing, in: Proceedings of the 16th ACM Conference on Embedded Networked Sensor Systems, 2018, pp. 315−316.

[57] S. Dabiri, K. Heaslip, Inferring transportation modes from GPS trajectories using a convolutional neural network, Transportation Research Part C: Emerging Technologies 86 (2018) 360−371.

[58] S. Shaheen, A. Cohen, Mobility on demand (MOD) and mobility as a service (MaaS): early understanding of shared mobility impacts and public transit partnerships, Demand for Emerging Transportation Systems (2020) 37−59.

[59] S. Jang, V. Caiati, S. Rasouli, H. Timmermans, K. Choi, Does MaaS contribute to sustainable transportation? A Mode Choice Perspective 15 (2021) 351−363.

[60] T. Storme, J. De Vos, L. De Paepe, F. Witlox, Limitations to the car-substitution effect of MaaS, Findings from a Belgian Pilot Study 131 (2020) 196−205.

[61] S. Lewis, W. Ecology, Neighborhood density and travel mode: new survey findings for high densities, International Journal of Sustainable Development & World Ecology 25 (2018) 152−165.

[62] T.A.H. Nguyen, M. Chikaraishi, H. Seya, A. Fujiwara, J. Zhang, I. Research, Elderly's heterogeneous responses to topographical factors in travel mode choice within a hilly neighborhood: an analysis based on combined GPS and paper-based surveys, European Journal of Transport and Infrastructure Research 17 (2017).

[63] Y. Huang, L. Gao, A. Ni, X. Liu, Analysis of travel mode choice and trip chain pattern relationships based on multi-day GPS data: A case study in Shanghai, China, Journal of Transport Geography 93 (2021), 103070.

[64] Z.A. Lari, A. Golroo, Automated transportation mode detection using smart phone applications via machine learning: case study mega city of Tehran, in: Proceedings of the Transportation Research Board 94th Annual Meeting, Washington, DC, USA, 2015, pp. 11−15.

[65] H. Zhang, X. Song, Y. Long, T. Xia, K. Fang, J. Zheng, et al., Mobile phone GPS data in urban bicycle-sharing: layout optimization and emissions reduction analysis, Applied Energy 242 (2019) 138−147.

[66] H. Zhang, J. Chen, W. Li, X. Song, R. Shibasaki, Mobile phone GPS data in urban ride-sharing: an assessment method for emission reduction potential, Applied Energy 269 (2020) 115038.

[67] L. Ding, N. Zhang, A travel mode choice model using individual grouping based on cluster analysis, Procedia Engineering 137 (2016) 786–795.

[68] P. Lanzini, S.A. Khan, Shedding light on the psychological and behavioral determinants of travel mode choice: a meta-analysis, Transportation Research Part F: Traffic Psychology and Behaviour 48 (2017) 13–27.

CHAPTER EIGHT

Trajectory super-resolution methods

Xudong Shen[1], Dou Huang[1], Peiran Li[1], Ning Xu[2]
[1]Center for Spatial Information Science, The University of Tokyo, Kashiwa-shi, Chiba, Japan
[2]Beijing Key Laboratory of Urban Oil and Gas Distribution Technology, China University of Petroleum Beijing, Beijing, China

1. Introduction

Recent years, with the development of global positioning systems (GPS), the amount of trajectory data collected is significantly improved. Therefore research on data mining related to trajectory is gradually rising, which has attracted attention in computer science, sociology, geography and many other fields [1], and lead to many different real-world applications, for example, traffic jam detection [2−4], automatic driving [5,6], navigation route planning [7,8], and mobility modeling [9]. All such applications require high-quality and large-scale trajectory datasets. However, in reality, it is hard to get enough high-quality trajectories. On the one hand, frequent positioning will consume lots of power, so most of GPS devices have a limited positioning rate. On the other hand, considered personal privacy, most of the users will refuse to give out their detailed trajectory data and only give rough data. These trajectories with a low sample rate cannot express the route in detail and increase the uncertainty between two sample points, which will have a bad side effect on those applications that need detailed trajectories, lead to a bad analysis result. Therefore, it is necessary to improve the quality of current datasets in order to support related researches. Fig. 8.1 shows the difference between the two trajectories.

The sampling rate of the GPS trajectory dataset has two aspects since it is spatiotemporal data. The first aspect is the spatial sampling rate, or the number of users distributed on observed areas. The second aspect is the temporal sampling rate or the time interval of collected GPS data. On the one hand, improving the spatial sampling rate is essential since the currently collected GPS trajectory dataset can only represent a tiny percentage of people living in an area. On the other hand, low sampling rate GPS trajectory data often

Handbook of Mobility Data Mining, Volume 1
ISBN: 978-0-443-18428-4
https://doi.org/10.1016/B978-0-443-18428-4.00010-4

139

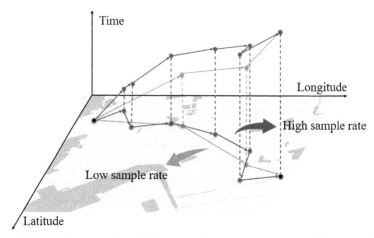

Figure 8.1 A spatiotemporal graph of contrast between trajectory with low sample rate (orange, light gray in print) and high sample rate (blue, dark gray in print). Usually, we can access some GPS trajectory data with low sampling rate, so the problem is how to efficiently generate a finer-grained inference without external information, such as road network?.

lost many detailed movement information, which will damage the performance of data-driven methods.

We only consider the temporal sampling rate of GPS trajectory data in this paper. There are two branches of existing methods that aim to tackle the issue mentioned before. The first branch is trajectory completion, and the second branch is trajectory generation.

Among these methods, there are two distinct options depending on whether the map data, such as road networks, is accessible. In the first option, the trajectories are mapped to road segments, improving the trajectory with such prior knowledge. As for the second option, the map information is not accessible as input, trying to improve the trajectory in free space. Comparing the two options, the formal can give a more relevant trajectory but take more computation resources, the latter is more challenging to solve but also more prevalent in practice. This chapter focuses on compare methods for the second option.

When it comes to enhancing the quality of existing trajectory datasets, most current research focuses on trajectory completion. By using information acquired from GPS trajectory data or other external data sources, this technique improves sparse and imperfect trajectories. Most previous study has focused on historical experience, inferring the missing pieces via simple mathematical technique. Recently, there have been researches using heuristic search algorithms or complex probability models [10]. Their approach focuses on modeling the transition pattern between locations. With the extensive use of the neural network, considerable research also focuses on utilizing its excellent modeling ability to extract the feature of trajectories. In this respect, recurrent neural networks (RNN) are widely used. Numerous researchers have proposed many different deep learning models and proved their efficiency. However, there is some deficiency of this approach. Firstly, there may be some minor deviation in trajectory complement.

If the deviation of all trajectories gets accumulated, a significant aggregation error occurs, which has a detrimental effect on the total dataset quality improvement. Besides, in reality, we discovered that there are only a few incomplete trajectories in actuality. The poor quality of the trajectory dataset is due to the fact that the majority of the trajectories have a low sample rate. That is to say, the time interval between location records is too lengthy, which is a crucial shortcoming for data mining-related researches. Finally, after trajectory compliment, the information density of the trajectory remains unchanged, which is also a shortcoming.

As for trajectory generation, this kind of study focuses on extracting features from a limited quantity of existing high-quality trajectory data and massively creating high-quality trajectory data with a high sample rate. There has also been a surge in related research in recent years. Some researchers use a random mobility model in conjunction with realistic road topology, while others employ mobility prediction models, especially sequential models such as Markov Chain. Deep learning techniques are also used in this case. For instance, RNNs, Generative Adversarial Networks (GAN) [11], and several versions of their variants are used. However, some of the generated trajectories are implausible, which will have an effect on the result of data mining researches conducted on these trajectories. Additionally, for some researches, the generated trajectory cannot be used in lieu of real-world trajectories.

In the computer vision (CV) field, super-resolution techniques [12] allow researchers to produce a collection of high-resolution images from a sequence of low-resolution frames. The fundamental concept is to fuse a sequence of low-resolution noisy blurred images to produce a higher resolution image or sequence. Inspired by this idea, we transfer the sense into trajectory super-resolution. Under this circumstance, trajectory super-resolution means improving the resolution of the existing trajectory, for example, to raise the sampling rate of trajectory from sample every

10 minutes to 3 minutes. With the help of super-resolution, we can improve the information density of the trajectory, allowing for extraction more valuable information from the trajectory data.

Additionally, considerable study has been conducted on trajectory super-resolution. However, majority of these researches concentrate on trajectories of particles [13], cells [14], or missiles [15]. Their trajectory is distinct from that of human mobility trajectories, and it is hard to extend their usage in this field directly.

In comparison with trajectory complement, trajectory generation, and trajectory super-resolution, trajectory super-resolution can better complete trajectory information for analysis and data mining. Here we focus on trajectory super-resolution methods. We tested them on two different datasets and used different metrics to evaluate their performance. Finally illustrate the efficiency of different models via a series of experiments.

The rest of the paper is organized as follows. In section 3, we discussed related work. Section 4 introduced the preliminary. In section 5, we introduced the data we used, its preprocessing and the evaluation metrics in detail. Section 6 introduced three different methods we compared in detail. The experiments and the results are shown and discussed in section 7. Finally, we conclude the paper in section 8.

2. Related work

Related research includes trajectory complication, generative, and super-resolution. We will discuss them here separately.

2.1 Trajectory completion

Numerous GPS devices would be prone to failure for a variety of reasons, resulting in missing data throughout the recording trajectory, and leading to a sparse and incomplete trajectory. Many researchers concentrated their efforts on improving existing trajectory datasets' quality via trajectory completion methods.

For example, some of these methods based on past knowledge [16–18], attempt to infer the missing segment of the trajectory. Shen G [19]. use a specially designed algorithm, which computes the area between two trajectories and combines the K-modes algorithm to complete missing trajectories. Recently most of the approaches used the deep learning model. Kim [20] uses RNN-based LSTM architecture to predict locations of a trajectory. Wang H [21] represents the GPS trajectory as a 2D image and uses

DNN to extract the feature. Nawaz A [22]. proposed a bidirectional conventional recurrent encoder-decoder architecture and interfaced attention mechanism to enhance the model performance. Wang J [23] implementing a subsequence to sequence to capture spatiotemporal correlation and integrating Kalman filter to reduce the prediction uncertainty.

These solutions, however, can only complete the incomplete portion of the trajectory. The information density remains unchanged after these processes.

2.2 Trajectory generation

Another approach to fulfill the demand is via trajectory generation. The generation model has attracted considerable interest due to its ability to extract existing data features and approximate complex distributions. Some methods use historic knowledge [24], this kind of method learns trajectory features from the previous dataset and generates additional comparable trajectories. Moreover, some of the methods use deep learning methods for generation. A traditional generation model is AutoEncoder (AE) [25], it has an encoder module and a decoder module. The encoder maps the input into code, and a decoder converts the code to reconstruct the input. Occasionally, however, the decoder may fail to generate reasonable trajectories due to an inability to learn the relation between input noise and trajectories. An improvement of AE is Variational AutoEncoder (VAE) [26], it sampled on the noise of input distribution and can approximate an effective result. On this basis, Huang D [27]. constructs plausible trajectories for human mobility by combining a VAE with a seq2seq model. Generative Adversarial Network (GAN) [11] is also a popular generation model that is capable of extracting data distributions and estimating probability. In this way, Wang X [28] uses a generation model based on a specifically designed two-stage GAN that takes into account the trajectory's geographical and sequential characteristics. Their model not only reveals the distribution similarities but also has a high degree of accuracy in matching road networks.

2.3 Super-resolution

Recently, super-resolution has become a popular research in CV field. Image processing researchers try to reconstruct high-resolution images from a sequence of low-resolution images [29,30]. This idea has also been extended into trajectories. For example, Gregory G [31] use superresolution method for dynamic cells' trajectory. Tan Q [32] proposed a novel algorithm for super-resolution Synthetic Aperture Radar (SAR) in curve trajectory. Liangkui L [15] proposed a QPSO-based algorithm for ballistic trajectories. However, most of their research focuses on trajectories in distinct fields and cannot be applied directly to human mobility trajectories.

To our knowledge, there are very few researches apply the deep learning method for trajectory super-resolution. Here we adapt some methods to let them fit this task.

3. Preliminary

This section introduces the notations we used in this paper and gives out a formal definition of the problem.

Definition of Location. Generally speaking, a location point is a pair of coordinate value latitude and longitude $p = < x, y, t >$. Here t is the sample timestamp.

Definition of Trajectory. A GPS trajectory can be represented as a series of coordinates $T = (< x_1, y_1, t_1 >, < x_2, y_2, t_2 >, \cdots, < x_n, y_n, t_n >)$. Here $< x_i, y_i, t_i >$ is a sample point, where x_i and y_i are latitude and longitude of an object at time instance t_i. Formally, this series of coordinates are in time order, $1 \leq i \leq n$.

Here longitude and latitude are real numbers. Time is denoted by the Unix time stamp and is accurate to seconds.

Definition of Region cell. The entire geographical research area is divided into a set of region cells, denoted by C. Every cell $c \in C$ has the same length and width. Each location P in trajectory T belong to certain cell c. In this case, each trajectory can be represent as a series of region cell ID, $T = (c_1, c_2, \cdots, c_n)$.

Transferring continuous measurements into distinct cells is a frequent prepossessing approach. Using cells can alleviate the complexity of directly modeling numerical coordinate sequence to some extends, since it is easier to perform computation over discrete cells. As a result, we partitioned the geographical research space into cells.

Definition of Sampling interval. The sampling interval Δt is the time difference between two continuous sampled coordinates of the user, $\Delta t = t_n - t_{n-1}$. Usually, it depends on the sample rate of the devices.

Definition of low-quality trajectory. A series of coordinates with a low sampling interval Δt.

Definition of high-quality trajectory. A series of coordinates with a high sampling interval Δt.

Table 8.1 Symbols and descriptions.

Symbols	Descriptions
P	A location point
C	A cell in research area
N	Number of sample points
T	Original trajectory
T'	High-resolution trajectory
Δt	Sample time interval
$\mathcal{T} = (T_1, T_2, \cdots, T_n)$	Original trajectory dataset
$\mathcal{T}' = (T'_1, T'_2, \cdots, T'_n)$	High-resolution trajectory dataset

Obviously, high-quality trajectory contains more information than low-quality trajectories, which means we can mine more valuable information from them. However, in reality, most of the trajectory datasets are of low-quality.

Definition of trajectory dataset. Trajectory dataset is consists of a series of trajectories, represent as $\mathcal{T} = (T_1, T_2, \cdots, T_n)$. Here n is the number of trajectories.

Problem Definition. The aim is to improve the resolution of the given trajectory dataset. Given a low-quality trajectory dataset $\mathcal{T}$ with a low sample rate, we focuses on improving the resolution of trajectories. That is to say, for each trajectories T in the dataset, we will improve its resolution and get T', here we have $m > n$, which means the sample interval Δt of trajectory T is bigger than $\Delta t'$ of trajectory T'. Different from trajectory completion and generation, this approach improve the information density of given trajectory. Table 8.1 summarizes all the symbols.

4. Data description

To get the performance of different methods, we employ two distinct datasets. One is the Didi taxi trajectory data. It is open-source, collected in Xian city in China. The other is population mobility data from ZDC, which collected mobility data in Tokyo, Japan. The statistic of the two datasets is shown in Table 8.2. The bulk of the trajectory lengths in both datasets are shorter than 1 hour. With regard to the Didi taxi trajectory dataset, its quality is superb, its resolution is very high, and the sample rate is every 2–5 s. Thus we first resample on these trajectories, sampled about every 10 min to mimic a low-resolution trajectory. Simultaneously, we retain original high-resolution trajectories in order to compare them with the

Table 8.2 Statistics of two datasets.

Dataset	Didi	ZDC
Duration	7 days	7 days
GPS points	35,122,118	21,463,488
Trajectories	63,897	108,399
Sample interval	2 ~ 5 s	2 ~ 10 min

output of different models. As for the ZDC mobility dataset, the sample rate is about 2–10 min. Here we also resampled about every 10 min. We will compare the trajectories improved by different models with the original ones later. To facilitate analysis, we assume all trajectories have the same time period unit(1 h), and we will evaluate the performance on different sample intervals.

4.1 Data preprocessing

We split the study area into two-dimensional grids of equal length and breadth. As mentioned above, we put every trajectory on cells and get a cell ID list to represent the trajectory.

Due to the fact that the neural network requires a fixed-length input, we need to do additional special processing on trajectories. Here is the strategy to put all the trajectories in a fixed-length size n. If the processed mesh list exceeds length n, then drop some grid ID in this trajectory randomly until the length is equal to size n. If the length is less than size n, then repeat the first and last grid ID in the list until the length is equal to the specified size n. Here, we take processed trajectories as ground truth and resample on these fixed-length trajectories to simulate a low sample rate condition.

4.2 Evaluation metrics

To better evaluate the performance of different models, we use metrics both in macroview and microview.

4.2.1 Metrics of microview

The microview is used for evaluate the similarity of two trajectories. By comparing truth trajectory with predicted trajectory, and we can get their similarity. Here we use normalized Dynamic Time Warping (nDTW) [33] and Average Displacement Error (ADE) to evaluate the similarity of a single trajectory.

DTW is a robust distance measure for time series, allowing similar shapes to match even if they are out of shape in time series.

$$D[i][j] = \begin{cases} 0, & \text{if } i = 1 \wedge j = 1 \\ \infty & \text{if } i = 1 \vee j = 1 \\ \text{dist}\left(p_i, \widetilde{p}_j\right) + \min(D[j-1][i], \\ D[j][i-1], D[j-1][i-1]) & \text{otherwise} \end{cases} \quad (8.1)$$

Here, $D[i][j]$ is DTW and $1 \leq i \leq k_1$, $1 \leq i \leq k_2$ [34]. nDTW is an improvement of DTW and is directly derived from it. By normalizing DTW by a factor of $\frac{1}{T_{len}}$, where T_{len} is the length of generated trajectory.

Average Displacement Error(ADE) [35] is another benchmark metric in microview. It measures the Euclidean distance between predicted meshes and actual meshes of all the trajectories.

$$ADE = \sum_{j=1}^{N} \frac{\sum_{i=1}^{n} \left(\widehat{x}_i^j - x_i^j\right)^2 - \left(\widehat{y}_i^j - y_i^j\right)^2}{N} \quad (8.2)$$

Here, n is the number of steps in trajectory, and N is the number of trajectories in total.

4.2.2 Metrics of macroview

At the macrolevel, the goal is to evaluate the distribution of all trajectories throughout the whole research area. By comparing the overall distribution of the whole predicted trajectory dataset with ground truth, we can get the similarity of the two distributions. Here we use a Mob similarity method provided by Y. Yao [36].

In this method, they first defined three operations: add, shift, and delete to transform prediction mobility pattern to truth mobility pattern, and each operation has a different cost. Then, this method uses several indicators to evaluate the similarity of two mobility matrices, including Manhattan distance (MD), normalized Manhattan distance (NMD), shift proportion (SP), normalized mass angle (NMA), and normalized structural angle (NSA). Followed are the equations for these indicators.

$$MD(X, Y) = V(S_X \rightarrow S_Y) * w \quad (8.3)$$

$$NMD(X, Y) = 1 - \frac{V(S_X \rightarrow S_Y)}{V(\varnothing \rightarrow S_X) + V(\varnothing \rightarrow S_Y)} \tag{8.4}$$

$$SP(X, Y) = \frac{V_{\text{shift}}(S_X \rightarrow S_Y)}{V_{\text{shift}}(S_X \rightarrow S_Y) + V_{\text{add/delete}}(S_X \rightarrow S_Y)} \tag{8.5}$$

$$NMA = 1 - \frac{\arccos \frac{V(\varnothing \rightarrow S_X)^2 + V(\varnothing \rightarrow S_Y)^2 - V(S_X \rightarrow S_Y)^2}{2V(\varnothing \rightarrow S_X) * V(\varnothing \rightarrow S_Y)}}{\pi} \tag{8.6}$$

$$NSA = 1 - \frac{\arccos \frac{V(\varnothing \rightarrow S_{X'})^2 + V(\varnothing \rightarrow S_{Y'})^2 - V(S_{X'} \rightarrow S_{Y'})^2}{2V(\varnothing \rightarrow S_{X'}) * V(\varnothing \rightarrow S_{Y'})}}{\pi} \tag{8.7}$$

Here S_X and S_X means two different vector graphs, and operation $\rightarrow$ indicate transform operation from two different vector sets, w is the width of the mesh or cell. V reflects the least cost from this transform, $V_{\text{add/delete}}$ and V_{shift} indicate the total cost of add, delete and shift operation.

5. Baseline methods

5.1 Method 1—Deepmove: predicting human mobility with attentional recurrent networks [37]

Fig. 8.2 presents the architecture of Deepmove. It has three key components: (1) feature extracting and embedding; (2) recurrent module and historical attention; and (3) prediction.

For feature extracting and embedding component, trajectories information in two parts are utilized: current trajectory and historical trajectory. The recurrent layer processes the current trajectory to describe complex sequential information. The historical attention module manages the trajectory history to extract the mobility's regularity. The multimodel embedding module must first embed all trajectories prior to this. As mobility transitions are driven by numerous variables, such as time of day and user desire, they are subject to change. Consequently, a multimodal embedding module is utilized to concurrently embed the spatiotemporal data and the personal information into dense representations in order to simulate the complex transitions. In practice, all the available features of one trajectory point including time, location, user ID can be numbered. The numbered features are then converted to one-hot vectors and sent into the multimodel embedding module.

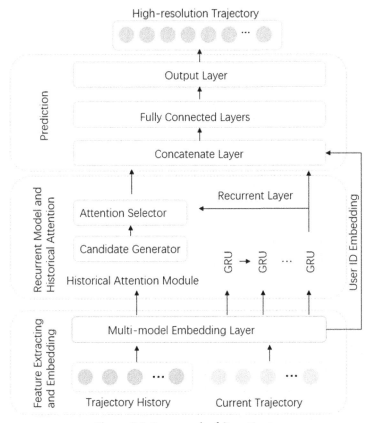

Figure 8.2 Framework of DeepMove.

For recurrent module and historical attention, the recurrent module tries to capture the complicated sequential information or long-range dependencies contained in present trajectory. Due to its computational efficiency and lack of performance degradation, GRU is utilized as the fundamental recurrent unit in this context. The recurrent layer takes the spatiotemporal vector sequence embedded by the multimodel embedding layer as input and outputs the hidden state step by step. The output hidden state goes to the historical attention module and prediction module at each phase. The parallel to the recurrent module is the historical attention module, which is intended to extract mobility regularity from the extensive history data. It receives the historical trajectory as input and returns the most relevant context vector in response to a query vector from the recurrent module.

For prediction, this module is the final component that incorporates the context from other modules to perform the prediction job. It is composed of a concatenate layer, many fully connected layers and an output layer. The concatenate layer combines all of the characteristics from the historical attention module, the recurrent module, and the embedding module into a single vector. After the concatenate layer, fully connected layers transform the feature vector into a vector that is both smaller and more expressive. Here, we adapted the output layer to give out the full trajectory with high resolution. It is possible to make this adaption for the network have enough trajectory information.

5.2 Method 2—convolutional neural network for trajectory prediction [38]

The structure of this method is shown in Fig. 8.3. In contrast to LSTM-based networks, this model handles temporal dependencies using highly

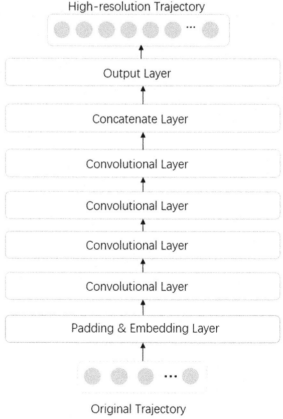

Figure 8.3 Framework of CNN.

parallelizable convolutional layers, for CNN has a straightforward sequence-to-sequence design. As input, trajectory histories are embedded to a given size inside a fully connection layer. Several convolutional layers are used to maintain temporal consistency. The information from the final convolutional layer is then concatenated and fed through a fully connected layer to produce all predicted locations simultaneously.

Here, the predicted trajectory output is continuous rather than discrete, and the architecture forecasts all future time steps simultaneously. The network can be constructed with sufficient depth to extract the context from each time step of the observed trajectory.

In addition, unlike LSTM-based designs that use a recurrent function to calculate sequentially, all the computations in the proposed model are feed-forward in nature, resulting in a large performance improvement in terms of inference time. Additionally, the convolutions can be easily parallelized.

5.3 Method 3—TrajVAE: a variational AutoEncoder model for trajectory generation [39]

For this method, a trajectory generation model based on VAE is designed, named TrajVAE, which can effectively extract the feature of existing trajectories and then convert a noise into similar trajectories. The model structure of TrajVAE is shown in Fig. 8.4.

TrajVAE consists of two segments: Encoder and Decoder. Encoder aims to capture the distribution of training data and transfer it to a latent vector with a lower dimension. Then, Decoder accepts as input the latent vector and turns it back to data. A well-trained Decoder may also be

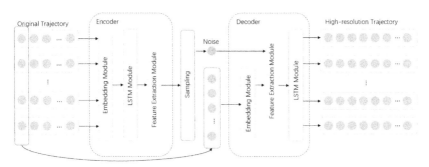

Figure 8.4 Framework of TrajVAE.

employed as a generator capable of decoding a noise sampled from a certain distribution into a sample. Here Long Short Term Memory (LSTM) is capable of learning short and long-term dependencies, making it an effective and scalable model for trajectory generation issues, and the original LSTM architecture has been significantly enhanced. Here, the basic LSTM model is employed in both the Encoder and Decoder for general-purpose applications, and it is simple to adapt to additional LSTM versions. Here, we also have adapted the output of the Decoder to fit this task.

6. Experiments and results

In this section, we compare the performance of different methods from several experiments and with different metrics.

The performance of all models has been presented in Table 8.3 and Table 8.4. Table 8.3 use micro views for evaluation and Table 8.4 use macroviews. It can be observed that:

As shown in Table 8.3, we use metrics in microviews for evaluation. Overall speaking, TrajVAE outperforms DeepMove and CNN on both two datasets. This is because the network structure of DeepMove is simple and can't extract the feature of trajectory effectively. For CNN, the convolution operations can't exploit the high spatial and temporal correlation of trajectory. To some extent, TrajVAE improved on these aspects.

In Table 8.4, we tested on the different time intervals and used macro metrics to evaluate the similarity of overall trajectory distribution. The conclusion is similar. TrajVAE performed better than DeepMove and CNN in most cases. However, the model DeepMove performed better than the other model under some circumstances.

Generally speaking, the performance on the Didi dataset is better than on the ZDC dataset. This is because the research area of the Didi dataset is smaller than on the ZDC dataset, and there are fewer grid cells.

Table 8.3 Comparison between different models on two datasets in microview.

Model	Didi		ZDC	
	nDTW	ADE	nDTW	ADE
DeepMove	1.0400	4.4483	1.6558	7.0617
CNN	0.9905	4.2890	1.4940	6.1590
TrajVAE	0.7244	2.9002	1.2291	5.1793

Table 8.4 Comparison between different models on two datasets in macroview.

Metrics	Sample rate	10 min			20 min			30 min		
	Dataset	DM	TrajVAE	CNN	DM	TrajVAE	CNN	DM	TrajVAE	CNN
SP	Didi	0.8889	0.9414	0.9182	0.9057	0.9245	0.9163	0.9381	0.8910	0.9256
	ZDC	0.9436	0.8720	0.9096	0.9317	0.9019	0.9315	0.9470	0.9161	0.9538
MD	Didi	13878	7680	12731	10344	6718	10984	6414	5663	6714
	ZDC	21686	13506	15607	17081	11233	15672	10626	9254	10172
NMD	Didi	0.6918	0.8069	0.7069	0.7389	0.8183	0.7260	0.8069	0.8304	0.7977
	ZDC	0.7050	0.7711	0.7625	0.7270	0.7868	0.7438	0.7881	0.8041	0.7970
NMA	Didi	0.8467	0.8921	0.8448	0.8559	0.8941	0.8499	0.8800	0.8969	0.8738
	ZDC	0.8596	0.8530	0.8636	0.8597	0.8634	0.8644	0.8739	0.8753	0.8800
RRNSA	Didi	0.8321	0.8907	0.8357	0.8507	0.8920	0.8446	0.8800	0.8969	0.8738
	ZDC	0.8541	0.8451	0.8588	0.8579	0.8594	0.8633	0.8739	0.8753	0.8800

7. Conclusion and discussion

In this chapter, we focus on improving the resolution of trajectory to improve the quality of trajectory and get a high-quality dataset. We compared three different methods, use two different datasets for evaluation, and use two metrics both in microview and macroview to evaluate the performance.

Future efforts might be made to enhance the performance on tiny grids and the degree of accuracy. In addition to the fact that existing approaches primarily rely on spatiotemporal correlation, other information (such as points of interest and life patterns) may be taken into account for human mobility data. These details are beneficial for long-term trajectories.

References

[1] Y. Zheng, Trajectory data mining: an overview, ACM Transactions on Intelligent Systems and Technology (TIST) 6 (3) (2015) 1–41.

[2] Z. Wang, M. Lu, X. Yuan, J. Zhang, H.V.D. Wetering, Visual traffic jam analysis based on trajectory data, IEEE Transactions on Visualization and Computer Graphics 19 (12) (2013) 2159–2168.

[3] Y. Wang, K. Qin, Y. Chen, and P. Zhao, "Detecting anomalous trajectories and behavior patterns using hierarchical clustering from taxi gps data," ISPRS International Journal of Geo-Information, vol. 7, no. 1, p. 25, 2018. [Online]. Available: https://www.mdpi.com/2220-9964/7/1/25.

[4] M. Kohan, J.M. Ale, Discovering traffic congestion through traffic flow patterns generated by moving object trajectories, Computers, Environment and Urban Systems 80 (2020) 101426 [Online]. Available: https://www.sciencedirect.com/science/article/pii/S0198971518305684.

[5] C. Zhang, D. Chu, N. Lyu, and C. Wu, "Trajectory planning and tracking for autonomous vehicle considering human driver personality," in 2019 3rd Conference on Vehicle Control and Intelligence (CVCI), Conference Proceedings, pp. 1–6.

[6] T. Peng, L. Su, R. Zhang, Z. Guan, H. Zhao, Z. Qiu, C. Zong, H. Xu, A new safe lane-change trajectory model and collision avoidance control method for automatic driving vehicles, Expert Systems with Applications 141 (2020) 112953 [Online]. Available: https://www.sciencedirect.com/science/article/pii/S0957417419306712.

[7] J. A. Preiss, K. Hausman, G. S. Sukhatme, and S. Weiss, "Trajectory optimization for self-calibration and navigation," Conference Proceedings.

[8] H. Yang, J. Qi, Y. Miao, H. Sun, J. Li, A new robot navigation algorithm based on a double-layer ant algorithm and trajectory optimization, IEEE Transactions on Industrial Electronics 66 (11) (2019) 8557–8566.

[9] Z. Yang, J. Hu, Y. Shu, P. Cheng, J. Chen, T. Moscibroda, Mobility modeling and prediction in bike-sharing systems, in: Proceedings of the 14th Annual International Conference on Mobile Systems, Applications, and Services, 2016, pp. 165–178.

[10] Z. Chen, H.T. Shen, X. Zhou, Discovering popular routes from trajectories, in: 2011 IEEE 27th International Conference on Data Engineering, IEEE, 2011, pp. 900–911.

[11] I. Goodfellow, J. Pouget-Abadie, M. Mirza, B. Xu, D. Warde-Farley, S. Ozair, A. Courville, Y. Bengio, Generative adversarial nets, Advances in Neural Information Processing Systems 27 (2014).

[12] S. Farsiu, D. Robinson, M. Elad, P. Milanfar, Advances and challenges in super-resolution, International Journal of Imaging Systems and Technology 14 (2) (2004) 47−57.

[13] E.M. Puchner, J.M. Walter, R. Kasper, B. Huang, W.A. Lim, Counting molecules in single organelles with superresolution microscopy allows tracking of the endosome maturation trajectory, Proceedings of the National Academy of Sciences 110 (40) (2013) 16 015−016 020.

[14] Š. Bálint, I.V. Vilanova, Á.S. Álvarez, M. Lakadamyali, Correlative live-cell and super-resolution microscopy reveals cargo transport dynamics at microtubule intersections, Proceedings of the National Academy of Sciences 110 (9) (2013) 3375−3380.

[15] L. Lin, H. Xu, D. Xu, W. An, K. Xie, Qpso-based algorithm of cso joint infrared super-resolution and trajectory estimation, Journal of Systems Engineering and Electronics 22 (3) (2011) 405−411.

[16] Z. Zhang, W. Rao, X. Di, P. Zhao, X. Xu, F.B. Abdesslem, Frequent Pattern-Based Trajectory Completion, 2018, pp. 311−312 [Online]. Available: https://doi.org/10.1145/3274783.3275158.

[17] Y. Li, Y. Li, D. Gunopulos, L. Guibas, Knowledge-based Trajectory Completion from Sparse Gps Samples, 2016, p. Article 33 [Online]. Available: https://doi.org/10.1145/2996913.2996924.

[18] K. Zheng, Y. Zheng, X. Xie, X. Zhou, Reducing uncertainty of low-sampling-rate trajectories, in: 2012 IEEE 28th International Conference on Data Engineering, IEEE, 2012, pp. 1144−1155.

[19] G. Shen, C. Zhang, B. Tang, and R. Yuan, "An area-based method for missing trajectory completion: a stz algorithm," in 2015 8th International Symposium on Computational Intelligence and Design (ISCID), Vol. 2, Conference Proceedings, pp. 184−188.

[20] B. Kim, C.M. Kang, J. Kim, S.H. Lee, C.C. Chung, J.W. Choi, Probabilistic vehicle trajectory prediction over occupancy grid map via recurrent neural network, in: 2017 IEEE 20th International Conference on Intelligent Transportation Systems (ITSC), IEEE, 2017, pp. 399−404.

[21] H. Wang, G. Liu, J. Duan, L. Zhang, Detecting transportation modes using deep neural network, IEICE - Transactions on Info and Systems 100 (5) (2017) 1132−1135.

[22] A. Nawaz, Z. Huang, S. Wang, A. Akbar, H. AlSalman, A. Gumaei, Gps trajectory completion using end-to-end bidirectional convolutional recurrent encoder-decoder architecture with attention mechanism, Sensors 20 (18) (2020) 5143 [Online]. Available: https://www.mdpi.com/1424-8220/20/18/5143.

[23] J. Wang, N. Wu, X. Lu, W.X. Zhao, K. Feng, Deep trajectory recovery with fine-grained calibration using kalman filter, IEEE Transactions on Knowledge and Data Engineering 33 (3) (2021) 921−934.

[24] L. Zhao, Y. Liu, A. Al-Dubai, Z. Tan, G. Min, and L. Xu, "A learning-based vehicle-trajectory generation method for vehicular networking," in 2019 IEEE 21st International Conference on High Performance Computing and Communications; IEEE 17th International Conference on Smart City; IEEE 5th International Conference on Data Science and Systems (HPCC/SmartCity/DSS), Conference Proceedings, pp. 519−526.

[25] A. Ng, "Sparse Autoencoder," CS294A Lecture notes vol. 72, 2011, pp. 1−19.

[26] C. Doersch, Tutorial on Variational Autoencoders, 2016 arXiv:1606.05908, June 01, 2016 [Online]. Available: https://ui.adsabs.harvard.edu/abs/2016arXiv160605908D.

[27] D. Huang, X. Song, Z. Fan, R. Jiang, R. Shibasaki, Y. Zhang, H. Wang, and Y. Kato, "A variational autoencoder based generative model of urban human mobility," in 2019 IEEE Conference on Multimedia Information Processing and Retrieval (MIPR), Conference Proceedings, pp. 425−430.

[28] X. Wang, X. Liu, Z. Lu, H. Yang, Large scale gps trajectory generation using map based on two stage gan, Journal of Data Science 19 (1) (2021) 126−141.

[29] E. Shechtman, Y. Caspi, M. Irani, Space-time super-resolution, IEEE Transactions on Pattern Analysis and Machine Intelligence 27 (4) (2005) 531−545.

[30] O. Shahar, A. Faktor, M. Irani, Space-time Super-resolution from a Single Video, IEEE, 2011.

[31] G. Giannone, E. Hosy, F. Levet, A. Constals, K. Schulze, A.I. Sobolevsky, M.P. Rosconi, E. Gouaux, R. Tampé, D. Choquet, et al., Dynamic superresolution imaging of endogenous proteins on living cells at ultra-high density, Biophysical Journal 99 (4) (2010) 1303−1310.

[32] T. Qu, Y. Zhang, J. Wu, A novel afncs algorithm for super-resolution sar in curve trajectory, Multimedia Systems 27 (4) (2021) 837−844.

[33] E. Keogh, Exact Indexing of Dynamic Time Warping, Morgan Kaufmann, San Francisco, 2002, pp. 406−417 [Online]. Available: https://www.sciencedirect.com/ science/article/pii/B9781558608696500433.

[34] J.B. Kruskal, An overview of sequence comparison: time warps, string edits, and macromolecules, SIAM Review 25 (2) (1983) 201−237.

[35] A. Sadeghian, V. Kosaraju, A. Gupta, S. Savarese, A. Alahi, Trajnet: Towards a Benchmark for Human Trajectory Prediction, 2018 *arXiv preprint.*

[36] Y. Yao, H. Zhang, J. Chen, W. Li, M. Shibasaki, R. Shibasaki, X. Song, Mobsimilarity: Vector Graph Optimization for Mobility Tableau Comparison, 2021 arXiv: 2104.13139, April 01, 2021 [Online]. Available: https://ui.adsabs.harvard.edu/abs/ 2021arXiv210413139Y.

[37] J. Feng, Y. Li, C. Zhang, F. Sun, F. Meng, A. Guo, D. Jin, Deepmove: predicting human mobility with attentional recurrent networks, in: Proceedings of the 2018 World Wide Web Conference, 2018, pp. 1459−1468.

[38] N. Nikhil, B.T. Morris, Convolutional Neural Network for Trajectory Prediction, 2018 *arXiv preprint arXiv:1809.00696.*

[39] X. Chen, J. Xu, R. Zhou, W. Chen, J. Fang, C. Liu, Trajvae: a variational autoencoder model for trajectory generation, Neurocomputing 428 (2021) 332−339.

CHAPTER NINE

Map-matching for low accuracy trajectory data

Yuhao Yao[1], Haoran Zhang[2]

[1]Center for Spatial Information Science, The University of Tokyo, Kashiwa-shi, Chiba, Japan
[2]School of Urban Planning and Design, Peking University, Shenzhen, China

1. Introduction

Map-matching is a process in which the orderly GPS position sequence of vehicles is associated with the road network of an electronic map, and the sampling sequence under the GPS coordinate is converted into sequence under the coordinate of the road network (Fig. 9.1).

For low accuracy trajectory data, map-matching means estimating the ground truth position on the road network based on the corresponding possible position region. Different from accurate GPS map-matching, the distance between the known position and the ground truth position is usually very large, which makes it very complex to estimate the real position.

Some researchers interpolate the missing location information due to long time intervals based on spatial-temporal correlations among data. They assume that the relationship between the missing points and the given points could be described as a simple mathematical model such as a Gaussian function. For interpolation, features like distances and time span between the missing point and its contextual points are utilized to measure weights and estimate the missing point's position [1−4].

Some researchers also utilize artificial intelligence to learn the latent pattern of human mobility to generate the missing records. Historical trajectories are utilized to explore the characteristics of human movement behavior, which greatly improve various models. For instance, Fan et al. [5] proposed a collaborative filtering method based on the LDA topic model to infer the movement of people. Liu et al. [6] utilized a back propagation neural network based on the gyration radius as an indicator to estimate the mobile phone user's position. Li et al. [7] proposed a multi-criteria data partitioning technique to measure the similarity among individuals for the reconstruction model.

Handbook of Mobility Data Mining, Volume 1
ISBN: 978-0-443-18428-4
https://doi.org/10.1016/B978-0-443-18428-4.00007-4
157

Fore map-matching, there is a basic assumption that people always move on the road network [8−10]. Then each location point in the trajectory corresponds with a road segment in the road network, and these road segments form the complete trajectory. To find the corresponding road segment, Jagadeesh et al. [11] utilized a Hidden Markov Model to generate coarse map-matched trajectories and identified it based on a pretraining route selecting a model to get a more accurate result. Xiao et al. [12] reconstruct trajectories from CDR based on a conditional random field model, in which the contextual relationships between different trajectory points are utilized as indicator features.

Assume that the road network is G, the time interval of the low accuracy data is T, a trip segment in moving mode M of an individual u starting at time t as $R(u, t, M) = \{r_0, r_1, ..., r_n\}$, the corresponding ground truth position sequence is $P(u, t) = \{p_0, p_1, ..., p_n\}$, p_i is the position of u at $t + T*i$, where $p_i \in G$, $0 \leq i \leq n$. We need to estimate $P(u, t)$ based on $R(u, t, M)$.

After map-matching, a sparse trajectory with original low accuracy data time interval T has been obtained. However, the original low accuracy data time interval is usually relatively large, which makes the route between every two points still unclear. Therefore, we need to interpolate the sparse trajectory into a fine trajectory. That is, for a coarse position sequence $P(u, t) = \{(p_0, t), (p_1, t + T), ..., (p_n, t + T * n)\}$, p_i is the position of u at $t + T*i$, where $p_i \in G$, $0 \leq i \leq n$, we need to estimate a fine position sequence as $P'(u, t) = \{(p_0', t_0), (p_1', t_0), ..., (p_m', t_m)\}$, p_i' is the position of u at t_i, where $p_i' \in G$, $(p_i', p_{i+1}') \in G$, $0 \leq i \leq m$.

2. Traditional map-matching method

The existing map-matching algorithms could be divided into four categories: *geometry, topology, probability,* and *advanced.*

- *Geometry*: The geometric information of known points, such as the moving distance and angle of turn of trajectory, is considered in the algorithm.
- *Topology*: Topology-based algorithm utilizes road topology information to control the result [13].
- *Probability*: The probability method matches the points based on the probability of the case.
- *Advanced*: Advanced algorithms often consider the utilization of comprehensive information, such as *Kalman filter, Fuzzy Logic Model, Hidden Markov Hodel,* and so on [14,15].

According to the range of sampling points, map-matching algorithms could also be divided into two types: *local/incremental algorithm* and *global algorithm*.

- *Local/Incremental Algorithm*: Local/Incremental algorithm is a greedy algorithm, which just determines one matching point at one time, and the next point starts from the determined matching point [16]. These methods find the local optimum point or edge according to the similarity of moving distance and moving direction.

- *Global Algorithm*: The global algorithm aims to find a matching trajectory that is closest to the sampling trajectory based on the road network. To measure the similarity between the sample trajectory and the matching trajectory, algorithms like *Frechet Distance* or *Weak Frechet Distance* are usually applied [17]. Some other algorithms are also popular, like *Space-time Matching Algorithm, Voting Algorithm,* and so on [18−20].

Generally speaking, among all these methods, Hidden Markov Model-based methods have the best performance. They assume the ground truth position in road networks as hidden states and utilize both geometry and topology information as observable information to form a Hidden Markov Model and decode the target sequence. As an advanced global algorithm, these methods could achieve more than 90% accuracy.

Normal Hidden Markov Model-based map-matching methods believe that for a given GPS position, the corresponding ground truth position is usually the closest point in one of the road segments around. Therefore, the candidate position set could be regarded as hidden states. The least time cost of paths between two continuous points is usually assumed as the indicator of transfer probability, and the distance between the possible point and original GPS position is usually assumed as the indicator of emission probability.

Obviously, most of the HMM-based traditional map-matching methods cannot be directly applied to low accuracy data because of the difference between low accuracy data and GPS. The large sampling time interval and possible distance between known position and ground truth make most of the useful features as observable states lost, such as the moving direction, the stop interval, the angle of turn, etc.

3. Multi-steps least cost algorithm

We propose a *Multi-Steps Least Cost Algorithm* to solve both the map-matching problem and the interpolation problem. To introduce it, we first introduce two indicator factors for map-matching, then we introduce the basic *Dijkstra algorithm*, we build a Hidden Markov Model for the map-matching problem, and finally simplify it into a multi-step shortest path problem, which could be solved by our method.

3.1 Indicator factors

For a given position Y as the center of the possible range, assume that the nodes of the road network in its coverage area with radius R are nodes set $S = \{node_0, node_1, ..., node_n\}$. In consideration that due to the information loss, restoring the precise position of the mobile terminator holder as what GPS can is impossible, we assume that every time when the low accuracy data is generated, the device holder is at one node of the road network. Therefore, it is possible for all the nodes in S to be a candidate ground truth position of the mobile terminator holder. Since observable attributions of low accuracy data sequences are too limited, the probability of each node to be the ground truth is mainly indicated by two factors.

The first one is the connecting probability, which is associated with the distance between the node and the center of the possible range.

The second one is the least impedance (usually the least time cost) of the paths between two continuous points. Two nodes that are easy to move from one to the other are obviously more reasonable than two nodes that are nearly impassable.

To calculate the impedance, traditional GPS map-matching methods usually utilize the length of the path. Some methods also assign average speed to each road segment based on its road type and calculate the time cost, which is more reasonable. *Dijkstra Algorithm* is applied to find the least impedance path between two points.

However, those methods ignore an important feature, which is the moving mode of the device holder. For GPS data, using the length of the road to divide the assigned average speed as impedance may be reasonable because GPS data is usually collected by vehicles, which need to obey the speed limit of the road and have different speeds on different roads. When it comes to low-accuracy data, things are different.

While the mobile terminator device holder is driving or taking motor vehicles, of course, the time cost of the trip could be calculated by the road length and assigned speed. But when the device holder is taking a nonmotorized way, the type of the road almost does not affect the holder's moving speed. For instance, if the device holder needs to move from A to B. There are two routes for the holder to choose: one is a small direct path with a length of 0.2 km, and the other is the main road but needs to take a big turn, of which the length is 0.5 km. We assume the average speed for vehicles on a small path is 20 km/h and on the main road is 60 km/h. If the moving mode of the device holder is the *motor* type, obviously, he will choose the main road because the time cost is 0.5 km/(60 km/h), nearly 30 s, while a small path will take 0.2 km/(20 km/h) nearly 36 s. But if his moving mode is a *non-motorized* type, of which the moving speed is a constant value, such as 5 km/h, he will choose the small path, which is shorter with no doubt. In addition, if the mobile terminator device holder is in *metro* mode, he must move on the metro line, which will be far away from the route of the shortest path.

Therefore, we apply a different strategy for different moving modes:

- *Non-motorized* Mode: For this moving mode, we utilize the whole road network and just utilize the length of the road as the road impedance.
- *Metro* Mode: For this moving mode, we extract metro lines from the road network to compose the metro road network. We just utilize the length of the road as the road impedance. When the time interval is not large, the cost will not affect too much because usually, there is just one route that could be selected.
- *Motor* Mode: For this moving mode, we first remove all roads with road types that cannot find the corresponding speed limitation, such as *path*, and *pedestrian*, to form the motor road network. Because these road types are not for vehicles but just for pedestrians. Then we assign the speed limit as the average speed to each road type. The speed limitation of each road type varies in different countries.

Assume that the length of the road is L, the speed limit of the road is V, and the basic impedance I of the road is:

$$I = \frac{L}{V} \# \tag{3.1}$$

However, the impedance of the road should not be constant. This kind of calculation method ignores the load of the road. When the number of vehicles on the road is smaller than the capacity of the road, which means there is no traffic jam on this road, vehicles can move an average speed, and the impedance makes sense. Once on some core roads, especially during the commute time, the vehicles are too much that exceed the capacity of the road, the average speed will dramatically dropdown. If we simply utilize this impedance as the indicator for map–matching and interpolation, the result will be that all vehicles prefer to select several core roads ignoring the number of vehicles on this road, and the number of vehicles on these roads will seriously exceed the ground truth number.

To solve it, we combine the impedance with *The Bureau of Public Roads Function*. *The Bureau of Public Roads (BPR) Function* is utilized to calculate the free travel time of road sections. In the traffic assignment stage of the stages for traffic planning, the time impedance of a certain road section should be considered to allocate the traffic flow. The correction of road travel time can be determined according to the relationship between travel time and road traffic volume, i.e., the road impedance function.

The BPR function could be described as:

$$t_i = t_{i0} * \left(1 + \alpha \left(\frac{Q}{C} \right)^{\beta} \right) \#$$

(3.2)

Where t_i is the actual time cost required to pass through the road section. t_{i0} is the free time cost of the road section, i.e., assume that there is no other vehicle on the road. Q is the traffic volume passing through the road section at that time. C is the actual traffic capacity of the road section. α and β are the undetermined parameters of the model, of which the recommended values are respectively 0.15 and 4. However, since the traffic environment varies in different countries, the value should be determined according to the actual situation.

In consideration that the actual capacity of each road section is unknown from the road network, but the number of lines in each road is known, which is related to the capacity, we utilize the number of lines multiply a coefficient to replace the capacity. The coefficient could be merged into α. To save calculating time, we save the temporal traffic volume in Q(*road, timewindow*). Every time when a new trajectory is determined, the traffic volume will be updated. In this case, at first, Q for each road is empty, and the route will be chosen for free. With more and more trips interpolated at that time, route choosing will be seriously affected by traffic volume. In this way, we do not need to calculate it twice to get the traffic volume first and reallocate the volume then. Although in this way, the trajectory for an individual may not be close to the ground truth because, which trip is earlier is random, the aggregated statistic data will be close to the ground truth like traffic volume.

The new impedance function could be constructed as:

$$I = \frac{L}{V} * \left(1 + \left(\frac{Q}{\alpha C} \right)^{\beta} \right) \#$$

(3.3)

Parameters α and β is determined by the dataset scale.

3.2 Dijkstra algorithm

The Dijkstra algorithm was proposed by the Dutch computer scientist Dijkstra in 1959. It is the shortest path algorithm from one vertex to other vertices, which solves the shortest path problem in weighted graphs with nonnegative weights from a single source. The main feature of Dijkstra algorithm is that it starts from the starting point and utilizes the greedy algorithm strategy. Each time, it traverses the neighbor node of the nearest vertex, which is not visited from the starting point until it extends to the endpoint.

Assume that $G = (V, E)$ is the graph, where V is the set of vertices, E is the set of edges, $E(v_i, v_j)$ means the distance between vertex v_i and vertex v_j, the start point is v_0. Prepare a set S to represent the vertices that have been checked, then $V-S$ is the vertices that have not been checked. We utilize a vector $dist$ to store the distance between the points and a vector $path$ to store the passed by vertices, which could be utilized to interpret what the shortest path is. The process of the Dijkstra Algorithm could be described as follows:

- Step 1: Initialize S as $\{v_0\}$. For vertex v_i in $V-S$, if $E(v_0, v_i)$ exists, set $dist(v_i) = E(v_0, v_i)$ and record v_0 into $path(v_i)$; else set it NAN.
- Step 2: For any point in S, obtain the distance between it and any point in $V-S$ from $dist$. Select the point with the smallest distance and record it, which is the new point for the shortest path that could be determined. Assume the last vertex as min, and put min into S.
- Step 3: Set min in Step 2 as the intermediate node, find all the vertices in $V-S$, and set it as K to check whether:

$$dist(min) + E(min, K) < dist(K)\# \tag{3.4}$$

If so, update $dist(K)$ into the value of $dist(min) + E(min, K)$, and $path(K)$ records min.

- Step 4: Repeat Step 2 and Step 3 until S has all the vertices or there is no new route.

Finally, we get the shortest path of v_n by $path(v_n)$ and shortest distance $dis(v_n)$.

3.3 Original Hidden Markov Model

For the traditional HMM-based map-matching method, the two features mentioned in 3.1 could be described as two indicators of transfer probability and emission probability.

Assume that the road network is G, the time interval of the low accuracy data is T, and a low accuracy data trip segment in moving mode M of an individual u starts at time t as R $(u, t, M) = \{r_0, r_1, \ldots, r_n\}$.

Define a function $F_t(x)$ and $F_p(x)$ to normalize the path cost and the connecting probability. The smaller the path cost is, the larger the F_t will be. The larger the probability is, the larger the F_p will be.

Then the process of the original Hidden Markov Model will be:

- Assign the closest node in the road network for start and end position as ground truth position for the start point and end point, then for middle-low accuracy data set $R' = \{ r_1, \ldots, r_{n-1}\}$, we find the nodes set $S_i = \{node_0, node_1, \ldots, node_n\}$ that are in the coverage area with radius R of r_i, where $1 \leq i \leq n - 1$. Set $S_0 = \{node_{start}\}$ and $S_n = \{node_{end}\}$.

- For each node pair $(node_j, node_k)$, where $node_j \in S_i$, $node_k \in S_{i+1}$, $0 \leq i \leq n - 1$, calculate the least time cost $\Delta t(j, k)$ by $Dijkstra\ Algorithm$.

- For $node_j \in S_i$, $0 \leq i \leq n$, calculate the probability of $node_j$ to connect to the position in r_i as P_j.

- Decode the best ground truth position sequence $\{node_0, node_1, \ldots, node_n\}$ to fit the low accuracy data sequence, in which:

$$\{node_0, node_1, \ldots, node_n\} = argmax\big(F_t(\Delta t(0, 1)) * F_p(P_1) * F_t(\Delta t(1, 2))$$
$$*\ldots*F_t(\Delta t(n - 2, n - 1)) * F_p(P_{n-1})$$
$$*F_t(\Delta t(n - 1, n)))\big)$$

$$(3.5)$$

3.4 Model simplifying

The Hidden Markov Model defined in Section 3.3 already has the ability to solve the low accuracy data map-matching problem. However, we may find that it has several limitations:

- Need to build two normalization functions for two indicator factors, which will increase the complexity of model training but has little help for improving accuracy.

- $Dijkstra\ Algorithm$ is frequently applied to find the least cost route, which may have lots of replication computation and is not efficient.

- Interpolation step shares the same method in calculating the least cost route, which could be done together.

To address these limitations, we start to simplify the Hidden Markov Model. First, we do a logarithm for (4.5) to get:

$$\{node_0,\ node_1,\ \dots,\ node_n\} = argmax\big(\log\big(F_t(\Delta t(0,1))$$
$$*F_p(P_1)*F_t(\Delta t(1,2))* \dots *F_t(\Delta t(n-2,n-1))$$
$$*F_p(P_{n-1})*F_t(\Delta t(n-1,n))\big)\big)$$
$$= argmax\big(\log(F_t(\Delta t(0,1))) + \log\big(F_p(P_1)\big)$$
$$+ \log(F_t(\Delta t(1,2))) + \dots$$
$$+ \log(F_t(\Delta t(n-2,n-1))) + \log\big(F_p(P_{n-1})\big)$$
$$+ \log(F_t(\Delta t(n-1,n)))\big)$$

$$(3.6)$$

Define two functions $F_t{'}(x)$ and $F_p{'}(x)$, which have a negative correlation with x, to make the equation still hold as:

$$\{node_0,\ node_1,\ \dots,\ node_n\} = argmin\Big(F_t'(\log(F_t(\Delta t(0,1)))$$
$$\times\ ) + F_p'\big(\log\big(F_p(p_1)\big)\big) + F_t'(\log(F_t(\Delta t(1,2)))$$
$$\times\ ) + \dots + F_t'(\log(F_t(\Delta t(n-2,n-1)))) + F_p'\big(\log\big(F_p(p_{n-1})\big)$$
$$\times\ ) + F_t'(\log(F_t(\Delta t(n-1,n))))\Big)$$

$$(3.7)$$

Based on (3.7), the Hidden Markov Model decoding problem is transferred into a kind of multi-steps shortest path problem, as Fig. 9.1 shows:

For a given graph G, start node $node_{start}$, end node $node_{end}$, nodes set $S_i = \{node_0,\ node_1,\ \dots,\ node_k\}$ from a given nodes set sequence $S = \{S_1, S_2,\ \dots,\ S_{n-1}\}$, the road impedance cost of $node_j$ to $node_k$ is $F_t'(\log(F_t(\Delta t(j,k))))$, the first time passing $\forall\ node_l \in S_i$, $1 \le i \le n-1$ need extra probability cost $F_p'\big(\log\big(F_p(p_l)\big)\big)$.

In order to save the calculating time, every time processing the shortest path problem, we do not utilize the whole road network; instead, we create

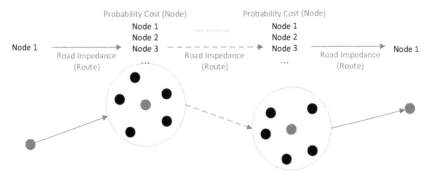

Figure 9.1 Multi-steps Shortest Path Problem of Map-matching and Interpolation.

a subroad network as follows: We calculate the centroid of the start nodes cluster plus end nodes cluster as the center of the circle, and then we utilize the maximum distance between this centroid and any node in start nodes cluster or end nodes cluster plus 2 km as the radius to create the circle. We utilize all the nodes and edges in this circle from the road network to create the subroad network.

To further simplify the problem, we define:

$$F'_t(\log(F_t(\Delta t(i,j)))) = \Delta t(i,j) \# \tag{3.8}$$

$$F'_p(\log(F_p(p_i))) = \frac{\alpha}{1 + \beta * p_i} \# \tag{3.9}$$

where α and β are the undetermined parameters. α controls the influence of connecting probability indicators. β controls the difference between large connecting probability and small connecting probability. These two parameters are mainly determined by sampling interval because it controls the average time cost between two nodes.

Then, the problem of map-matching and interpolation could be solved together by a multi-step Dijkstra algorithm as follow:

Assume that $G = (V, E)$ is the graph, where V is the set of vertices, E is the set of edges, Δt (v_i, v_j) is the cost between vertex v_i and vertex v_j. Start vertex set is $C_0 = \{v_{start}\}$, End vertex set is $C_n = \{v_{end}\}$, middle nodes set $C_i = \{v_0, v_1, \ldots, v_k\}$ from a given nodes set sequence $C = \{C_1, C_2, \ldots, C_{n-1}\}$ need to be passed. Utilize C_{last} to present the last nodes cluster that needs to pass and C_{next} to present the next nodes cluster that needs to pass. Prepare a set S to represent the vertices that have been checked, then $V-S$ is the vertices that have not been checked. We utilize a vector *dist* to store the cost between the points, a vector *path* to store the passed by vertices, which interprets what the shortest path is, and a vector *time* to store the arriving time for vertices.

- Step 1: Initialize S as $\{v_{start}\}$. $C_{last} = C_0$, $C_{next} = C_2$. Construct the subgraph $G' \in G$ between C_{last} and C_{next} as the temporal graph. For vertex v_i in $V-S$, if Δt (v_0, v_i) exists, set $dist(v_i) = \Delta t$ (v_0, v_i) and record v_0 into $path(v_i)$; else set it NAN.

- Step 2: For any point in S, obtain the distance between it and any point in $V-S$ from *dist*. Select the point with the least cost and record it, which is the new point for the shortest path that could be determined. Assume the last vertex as *min*, and put min into S.

- Step 3: Set min in Step 2 as the intermediate node, find all the vertices in $V-S$, and set it as K to check whether $dist(min) + \Delta t(min, K) < dist$ (K). If so, update $dist(K)$ into the value of $dist(min) + E(min, K)$, and $path(K)$ records min.
- Step 4: Repeat Step 2 and Step 3 until $C_{next} \in S$ there is no new route.
- Step 5: If $C_{next} = C_n$, Finish. For v_i in C_{next} and corresponding v_j in C_{last}, for v_k in $path(v_i) - path(v_j)$, record $t_k = t_j + \left(t_i - t_j\right) * \frac{dist(v_k) - dist(v_j)}{dist(v_i) - dist(v_j)}$ into $time(v_k)$. Update $dist(v_i) = dist(v_i) + \frac{\alpha}{1+\beta * p_i}$. For v_i in $S - C_{last}$, initialize $dist(v_i) = \{\}$ and $path(v_i) = \{\}$. Initialize S as C_{last}. $C_{last} = C_{next}$, $C_{next} = C_{next+1}$, Go back to Step 2.

The map-matched and interpolated path is $(path(v_{end}), time(v_{end}))$.

The pseudo-code is as follows:

```
Multi-Steps Range Dijkstra.
    Input: graph G with vertices sets V and edges E
    start vertex v_start, start time t_start, end vertex v_end, end time t_end
    middle connected position sequence C, corresponding time sequence T
    nodes set in the coverage area of each position function R
    road impedance indicator function Δt and connecting probability indicator
function P.
    Output: moving path and corresponding time sequence
    d[v_start] ← 0
    path[v_start] ← v
    last[v_start] ← v
    for each v ∈ V - {v_start}
        do d[v] ← ∞
    path[v] ← ∅
        end.
    S ← {v_start}
    For each c ∈ C, corresponding t ∈ T.
        do while (V−S) ∩ R(c) ≠ ∅
            do u ← Extract-Min(V−S).
            S ← S ∪ {u}
            for each v ∈ Adj(u)
                do if d[v] > d[u] + Δt (u, v)
                    then d[v] = d[u] + Δt (u, v), path[v] ← path[u]+u, last[v] ← last[u]
                end.
            end
        for each v ∈ R[c]
        do for each k ∈ path[v]
```

(Continued)

(cont'd)

do   time[v][k] ← time[v][last[k]]+(t-time[v][last[k]])*(d[k]-d[last[k]])/(d[v]-d[last
[k])
   end
   end
   for each v ∈ R[c]
   do d[v] ← d[v]+P[v]
   for each v ∈ V - R[c]
     do d[v] ← ∞
   path[v] ← ∅
     end.
     S ← R[c]
   end
   do while (V−S)∩{v_{end}}≠∅
     do u ← Extract-Min(V−S)
     S ← S∪{u}
   for each v ∈ Adj(u)
     do if d[v] > d[u] + Δt (u, v)
       then d[v] = d[u] + Δt (u, v), path[v] ← path[u]+u, last[v] ← last[u]
     end
   end
   for each v ∈ R[c]
   do for each k ∈ path[v]
   do   time[v][k] ← time[v][last[k]]+(t-time[v][last[k]])*(d[k]-d[last[k]])/(d[v]-d
[last[k])
   end
   end
   return path[v_{end}], time[v_{end}]

4. Real world application

In this section, we map-match CDR data (the position of the cell tower could be regarded as the possible vehicle position) and compare the result with the map-matched GPS data as ground truth to validate the performance of the introduced method.

The GPS data is a part of *Konzatu-Tokei(R)* provided by *Zenrin DataCom INC. Konzatsu-Tokei (R)* Data refers to people flow data collected by individual's location data sent from a mobile phones under utilizers' consent, through Applications provided by *NTT DOCOMO, INC.* These data are processed collectively and statistically in order to conceal private information. Original location data is GPS data (latitude, longitude) sent in about every 5 min and does not include the information to specify an individual. We randomly select 10,000 users in 1 month (each user may not be available every day).

The road network we use is extracted from *OpenStreetMap (OSM)*. OSM is an online map collaboration project, which aims to create a world map with free content that can be edited by everyone.

We first validate the similarity between the map-matched whole-day trajectory from CDR data and the ground truth trajectory.

To measure the similarity, we utilize three metrics:

· *Non-Coincidence Ratio*: We compare the map-matched trajectory with the ground truth trajectory and record the length of the noncoincidence part in the estimated trajectory to divide the total length of the estimated trajectory as *Non-Coincidence Ratio*.

· *Average Dynamic Time Warping (DTW) Distance*: *DTW Distance* is a value to measure the similarity of two-time series with different lengths. To measure the average *DTW Distance* between estimated trajectory A and ground truth trajectory B, we map points in A to points in B in time sequence by dynamic programming to ensure the total distance is the shortest one, then calculate the average distance between each node pair.

· *Fréchet Distance*: *Fréchet Distance* is a value to measure the space similarity between two paths, proposed by French mathematician *Maurice René Fréchet* in 1906. To measure *Fréchet Distance* between estimated trajectory A and ground truth trajectory B, we first find the shortest distance for each point in A with B, then find the maximum one in these shortest distances as *Fréchet Distance*.

To validate the map-matched result, the baseline method we use is as follows:

· *Nearest Shortest*: In this method, we assume that the ground truth position of each CDR is the closest node in the road network to the cell tower. Then we directly apply *Dijkstra Algorithm* to interpolate the trajectory, of which the road impedance is set as the time cost.

· *OD Shortest*: In this method, we assume that the device holder always moves on the shortest path between origin and destination. Therefore, we assume the closest node in the road network to the cell tower is the ground truth position of origin and destination. Then for each trip segment, we ignore the middle CDR and directly apply *Dijkstra Algorithm* to interpolate the trajectory just for origin and destination, of which the road impedance is set as the time cost.

· *Map-matching of Hidden Markov Model*: In this method, we utilize a classical HMM-based map-matching method [15] to map-match the CDR and utilize Dijkstra Algorithm to interpolate the trajectory, of which the road impedance is set as the time cost.

The cell tower density is nearly $40/\text{km}^2$. The average comparison result is shown in Table 9.1.

From the table, we can see that for three metrics, our method all has the best result. Especially, we may find that the result of the HMM-based map-matching method is similar to the nearest shortest method, that is because, in this method, the distance between the possible node and the cell tower is regarded as an important feature, so the model prefers to select a closer node and becomes similar with the nearest shortest method.

We also validate the accuracy of traffic volume and average speed estimation based on the simulation dataset. We aggregate the data from 1 month into 1 day in order to expand the traffic volume to avoid the traffic volume being too small. We set the time window as hourly. Assume that the ground truth traffic volume of road i in time window tw is $V_t(tw, i)$, while the estimated traffic volume is $V_e(tw, i)$, and the ground truth average speed of road i in time window tw is $S_t(tw, i)$, while the estimated average speed is $S_e(tw, i)$, we measure the accuracy by:

· Error rate of traffic volume:

$$Error\ Rate = \frac{\sum\sum\sum(|V_t(tw,\ i) - V_e(tw,\ i)|)}{\sum\sum\sum(V_t(tw,\ i))}\# \quad (4.1)$$

· Coefficient of determination of traffic volume:

$$r^2 = 1 - \frac{\sum\sum\sum(V_t(tw,\ i) - V_e(tw,\ i))^2}{\sum\sum\sum(V_t(tw,\ i) - \overline{V_t})^2}\# \quad (4.2)$$

· Error rate of average speed:

Table 9.1 Trajectory similarity in different methods.

	Non-coincidence ratio	Average DTW distance	Fréchet distance
Our method	47.89%	75.36 m	258.12 m
Nearest shortest	55.61%	113.29 m	435.13 m
OD shortest	59.23%	259.89 m	732.84 m
MM with HMM	53.37%	102.91 m	416.58 m

$$Error\ Rate\ = \frac{\sum\sum\sum(|S_t(tw,\ i) - S_e(tw,\ i)|)}{\sum\sum\sum(S_t(tw,\ i))}\#$$ (4.3)

· Coefficient of determination of average speed:

$$r^2 = 1 - \frac{\sum\sum\sum(S_t(tw,\ i) - S_e(tw,\ i))^2}{\sum\sum\sum(S_t(tw,\ i) - \overline{S_t})^2}\#$$ (4.4)

We validate the result under the sampling condition of 40/km² cell tower density and 5 min time interval. The baseline methods are the same as before. The result is shown in Table 9.2.

We could see that the result of our method still has the best performance. Even though for r^2 of traffic volume, the nearest shortest method has a better value, it does not matter because the difference is very small.

For average speed, we may find that even though the error rate is not high, the r^2 is less than optimal. That may be because, for some roads that are not the main road, the traffic volume is still not too large, so the average speed may have a big fluctuation.

We also analyze the result in different sampling conditions, as Table 9.3 shows.

From the table, we could find that when the cell tower density is not sparse, the density change will not affect the accuracy of traffic volume and average speed estimation too much, but once it is very dense, the error rate will sharply rise. That may be because when the density is dense, the connected cell tower is close to the ground truth and the ground truth path is the unique minimum cost route in the connected cell tower's coverage area. When the density change, the distance between the connected cell tower and ground truth position becomes large, and more routes will be competitive for the model to select, which will lead to lower accuracy.

We may also find that time interval affects the result seriously. That is because, on the one hand, when the time interval gets longer, much

Table 9.2 Accuracy of traffic volume estimation comparison.

	Traffic volume		Average speed	
	Error rate	r^2	Error rate	r^2
Our method	24.64%	0.9207	26.02%	0.5282
Nearest shortest	33.80%	0.9298	28.40%	0.5098
OD shortest	43.67%	0.7843	37.22%	0.4396
MM with HMM	31.34%	0.9223	26.96%	0.5119

Table 9.3 Accuracy of traffic volume estimation in different conditions.

	Traffic volume		Average speed	
	Error rate	r^2	Error rate	r^2
5 min, 120/km^2	23.82%	0.9216	24.30%	0.5801
5 min, 40/km^2	24.64%	0.9207	26.02%	0.5282
5 min, 10/km^2	26.67%	0.9080	28.40%	0.5098
5 min, 2.5/km^2	34.28%	0.8651	33.51%	0.4142
5 min, 0.5/km^2	45.76%	0.7517	39.55%	0.4096
5 min, 40/km^2	24.64%	0.9207	26.02%	0.5282
10 min, 40/km^2	28.56%	0.8933	28.63%	0.4716
15 min, 40/km^2	37.80%	0.8705	31.46%	0.4474
30 min, 40/km^2	55.28%	0.8413	36.48%	0.4114
1 h, 40/km^2	79.71%	0.8136	46.85%	0.3544

important information will be lost. On the other hand, as we mentioned before that the accuracy of mode detection for *Motor* mode would be seriously affected, so the total number of device holders on the road is dramatically dropped.

We also demonstrate *Traffic Volume-Time Window* graph and *Average Speed-Time Window* graph for two representative cases, i.e., road segments in Fig. 9.2, in different sampling conditions to show the result more intuitively in Figs. 9.3 and 9.4.

From Figs. 9.3 and 9.4, we can see more clearly that when the time interval gets longer, the number of device holders on the road is dramatically dropped, and the average speed is influenced because the road lacks enough vehicles to calculate speed.

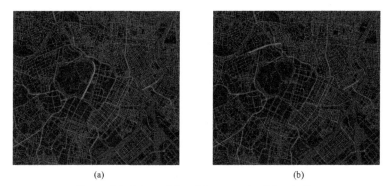

(a)   (b)

Figure 9.2 Selected Road Segment in Chiyoda Ku.

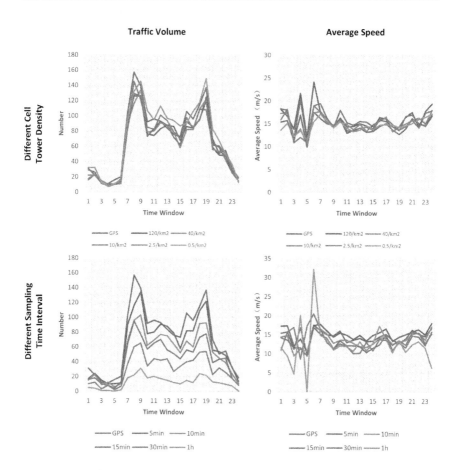

Figure 9.3 Traffic Volume versus Time Window and Average Speed versus Time Window for (A).

In the case of A, we select a road that is the main road without too many candidates in the same road type. The estimated traffic flow is very close to the ground truth. In the case of B, we select a road that has some candidate roads, so we can find the estimated traffic volume is much higher than the ground truth because in map-matching and interpolation steps, the assigned average speed is not so proper to calculate the time impedance, so in residents' real movement they may prefer another route instead, but in our estimation we assume they all select this road segment.

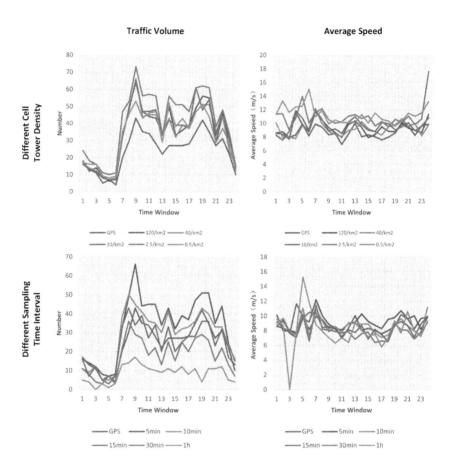

Figure 9.4 Traffic Volume versus Time Window and Average Speed versus Time Window for (B).

References

[1] M. Ficek, L. Kencl, Inter-Call Mobility model: a spatio-temporal refinement of call data records using a Gaussian mixture model, in: 2012 Proceedings IEEE INFOCOM, IEEE, 2012, pp. 469—477.

[2] S. Hoteit, S. Secci, S. Sobolevsky, G. Pujolle, C. Ratti, Estimating real human trajectories through mobile phone data, in: 2013 IEEE 14th International Conference on Mobile Data Management (MDM 2013), IEEE, Los Alamitos, 2013, pp. 148—153.

[3] S. Hoteit, S. Secci, S. Sobolevsky, C. Ratti, G. Pujolle, Estimating human trajectories and hotspots through mobile phone data, Computer Networks 64 (2014) 296—307.

[4] H. Yu, A. Russell, J. Mulholland, Z. Huang, Using cell phone location to assess misclassification errors in air pollution exposure estimation, Environmental Pollution 233 (2018) 261—266.

[5] Z. Fan, A. Arai, X. Song, A. Witayangkurn, H. Kanasugi, R. Shibasaki, A collaborative filtering approach to citywide human mobility completion from sparse call records, in:

S. Kambhampati (Ed.), Proceedings of the Twenty-Fifth International Joint Conference on Artificial Intelligence (IJCAI-16), AAAI Press, Palo Alto, 2016, pp. 2500−2506.

[6] Z. Liu, T. Ma, Y. Du, T. Pei, J. Yi, H. Peng, Mapping hourly dynamics of urban population using trajectories reconstructed from mobile phone records, Transactions in GIS 22 (2018) 494−513.

[7] M. Li, S. Gao, F. Lu, H. Zhang, Reconstruction of human movement trajectories from large-scale low-frequency mobile phone data, Computers, Environment and Urban Systems 77 (2019) 101346.

[8] G.R. Jagadeesh, T. Srikanthan, Probabilistic map-matching of sparse and noisy smartphone location data, in: 2015 IEEE 18th International Conference on Intelligent Transportation Systems (ITSC 2015), IEEE, Los Alamitos, 2015, pp. 812−817.

[9] J. Chen, M. Bierlaire, Probabilistic multimodal map-matching with rich smartphone data, Journal of Intelligent Transportation Systems 19 (2015) 134−148.

[10] E. Algizawy, T. Ogawa, A. El-Mahdy, Real-time large-scale map-matching using mobile phone data, ACM Transactions on Knowledge Discovery from Data 11 (2017) 52.

[11] G.R. Jagadeesh, T. Srikanthan, Online map-matching of noisy and sparse location data with hidden Markov and route choice models, IEEE Transactions on Intelligent Transportation Systems 18 (2017) 2423−2434.

[12] Z. Xiao, H. Wen, A. Markham, N. Trigoni, Lightweight map-matching for indoor localization using conditional random fields, in: IPSN'14: Proceedings of the 13th International Symposium on Information Processing in Sensor Networks, IEEE, Piscataway, 2014, pp. 131−142.

[13] A.U. Peker, O. Tosun, T. Acarman, Particle filter vehicle localization and map-matching using map topology, in: 2011 IEEE Intelligent Vehicles Symposium (IV), IEEE, 2011, pp. 248−253.

[14] C.E. White, D. Bernstein, A.L. Kornhauser, Some map matching algorithms for personal navigation assitants, Transportation Research Part C: Emerging Technologies 8 (1−6) (2000) 91−108.

[15] P. Newson, J. Krumm, Hidden Markov map matching through noise and sparseness, in: Proceedings of the 17th ACM SIGSPATIAL International Conference on Advances in Geographic Information Systems, ACM, 2009, pp. 336−343.

[16] K. Tanaka, K. Saeki, M. Minami, T. Ueda, LSH-RANSAC: incremental matching of large-size maps, IEICE - Transactions on Info and Systems E93-D (2010) 326−334.

[17] Y. Bang, J. Kim, K. Yu, An improved map-matching technique based on the Fréchet distance approach for pedestrian navigation services, Sensors 16 (2016) 1768.

[18] B. Kuijpers, B. Moelans, W. Othman, A. Vaisman, Uncertainty-based map matching: the space-time prism and k-shortest path algorithm, ISPRS International Journal of Geo-Information 5 (2016) 204.

[19] J. Yuan, Y. Zheng, C. Zhang, X. Xie, G. Sun, An interactive-voting based map matching algorithm, in: 2010 Eleventh International Conference on Mobile Data Management, IEEE, 2010, pp. 43−52.

[20] Y. Zhang, Y. He, An advanced interactive-voting based map matching algorithm for low-sampling-rate GPS data, in: 2018 IEEE 15th International Conference on Networking, Sensing and Control (ICNSC), IEEE, 2018, pp. 1−7.

CHAPTER TEN

Social information labeling for individual mobile phone user

Chen Zhiheng

Center for Spatial Information Science, The University of Tokyo, Kashiwa-shi, Chiba, Japan

1. Background

Tracking demographic dynamics is important in many fields, such as urban planning, placement of commercial advertising, emergency management, and so on [1,2]. The location function of mobile phones provides convenience for tracking demographic dynamics. Much research only tracks people's mobility without paying attention to their demographic and social information. Therefore, the goal of this research is to label anonymous users with social information for further tracking of demographic dynamics at fine time intervals and variable spatial scales. Since it is difficult to infer social information only from trajectory data [3], most studies choose to combine multi-source data for inference, such as SNS data [4] and individual-level user profiles. However, multi-source data often involves privacy and is not easy to access, so developing methods for inference using nonsensitive data is worth exploring. In summary, we put forward the idea of this study. We use nonsensitive government survey data to construct a Bayesian model to label social information for trajectory data.

2. Data description
2.1 Human mobility dataset

This chapter utilized a human mobility dataset named "Konzatsu-Tokei (R)" Data collected by NTT DOCOMO, INC. This dataset records location information sent by mobile phone, collected through applications provided by NTT DOCOMO INC under user's consent. The data is anonymized before publication to protect user privacy and therefore does not contain label information that could identify users. In our previous work [5,6], we used this dataset for life-pattern clustering and demographic information tracking, annotating users' home location (longitude and latitude) and age–gender (probability table) information. In this chapter, we selected users whose home location is within the Tokyo metropolis.

2.2 Administrative border dataset

This chapter employed the polygon shapefile of the Tokyo metropolis at home (translated as a block) level. This data was published in 2018 and recorded the name of the block for each polygon.

2.3 Social information dataset

We used a dataset named "chomonicx" from Zenrin Marketing Solutions Co., Ltd. Chomonicx is geodemographic data that classifies blocks all over Japan from the viewpoint of lifestyle by combining various statistical data such as census, estimation of the number of households by annual income class, and official land price. 219,055 blocks are classified into 38 clusters, and the social information characteristics of each category are counted, including family structure, household income, occupation, etc. This social information is recorded in the form of probabilistic proportions (e.g., 49% for men and 51% for women).

2.4 Prior dataset

To construct a Bayesian network to calculate conditional probabilities involving all variables, we collected a large amount of prior data from government statistics websites. These data contain joint statistics of two or more variables, and after transformation, we obtain conditional distribution probabilities between variables with dependencies.

3. Framework and case study

Taking users living in the Tokyo metropolis as a case study, we propose the research framework as shown in Fig. 10.1. First, we matched the social information with every user according to their home location to obtain the marginal probability matrix. We then constructed a Bayesian network using the prior dataset of conditional probabilities. In the labeling section, we generate a set of initial labels for each user and update the label by sampling with rotating variables. Finally, we can obtain individual-level social information labels and demographic dynamics with social information through further integration.

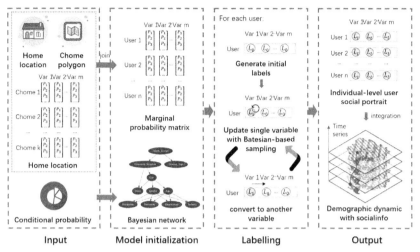

Figure 10.1 The framework of this study. *Credit: Chen Zhiheng.*

4. Methodology

4.1 Social information matching

We overlayed the home location point layer and administrative border data and used the "join attributes by location" function of QGIS to obtain the name of the block where the user lives. Using block names as the key, we then use the "join" function to match the marginal distribution (MD) of social information corresponding to blocks in the Chamonix data with each individual user.

4.2 Bayesian network

A Bayesian network is composed of random variables (nodes) and their conditional dependencies (arcs), which, together, form a directed acyclic graph (DAG) [7]. They are used to express the conditional dependencies relationship between various factors. Every arc is directed. If event B is conditionally dependent on A, A is called the parent node B, and the direction of the arc is from A to B. If there is no connection between events A and B, they are considered independent of each other. In Bayesian networks, each variable represents a node, and each node corresponds to a conditional probability table $P(X|Parent(X))$. The set of conditional probabilities of a Bayesian network shows the uncertainty of the correlation between the target event and the condition variable event [7]. The current popular method is to build a Bayesian network model from real data. Subject to Chamonix data, we adjusted the number of labels for each variable in the government survey data. Then we applied the package "pyAgrum" in python, inputting nodes,

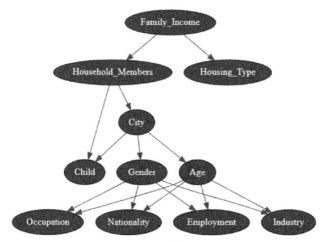

Figure 10.2 The Bayesian network of this study. *Credit: Chen Zhiheng.*

arcs, and conditional probability distributions (CPD) to create a Bayesian network (Fig. 10.2). There are a total of 11 variables in this network, where home location (City) is the observed variable, variables "Gender" and "Age" use probabilities inferred from our previous work, and other variables use government statistics.

4.3 Sampling

Input: The set of probability distribution functions for all individual variables $P = (p(x_1), p(x_2) \ldots, p(x_k))$, the number of samples drawn each time m, and the number of cycle times n.

Step 1: Fix observations (home location) and initialize other variables according to marginal distributions P to obtain an initial label set $x^{(0)}$.

$$x^{(0)} = \left(x_1^{(0)}, x_2^{(0)}, \ldots, x_k^{(0)}\right)$$

Step 2: For $i = 1$ to n and $j = 1$ to k, Choose a nonevidence variable and draw m samples according to its probability distribution function $p(x_j)$ to obtain a sample set X_j .

$$X_j = \left(x_{j,1}, x_{j,2}, \ldots, x_{j,m}\right)$$

Step 3: Resample the nonevidence variable x_j from its conditional probability $P\left(x_j | x_1^{(i)}, x_2^{(i)}, \ldots, x_{j-1}^{(i)}, x_{j+1}^{(i-1)}, \ldots, x_k^{(i-1)}\right)$ in the Bayesian network. If this sample is belonged to X_j, it can be assigned to $x_j^{(i)}$.

Step 4: Record the final sample as the label set of the user.

$$x^{(n)} = \left(x_1^{(n)}, x_2^{(n)}, \ldots, x_k^{(n)}\right)$$

5. Evaluation metrics

5.1 Evaluation by the marginal probability

For all users, we computed marginal distributions for each variable based on the inferred labels and compared the results with government statistics. We use the sum of the squares of the marginal probability differences of the same label as the metric to evaluate the performance of the model.

$$bias = \sum_i (GMP_i - SMP_i)^2$$

5.2 Evaluation by the joint probability

Since the ground truth, the joint probability distribution for all labels is not available, we qualify the results by comparing the average joint probability of users in different parameter combinations.

$$P_{joint} = \frac{1}{K} * \sum_k^K P_k(a, b, c, d \ldots)$$

6. Result

We tried six parameter combinations for n and m ((1, 10), (1, 5), (1, 15), (2, 10), (2, 5), (2, 15)). Among them, the parameter combination (1, 15) performs the best on the first metrics, and the parameter combinations (2, 10) and (2, 15) perform the best on the second metrics. According to the preference of the target, the corresponding parameter combination can be selected (Table 10.1).

We counted the proportion of all inferred labels among users. Fig. 10.3 shows the comparison of ground truth and inference statistics for each

Table 10.1 Evaluation for parameter combinations.

	n	m	bias	P_{joint}
Parameter combination 1	1	10	0.072	0.000011
Parameter combination 2	1	5	0.134	0.000009
Parameter combination 3	1	15	0.046	0.000011
Parameter combination 4	2	10	0.095	0.000013
Parameter combination 5	2	5	0.181	0.000011
Parameter combination 6	2	15	0.060	0.000013

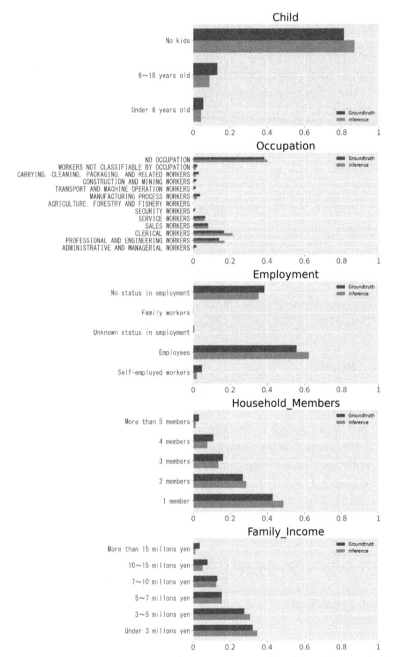

Figure 10.3 The ground truth and inference statistics of each variable. *Credit: Chen Zhiheng.*

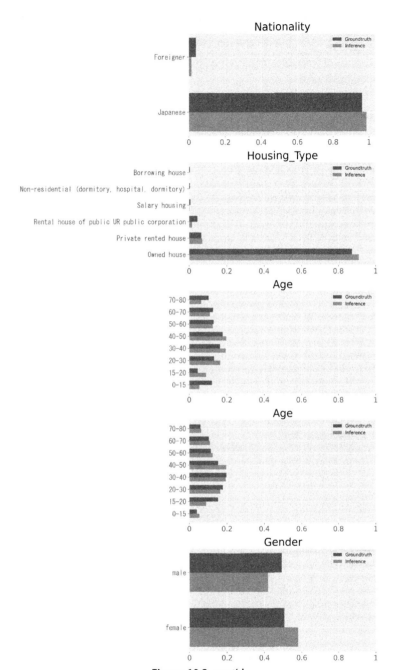

Figure 10.3 cont'd.

variable when the parameter combination is (2, 15). It can be seen that the inferred statistics are close to the real data on most variables. The errors in the age and gender variables are mainly due to the sample bias of the mobile phone location data.

References

[1] M.N. Alverti, K. Themistocleous, P.C. Kyriakidis, D.G. Hadjimitsis, A study of the interaction of human smart characteristics with demographic dynamics and built environment: the case of limassol, Cyprus, Smart Cities 3 (2020) 48—73, https://doi.org/10.3390/SMARTCITIES3010004.

[2] Q. Zhang, J. Wu, M. Zanella, W. Yang, A.K. Bashir, W. Fornaciari, Sema-IIoVT: Emergent Semantic-Based Trustworthy Information-Centric Fog System and Testbed for Intelligent Internet of Vehicles, IEEE Consumer Electronics Magazine, 2021, https://doi.org/10.1109/MCE.2021.3061067.

[3] A. Solomon, A. Bar, C. Yanai, B. Shapira, L. Rokach, Predict demographic information using Word2vec on spatial trajectories. UMAP 2018—Proceedings of the 26th Conference on User Modeling, Adaptation and Personalization, 2018, pp. 331—339, https://doi.org/10.1145/3209219.3209224.

[4] F. Xu, Z. Lin, T. Xia, D. Guo, Y. Li, SUME: semantic-enhanced urban mobility network embedding for user demographic inference, Proceedings of the ACM on Interactive, Mobile, Wearable and Ubiquitous Technologies 4 (3) (2020), https://doi.org/10.1145/3411807.

[5] P. Li, H. Zhang, W. Li, K. Yu, A.K. Bashir, A. Ali Al Zubi, J. Chen, X. Song, R. Shibasaki, IIoT based trustworthy demographic dynamics tracking with advanced bayesian learning, IEEE Transactions on Network Science and Engineering (2022) 1, https://doi.org/10.1109/TNSE.2022.3145572.

[6] W. Li, H. Zhang, J. Chen, P. Li, Y. Yao, X. Shi, M. Shibasaki, H.H. Kobayashi, X. Song, R. Shibasaki, Metagraph-based life pattern clustering with big human mobility data, IEEE Transactions on Big Data (2022) 1, https://doi.org/10.1109/TBDATA.2022.3155752.

[7] R. Renjith Raj, G. Venugopal, M.R. Rajkumar, Bayesian inference for parameter estimation in transient heat transfer experiments, Journal of Heat Transfer 137 (12) (2015), https://doi.org/10.1115/1.4030955/383788.

CHAPTER ELEVEN

Web-based spatio-temporal data visualization technology for urban digital twin

Qing Yu[1], Wen-Long Shang[2], Jinyu Chen[3], Haoran Zhang[4]
[1]Research Institute of Trustworthy Autonomous Systems, Southern University of Science and Technology, Shenzhen, Guangdong, China
[2]Beijing Key Laboratory of Traffic Engineering, College of Metropolitan Transportation, Beijing University of Technology, Beijing, People's Republic of China
[3]Center for Spatial Information Science, The University of Tokyo, Kashiwa-shi, Chiba, Japan
[4]School of Urban Planning and Design, Peking University, Shenzhen, China

1. Introduction

With the wide usage of smart mobile devices and the fast development of the Internet of Things (IoT) technology in recent years [1], GPS Positioning Data generated by individual users are collected began to grow explosively. Also known as "spatio-temporal big data" or "Track & Trace data" [2], these data are widely considered as a power source to support the construction of the next-generation smart city and have already triggered and motivated a large number of scientific research in relevant fields [3—9]. These Spatio-temporal big data typically require three aspects of information [10,11]: Who? When? Where? They can completely capture individuals' everyday activities and travel behavior in both temporal and spatial dimensions [12].

The emergence of large-scale Spatio-temporal big data has also brought about the demand for data visualization [13]. Data visualization figures can be used by researchers to express their perspectives and notion and have grown in importance as a tool for academics to extract relevant information from their data. Data-driven research may give valuable insights for comprehending the present situation of the urban system and assisting with urban management in the field of transportation [14,15], energy [16,17], human mobility [18], urban sustainability [19,20], emergency management [21,22], etc.

As a part of the Industry 4.0 wave, the concept of Digital Twin(DT) is emerged, which is defined as a virtual representation of an object or system

Handbook of Mobility Data Mining, Volume 1
ISBN: 978-0-443-18428-4
https://doi.org/10.1016/B978-0-443-18428-4.00002-5

that spans its lifecycle, is updated from real-time data, and uses simulation, machine learning and reasoning to help decision-making [23–25]. In urban areas, an urban DT is a digital version of a smart city that may be used to replicate and visualize real-world occurrences. It is frequently presented in the form of interactive platforms that can record and display real-time 3D Spatio-temporal data in order to model urban settings and data flows [26]. In fact, an urban DT can be regarded as a higher level of data visualization system with the integration of multiple interactive applications.

The emergence of web-based visualization technology has brought a new way to visualize Spatio-temporal big data. Meanwhile, the web-based application with the DT system deploying on a web page creates easy access dynamic and interactive experience for users. The organic combination of urban DT and visualization of Spatio-temporal big data is one of the important directions for future smart city decision-making, planning, and management [27].

In this chapter, we seek to address specific research questions regarding web-based visualization for Spatio-temporal big data:

- What are the advantages, key technologies, and common tools of web-based Spatio-temporal big data visualization?
- How to use web-based visualization technology to properly visualize spatiotemporal big data?

The best part of this chapter is organized as follows: Section 2 introduces the advantages, key technologies, and common tools of web-based visualization; Section 3 introduces the common form of Spatio-temporal data visualization; Section 4 introduces an example of Spatio-temporal data visualization using web-based technology; Section 5 draw the conclusions of our discussions.

2. Web-based data visualization technology

2.1 Advantages of web-based data visualization

The following difficulties exist in the visualization of Spatio-temporal big data:

- **Massive data:** Spatio-temporal big data usually involves a massive amount of data [28]. Real-time dynamic and interactive data visualization will occupy considerable computation resources and generates high requirements for visualization.
- **Various characteristics:** Spatio-temporal big data involves multiple types of data with different characteristics (taxi GPS data, bicycle-sharing

data, bus GPS data, etc.). Flexible visualization approaches are also required to show diverse types of data in a suitable manner.

- **GIS-based:** The spatial information of the data is the most important part, which means that the data visualization should be GIS-based, and a large part of data presentation and interaction should be on the map application.
- **Responsive interaction:** Spatio-temporal big data contains information in multi-dimensions. A better way to present the data is in the form of responsive interaction, which can help users perceive data.

To deal with these challenges, Web-based visualization technology have the following features that can well solve the above difficulties. The highlight advantages of Web-based visualization technology include follows:

- Web-based visualization technology can be built upon Web Map Service (OpenStreetMap, Mapbox, etc.), which supports rendering large geospatial data sets with interactive events. Also provides highly customizable and flexible APIs to present multiple forms of data visualization.
- Web-based applications are with high compatibility that can be easily accessed by any device by visiting the web page, which is helpful to promote among users.
- Web-based applications are based on JavaScript programming language, which has superior performance and great potential to integrate popular industries or algorithms like Machine Learning, Data Analysis, and Spatial data processing.

The above advantages make web-based data visualization become one of the most suitable technology for developing urban DT applications.

2.2 The key technology of web-based data visualization

2.2.1 HTML5 webpage standard

In recent years, web-based data visualization has become the mainstream of data visualization technology. It visually exhibits data figures on a web page so that users may readily access visualization figures via a web browser. Web-based data visualization is a type of webpage that is powered by the HTML5 standard [29]. HTML5 is the fifth version of HyperText Markup Language (HTML) for delivering website content on the World Wide Web, and it is regarded as one of the Internet's basic technologies.

The HTML5 webpage is usually supplemented by the Cascading Style Sheets (CSS) and JavaScript to support the animation and interactivity of webpage elements. In general, HTML determines the overall structure of the page; CSS determines the presentation style of the webpage contents, including layout, colors, and fonts; JavaScript provides the engine to enable programming and execute the code on the web page. Compared with Adobe Flash (the traditional way of webpage interaction), the HTML5 standard is safer, more efficient, and compatible [30,31].

2.2.2 WebGL 3D graphics rendering

Web Graphics Library (WebGL) is a standard that serves as a bridge between JavaScript and OpenGL (Open Graphics Library), allowing JavaScript to generate 3D graphical objects [32]. It also supports GPU-accelerated rendering of 3D scenes and models as part of the web page canvas in web browsers [33].

With the help of WebGL, web developers are able to present 3D objects (3D models, buildings, terrain, etc.) with live effects(sunlight, shadow, fog, etc.) on a WebGL maps to construct a highly realistic 3D city on the website. These features make WebGL becoming one of the most suited technology to build urban DT and visualize large-scale Spatio-temporal data.

2.2.3 JavaScript framework

A JavaScript framework is a prewritten collection of code designed to assist applications and provide features that plain JavaScript does not deliver on its own. JavaScript frameworks are designed to perform numerous functions and serve as the foundation of a web application [34]. The JavaScript framework allows for expanded functionality without the need to write code from scratch.

React, Angular, and Vue are the three most popular JavaScript frameworks [35–37]. Taking React as an example, it employs JSX rather than standard JavaScript to help in the handling of UI within the JavaScript code. One of React's benefits is that it employs the virtual document object paradigm (DOM). When a change is made to a React app, the diffing algorithm is used to compare the old DOM to the new in-memory and then update the altered part of the DOM. As a result, React is faster for web pages and applications with a lot of interactive elements.

React-based apps can only update the altered portion of the data without rerendering the entire dataset. This mechanism enables react apps to show larger amounts of data at a faster rendering speed with a quick response, which is especially useful when dealing with vast volumes of data visualization with interactivity.

2.2.4 Interaction between frontend and backend

In web development, the web application is usually separated into the web-page displaying contents (front-end) and the server storing the data and providing data access(back-end). For web-based data visualization, the design of interaction logic between the front-end and back-end will have a significant impact on the system function and response speed of the interaction. Generally, there are two types of settings: static web page and dynamic web page (Figs. 11.1 and 11.2).

Static web page: Prior to visualization, the massive dataset is computed and converted to a small dataset, keeping only the part that the user needs to visualize. It arranges all possible user interactions in advance, and all visualization results are already computed and saved. As a result, when a user conducts an interactive activity, the front-end merely needs to locate the associated data file and then update the visualization. This approach of thinking allows the data query to be completed ahead of time and eliminates the utilization of the back end.

Dynamic web page: When the user interacts with the visualized web page, the web page (front-end) sends the operation information of the interaction to the server (back-end). When the back-end receives the request, it implements the query on the database, obtains the result, and sends it back to the front end for visualization. Dynamic web pages allow interaction with real-time data queries. Compared to a static web page, dynamic web pages usually request data by sending query parameters to the back-end through an API. Each time a request is sent, the back-end must query the data and then deliver the data after the results have been gathered. As a result, dynamic

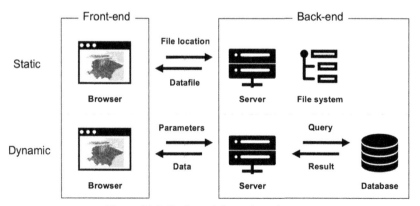

Figure 11.1 Static and dynamic web page.

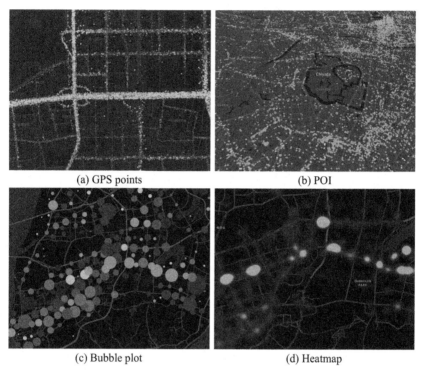

(a) GPS points   (b) POI

(c) Bubble plot   (d) Heatmap

Figure 11.2 Visualization of points. (A) GPS points. (B) POI. (C) Bubble plot. (D) Heatmap.

web pages may have a longer response time than static websites, but they may accomplish more flexible data interaction.

2.3 Web-based visualization tools

In JavaScript, there are already many mature libraries that can provide the integration of WebGL data visualization with web maps. Related tools are shown in Table 11.1. At present, these tools can be roughly divided into two categories. One is to provide the basic API interface for WebGL maps, which can display simple data information as layers on the map, such as Mapboxgl (based on Mapbox) [38], and leaflet (based on Open-StreetMap) [39]; The second category focus on the presentation of data, they are built upon the first category and further encapsulates the API to provide more advanced effects and visualization methods, such as Deck.gl [40], AntV-L7, ECharts.gl [41], etc.

Table 11.1 Popular Spatio-temporal data visualization libraries on JavaScript.

Library	Description
Mapbox.gl	Provides APIs for building interactive web maps and web applications on Mapbox.
React-map-gl	A suite of React components for Mapbox GL JS-compatible libraries.
Deck.gl	WebGL-powered framework for visual exploratory data analysis of large datasets.
Leaflet	Mobile-friendly interactive maps based on OpenStreetMap.
AntV-L7	Large-scale WebGL-powered geospatial data visualization analysis framework, which relies on mapbox GL or AMap to render base maps.
Maptalks.js	An open-source javascript library to create integrated 2D/3D maps with essential features for mapping projects.
ECharts.gl	WebGL-based data visualization tools provide multiple types of charts. Also provides integration of WebGL maps powered by mapbox or maptalks.

3. Visualization of data

In the urban digital twin, there are many types of data that need to be presented. The previously stated Web-based visualization tools also offer several forms of visualization. These visualization forms can be roughly divided into three types: Point, Line, and Region.

3.1 Point : GPS points, point of interests

Point data (scatter plot) is the simplest form of presentation and is often used to represent GPS points or Points of interest (POI) data (see Fig. 11.3).

In addition to spatial information, the marker size and color of the scatter plot can be used to represent additional dimensions of information (Figs. 11.3A and B). It is also called the bubble plot if there is a difference in the size of the data points (Fig. 11.3C). However, a bubble plot can only hold a limited amount of data. Too large bubbles may interfere with accurately identifying the location of the bubble center; some bubbles may also be too large to block and obscure smaller bubbles. If an extra dimension other than the location is to be displayed, color differences should be prioritized over size differences.

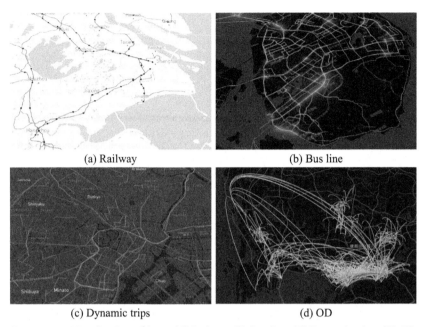

(a) Railway   (b) Bus line

(c) Dynamic trips   (d) OD

Figure 11.3 Visualization of lines. (A) Railway. (B) Bus line. (C) Dynamic trips. (D) OD.

Point data can also be visualized with a heatmap to represent the concentration of the data distribution (Fig. 11.3D). A heatmap is a thermal figure that has been smoothed and blurred. When creating a heatmap, three parameters are commonly included: point size, blur size, and colormap. The selection of parameters for a heat map can greatly affect the display; even the same dataset might be rendered substantially differently with various parameters.

3.2 Line: trajectory data, traffic line data, OD data

Lines are often used to represent trajectory data, traffic route data, and Origin-destination (OD) data (see Fig. 11.4). Lines are divided into Line segments (only with starting and ending points) and polylines (multiple points on the line) in terms of morphology, and static and dynamic lines in terms of display in terms of how they are displayed.

Static lines are usually suitable for traffic lines (bus, subway, or roads) and OD flows, and for line segments with only start and end points, the curvature can be added to them for better visualization (Fig. 11.4D). In some visualization tools, it is also possible to add dynamic light effects or arrows to the line to represent the direction of the flow.

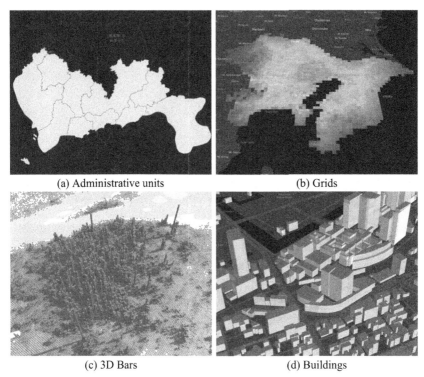

(a) Administrative units   (b) Grids

(c) 3D Bars   (d) Buildings

Figure 11.4 Visualization of regions. (A) Administrative units. (B) Grids. (C) 3D bars. (D) Buildings.

Dynamic Lines are animated lines that are used to show trajectories (Fig. 11.4C). Given a timestamp, the visualization tool calculates the trajectory's position and presents it with a trailing effect. It is feasible to create a time-controlled animation of the trajectory using this mechanism.

3.3 Region : AOI, buildings, grids, 3D bars

Region visualization is the polygon surfaces on the map, which is often used to represent polygon or multi-polygon data such as Areas of interest (AOI), administrative units, buildings, geospatial grids, 3D bars, etc. (see Fig. 11.5).

Region visualization is a common technique for geographic analysis involving location selection [6], spatial differentiation analysis [42,43], etc. When visualizing regions with areas of different sizes, the selection of spatial analyzing units may have a significant impact on the visualization outcomes, which is also known as the modifiable areal unit problem [44].

Figure 11.5 Dynamic trajectory visualization in 3D UrbanMOB.

One of the most common approaches to Spatio-temporal big data processing is to match and aggregate it into grids of the same size, as it provides a comparable and efficient way to process and present the data (Fig. 11.5B). Mapping the data to various hues of warm and cool tones and displaying the data on a grid-based map allows researchers to clearly understand how the data are distributed regionally and spatially and to conduct spatially relevant data analysis and discussion [45–47]. For the task of generating, calculating, matching, optimizing, and visualizing spatial mesh grids, we developed a Python package named TransBigData [11], which has already been used in a number of scientific publications [48–51].

By vertically extruding the polygon on 3D maps, the region may add another dimension to convey data. Extruding the grid data, for example, may provide the appearance of a 3D barplot (Fig. 11.5C), and the height of the data attribute value can be represented by the height of extruding.

Instead of using the detailed model object, buildings can be simplified and represented by the architectural outline using polygon extrude (Fig. 11.5D). This method of visualization in the urban DT system simplifies the building model, reduces resource consumption, and enables the visualization of large-scale buildings and the development of applications on top of them.

4. Case of web-based urban digital twin application: 3D UrbanMOB

This section introduces an example of a web-based urban digital twin application–3D UrbanMOB. As a submodule of the Small World AI (Spatial Multimodal ALL-World Artificial Intelligence) project [52], 3D Urban-MOB is a web-based digital twin visualization system with multiple solution-oriented applications. Small World AI incorporates several promising technologies that together help generate a near real-world scene in real time. In 2021, Small World AI received the R&D100 Award (the "Oscar of Innovation"), recognizing it as one of 2021s 100 most innovative and disruptive technologies, and the 2021 Smart 50 Awards in recognition of innovation and its potential impact on smart city technologies.

This section presents the feature, design concepts, and development details of 3D UrbanMOB. 3D UrbanMOB is developed based on JavaScript language and runs as a web-based data visualization application. The core structure of the system is developed based on React.js framework; the geographic information processing and analysis (WebGIS) module of the system adopts the technology combination of Deck.gl, React-map-gl, and Turf.js [53]. This technology Portfolio has also been used in multiple similar interactive visualization platforms [54–56].

4.1 Trajectory visualization

The human trajectory is the most basic data source in 3DUrbanMOB. Most applications are built based on trajectory data. With the support of the trips layer from Deck.gl, 3DUrbanMOB provides dynamic visualization for trajectory data. As time changes in the system, the user's trajectory is displayed with real-time animated lines with glowing effects.

This feature is supported by the interaction between three components: the hourly distribution bar plot, the playback control tool, and the base map. When the user selects a bar in the bar plot, the corresponding trajectory will be displayed on the map with animation. At the same time, a playback control tool appears on the interface, allowing the user to control the play, pause and speed up the trajectory movement, as well as drag the progress bar to specify a certain moment to observe the location of the individuals.

4.2 The active population inside a certain area

Buildings and POIs are the infrastructure data describing the city in the DT system. In practical applications, understanding the active population(the population generates activities or travel pass through) within a certain range of areas on the map can produce valuable information.

3DUrbanMOB provides the function of analyzing population characteristics in a certain area. By drawing an area on the map, the algorithm will extract the active population and passenger flow related to the selected area.

Methods for obtaining active population information in the region may be classified into two categories: based on key activity points and based on trajectories. Among them, the key activity point-based method is to extract the population information that has stayed and generates activities in the area, while the trajectory-based method is to filter out the trajectory passing through the area based on the spatial relationship between the trajectory and the selected area. The demographic information obtained from these two methods will have some differences with different application values Fig. 11.6.

4.3 Advertisement calculation

The selection of the proper place for offline billboards is extremely beneficial to brand promotion and the growth of the marketing market. The real-world influence of advertising models may be studied using urban building models in the DT system.

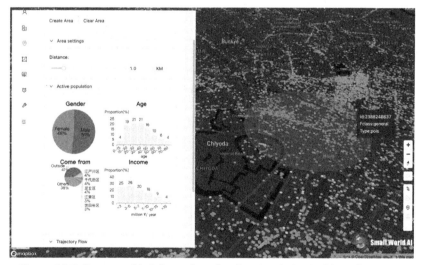

Figure 11.6 Demographic information of active population inside a given area.

3D UrbanMOB provides a tool to evaluate the visibility of outdoor advertising. By using the map-drawing tool, the width of the billboard and the top and bottom boundary information can be adjusted to set up the billboard at any location on the map.

The examination of the advertisement's visibility is divided into two steps: (1) The billboard resolution and average public visual acuity are used to compute the approximate visibility range of the advertisement; (2) The buildings within this range are screened, and the building occlusion is calculated to produce the fine visibility range of the advertisement.

The precise mapping from 3DUrbanMOB may serve as a reference base and theoretical foundation for offline billboard layout and commercial site selection investigations. The audience information of advertisements may be evaluated further in conjunction with the calculation of the active population to provide a complete evaluation of the advertising effectiveness Fig. 11.7.

4.4 Accessibility evaluation

The concept of accessibility is often used to measure the transportation performance of a certain geospatial region. The evaluation of accessibility is also one of the important topics in the field of urban transportation planning. 3D UrbanMOB provides a built-in Urban Accessibility Analysis System to assist decision-makers in promptly evaluating the accessibility improvements brought about by transportation infrastructure investment.

Figure 11.7 Visibility calculation of outdoor advertising billboard.

Figure 11.8 Accessibility evaluation with customized traffic lines.

The main functions of the system are as follows:

Accessibility calculation: Compute accessibility by using the built-in traffic network topology model to easily calculate the Average Travel Time of a certain area.

Custom traffic network: It allows users to draw any traffic line on the map. It also supports deploying stations and adjusting the operation speed of the traffic lines. The system can recalculate the average travel time and evaluate the improvement of accessibility Fig. 11.8.

5. Conclusion

In the era of big data, the emergence of Spatio-temporal data allows us to characterize a city's everyday activities in more detail. The urban digital twin is based on multi-source spatiotemporal big data, with a variety of real-world applications developed on top of data visualization technologies. The introduction of the urban digital twin can provide city planners with a brand new and powerful tool for designing next-generation smart cities.

The emergence of web-based visualization technology creates easy access to dynamic and interactive experiences to visualize Spatio-temporal big data. The organic combination of urban digital twin systems and web-based Spatio-temporal big data visualization is one of the important directions for future smart city decision-making, planning, and management.

This chapter introduces the advantages, key technologies, and common tools of web-based visualization, as well as the common form of visualization for different data. This chapter also presents an example of a web-based digital twin project called 3D UrbanMOB, including its feature, design concepts, and development details.

The web-based visualization technology is becoming increasingly important as researchers become more conscious of the necessity to use urban digital twins for monitoring, modeling, and assessment of urban events in the development of next-generation smart cities.

References

[1] Y. Yao, et al., Internet of Things positioning technology based intelligent delivery system, IEEE Transactions on Intelligent Transportation Systems (2022) 1—15.

[2] G. Harrison, S.M. Grant-Muller, F.C. Hodgson, New and emerging data forms in transportation planning and policy: opportunities and challenges for "Track and Trace" data, Transportation Research Part C: Emerging Technologies 117 (2020) 102672.

[3] J. Chen, et al., GPS data in urban online ride-hailing: a simulation method to evaluate impact of user scale on emission performance of system, Journal of Cleaner Production 287 (2021) 125567.

[4] H. Zhang, et al., Mobile phone GPS data in urban ride-sharing: an assessment method for emission reduction potential, Applied Energy 269 (2020) 115038.

[5] H. Zhang, et al., Epidemic versus economic performances of the COVID-19 lockdown: a big data driven analysis, Cities 120 (2022) 103502.

[6] J. Chen, et al., Roadmap to hydrogen society of Tokyo: locating priority of hydrogen facilities based on multiple big data fusion, Applied Energy 313 (2022) 118688.

[7] Q. Yu, et al., Mobile phone GPS data in urban customized bus: dynamic line design and emission reduction potentials analysis, Journal of Cleaner Production 272 (2020) 122471.

[8] Q. Yu, et al., Mobile phone data in urban bicycle-sharing: market-oriented sub-area division and spatial analysis on emission reduction potentials, Journal of Cleaner Production 254 (2020) 119974.

[9] Q. Yu, et al., GPS data in taxi-sharing system: analysis of potential demand and assessment of fuel consumption based on routing probability model, Applied Energy 314 (2022) 118923.

[10] Q. Yu, W. Li, D. Yang, Chapter 6—data-driven estimation for urban travel shareability, in: H. Zhang, X. Song, R. Shibasaki (Eds.), Big Data and Mobility as a Service, Elsevier, 2022, pp. 177—202.

[11] Q. Yu, J. Yuan, TransBigData: a Python package for transportation spatio-temporal big data processing, analysis and visualization, Journal of Open Source Software 7 (71) (2022) 4021.

[12] Q. Yu, et al., Mobile phone data in urban commuting: a network community detection-based framework to unveil the spatial structure of commuting demand, Journal of Advanced Transportation 2020 (2020) 15, 8835981.

[13] C. Yang, R. Jiang, R. Shibasaki, MaaS system visualization, in: Big Data and Mobility as a Service, Elsevier, 2022, pp. 245—263.

[14] H. Zhang, et al., Mobile phone GPS data in urban bicycle-sharing: layout optimization and emissions reduction analysis, Applied Energy 242 (2019) 138—147.

[15] S. Shekhar, et al., Data Mining and Visualization of Twin-Cities Traffic Data, 2001.

[16]   H. Zhang, et al., Battery electric vehicles in Japan: human mobile behavior based adoption potential analysis and policy target response, Applied Energy 220 (2018) 527—535.

[17]   H. Zhang, et al., Urban power load profiles under ageing transition integrated with future EVs charging, Advances in Applied Energy 1 (2021) 100007.

[18]   P. Li, et al., IIoT based trustworthy demographic dynamics tracking with advanced bayesian learning, IEEE Transactions on Network Science and Engineering (2022) 1.

[19]   Y. Sui, et al., Mining urban sustainable performance: spatio-temporal emission potential changes of urban transit buses in post-COVID-19 future, Applied Energy 280 (2020) 115966.

[20]   X. Song, et al., Mining urban sustainable performance: millions of GPS data reveal high-emission travel attraction in Tokyo, Journal of Cleaner Production 242 (2020) 118396.

[21]   X. Song, et al., Big Data and Emergency Management: Concepts, Methodologies, and Applications. IEEE Transactions on Big Data, 2020.

[22]   C. Fan, et al., Disaster City Digital Twin: a vision for integrating artificial and human intelligence for disaster management, International Journal of Information Management 56 (2021) 102049.

[23]   E. Negri, L. Fumagalli, M. Macchi, A review of the roles of digital twin in CPS-based production systems, Procedia Manufacturing 11 (2017) 939—948.

[24]   D. Jones, et al., Characterising the Digital Twin: a systematic literature review, CIRP Journal of Manufacturing Science and Technology 29 (2020) 36—52.

[25]   S. Dou, et al., Research on construction of spatio-temporal data visualization platform for GIS and BIM fusion, The International Archives of the Photogrammetry, Remote Sensing and Spatial Information Sciences 42 (2020) 555—563.

[26]   T. Deng, K. Zhang, Z.-J.M. Shen, A systematic review of a digital twin city: a new pattern of urban governance toward smart cities, Journal of Management Science and Engineering 6 (2) (2021) 125—134.

[27]   T. Seto, et al., Constructing a digital city on a web-3D platform: simultaneous and consistent generation of metadata and tile data from a multi-source raw dataset, in: Proceedings of the 3rd ACM SIGSPATIAL International Workshop on Advances in Resilient and Intelligent Cities, 2020.

[28]   H. Zhang, et al., 1.6 Million transactions replicate distributed PV market slowdown by COVID-19 lockdown, Applied Energy 283 (2021) 116341.

[29]   B. Lawson, R. Sharp, Introducing Html5, 2011 (New Riders).

[30]   J. Reyna, From flash to HTML5: the eLearning evolution, Training & Development 39 (5) (2012) 28—29.

[31]   J. Ozer, Video Compression for Flash, Apple Devices and HTML5, Doceo Publishing, 2011.

[32]   E. Angel, D. Shreiner, Interactive Computer Graphics with WebGL, Addison-Wesley Professional, 2014.

[33]   T. Parisi, Programming 3D Applications with HTML5 and WebGL: 3D Animation and Visualization for Web Pages, O'Reilly Media, Inc., 2014.

[34]   M. Kaluža, K. Troskot, B. Vukelić, Comparison of front-end frameworks for web applications development, Zbornik Veleučilišta u Rijeci 6 (1) (2018) 261—282.

[35]   S. Aggarwal, Modern web-development using reactjs, International Journal of Recent Research Aspects 5 (1) (2018) 133—137.

[36]   M.A. Jadhav, B.R. Sawant, A. Deshmukh, Single page application using angularjs, International Journal of Computer Science and Information Technologies 6 (3) (2015) 2876—2879.

[37]   Kyoreva, K. State of the art JavaScript application development with Vue. Js. in proceedings   of   international   conference   on   application   of   information   and

communication technology and statistics in economy and education (ICAICTSEE). 2017. International Conference on Application of Information and Communication ....

[38] B. Kastanakis, Mapbox Cookbook, Packt Publishing Ltd, 2016.

[39] P. Crickard III, Leaflet. Js Essentials, Packt Publishing Ltd, 2014.

[40] Y. Wang, Deck, Gl: Large-Scale Web-Based Visual Analytics Made Easy. arXiv Preprint arXiv:1910.08865, 2019.

[41] D. Li, et al., ECharts: a declarative framework for rapid construction of web-based visualization, Visual Informatics 2 (2) (2018) 136−146.

[42] H. Zhang, et al., A universal mobility-based indicator for regional health level, Cities 120 (2022) 103452.

[43] Z. Chen, et al., Using mobile phone big data to identify inequity of artificial light at night exposure: a case study in Tokyo, Cities 128 (2022) 103803.

[44] Y. Yao, et al., Modifiable Areal Unit Problem on Grided Mobile Crowd Sensing: Analysis and Restoration. IEEE Transactions on Mobile Computing, 2022.

[45] Y. Sui, et al., GPS data in urban online ride-hailing: a comparative analysis on fuel consumption and emissions, Journal of Cleaner Production 227 (2019) 495−505.

[46] W. Jiang, et al., GPS data in urban online ride-hailing: the technical potential analysis of demand prediction model, Journal of Cleaner Production 279 (2021) 123706.

[47] Q. Yu, et al., GPS data in urban bicycle-sharing: dynamic electric fence planning with assessment of resource-saving and potential energy consumption increasement, Applied Energy 322 (2022) 119533.

[48] Y. Hui, et al., Hotspots identification and classification of dockless bicycle sharing Service under electric fence circumstances, Journal of Advanced Transportation 2020 (2022) 16, 5218254.

[49] Y. Wu, et al., Analysis of the relationship between dockless bicycle-sharing and the metro: connection, competition, and complementation, Journal of Advanced Transportation 2020 (2022) 16, 5664004.

[50] Y. Li, et al., Taxi global positioning system data in urban road network: a methodology to identify key road clusters based on travel speed−traffic volume correlation, Transportation Research Record 2676 (1) (2022) 487−498.

[51] Q. Yu, et al., Mobile phone data in urban customized bus: a network-based hierarchical location selection method with an application to system layout design in the urban agglomeration, Sustainability 12 (15) (2020) 6203.

[52] Y. Jin, H. Zhang, S. Bharule, Modular metacognitive digital twin technologies for greener cities & cleaner mobility, Advances in Applied Energy 5 (2022) 100081.

[53] B. Hanson, C. Seeger, Mapping API's: Turf. Js in the Browser Console, 2018.

[54] Lo, R.Y.-H., N. Rao, and A. Sayara, Visualizing Linguistic Diversity in Vancouver.

[55] Chen, D., et al., A New City Map.

[56] S. DINKAR, A. SAINI, COVID-19 Tracker & Vaccination Monitoring, 2022.

Index

Note: 'Page numbers followed by "*f*" indicate figures and "*t*" indicate tables.'

A
Ablation study, 89–94, 92f, 93t
Administrative border dataset, 178
Artificial Neural Network, 125–126
Attentional recurrent networks, human
    mobility with, 148–150
Average displacement error (ADE), 147

B
Baseline methods, 148–152
    attentional recurrent networks, human
        mobility with, 148–150
    DeepMove, 148–150, 149f
    trajectory prediction, convolutional
        neural network for, 150–151, 150f
    TrajVAE, 151–152, 151f
Bayesian network, 125, 179–180, 180f
Big data, 1–2
Big mobility data
    mobility-as-a-service (MaaS), 15
    origin-destination (OD) matrices, 15–16
    origin-destination matrix similarity,
        27–31
        image-based measure, 28–29
        transforming distance-based, 29–31
        volume difference focused measure,
            27–28
    trajectory similarity, 16–25, 17f
        point-to-point distance metric, 17–19
        similarity function of trajectory, 19–25
        travel pattern similarity, 26–27

C
CDR, 6–7
Chebyshev distance, 18–19
Computer vision (CV), 141–142
Cross attention, 73–74
Cross scaling factors, 74–75
Crowd density error rate, 60–63, 61f, 63f

D
Dasymetric methods, 52

Data description, 177–178
Data preprocessing, 146
Decoding, 102–103
DeepMove, 148–150, 149f
Digital twin technology
    3D UrbanMOB, 195–198
    accessibility evaluation, 197–198, 198f
    advertisement calculation, 196–197,
        197f
    population, 196
    trajectory visualization, 195
    visualization of data, 191–194
    line, 192–193, 193f
    point data, 191–192
    region, 193–194, 194f
    web-based spatio-temporal data
        visualization technology, 186–190
        advantages of, 186–187
        frontend and backend, interaction
            between, 189–190, 189f–190f
        GIS-based, 187
        HTML5 webpage standard, 187–188
        JavaScript framework, 188
        massive data, 186
        responsive interaction, 187
        various characteristics, 186–187
        web-based visualization tools, 190,
            191t
        WebGL 3D graphics rendering, 188
Dijkstra algorithm, 163
Distributing error rate, 55–60, 56f,
    58f–60f
3D UrbanMOB, 195–198
    accessibility evaluation, 197–198, 198f
    advertisement calculation, 196–197, 197f
    population, 196
    trajectory visualization, 195
Dynamic time warping, 20–21

E
Edit distance
    with real penalty, 22–23

Edit distance (*Continued*)
on real sequence, 21–22
Environmental monitoring data, 8
Error analysis, 55–63
crowd density error rate, 60–63, 61f, 63f
distributing error rate, 55–60, 56f,
58f–60f
Euclidean distance, 17–18, 20
Evaluation metrics, 146–148
Event record, 7

F
Frechet distance, 23–24

G
Generative Adversarial Networks (GAN),
141
GIS-based, 187
Global positioning system (GPS), 68f, 139,
140f
ablation study, 89–94, 92f, 93t
cross attention, 73–74
cross scaling factors, 74–75
experimental setting, 75–81
human flow data, 75–77, 76t, 77f–78f
results, 82
vehicle flow data, 78
experiments, 75–94
feature extraction, 73
methodology, 71–75, 71f
population estimation, 69–70
preliminary, 71–72
problem define, 72–73
results, 82
human flow data, 82, 83t
vehicle flow data, 82, 84t
time horizon, predicting results on,
86–89, 89f–90f
transfer learning, 82–86
cross data, 85–86, 87t–88t
human flow data, 82–85, 85t
vehicle flow data, 85, 86t
vehicle flow estimation, 70
Ground truth data collection, 118–121,
118f–120f, 122f

H
Hausdorff distance, 23
Hidden Markov Model (HMM), 98–100,
125, 163–164
position state, 100
transferring speed state, 99–100, 99f
High-quality trajectory, 144
HTML5 webpage standard, 187–188
Human mobility dataset, 177–178
Human trip record, 5–6

I
Image-based measure, 28–29
Mean structural SIMilarity index
(MSSIM), 28–29
variants, 29

J
JavaScript framework, 188
Joint probability, 181

K
Kalman filter, 39–42

L
Levenshtein metric, 30–31
Locality in-between polylines, 25
Location, 144
Longest Common Subsequence (LCSS),
21
Low-quality trajectory, 144

M
Macroview metrics, 147–148
Manhattan distance, 18
Map-matching
multi-steps least cost algorithm, 159–168
Dijkstra algorithm, 163
Hidden Markov Model, 163–164
indicator factors, 160–162
model simplifying, 164–168, 165f
real world application, 168–173, 170t,
172f, 172t, 173f
traditional map-matching method,
158–159

Marginal probability, 181
Mean filter, 37—39
Mean structural SIMilarity index
    (MSSIM), 28—29
    variants, 29
Median filter, 37—39
Microview metrics, 146—147
Minkowski distance, 19
Mobile big data, 52—53
Mobile trajectory data, noise filter method
    for
    example of, 45—46, 46f
    Kalman filter, 39—42
    mean filter, 37—39
    median filter, 37—39
    origin, 36f
    Particle filter, 42—43
    road network matching, 44—45
    simple data cleaning, 37
Mobility-as-a-service (MaaS), 15
Mode detection, 98, 98f
Model simplifying, 164—168, 165f
Model training, 100—102
    supervised learning, 100—101
    unsupervised learning, 101—102
Modifiable areal unit problem (MAUP)
    dasymetric methods, 52
    definition, 51
    error analysis, 55—63
        crowd density error rate, 60—63, 61f,
        63f
        distributing error rate, 55—60, 56f,
        58f—60f
        mobile big data, 52—53
        position estimation, spatial error and
        temporal error in, 53f
        real case experiment, 63—64, 64t
Multi-steps least cost algorithm, 159—168
    Dijkstra algorithm, 163
    Hidden Markov Model, 163—164
    indicator factors, 160—162
    model simplifying, 164—168, 165f

O
One way distance, 24—25
Origin-destination (OD) matrices, 15—16,
    27—31

image-based measure, 28—29
transforming distance-based, 29—31
volume difference focused measure,
    27—28

P
Particle filter, 42—43
Point-to-point distance metric, 17—19
    Chebyshev distance, 18—19
    Euclidean distance, 17—18
    Manhattan distance, 18
    Minkowski distance, 19
Population estimation, 69—70
Position estimation, spatial error and
    temporal error in, 53f
Preliminary, 71—72
Prior dataset, 178

R
Random forest, 124—125
Real world application, 168—173, 170t,
    172f, 172t, 173f
Recurrent neural networks (RNN),
    140—141
Region cell, 144
Road network matching, 44—45

S
Sampling interval, 144
Short-trip density index
    linear regression, 110, 111f
    spatial lag regression, 110—114, 111t,
    113f
Short trips, spatial distributions of,
    105—107, 106f
Similarity function of trajectory, 19—25
    dynamic time warping, 20—21
    edit distance on real sequence, 21—22
    edit distance with real penalty, 22—23
    Euclidean distance, 20
    Frechet distance, 23—24
    Hausdorff distance, 23
    locality in-between polylines, 25
    Longest Common Subsequence (LCSS),
    21
    one way distance, 24—25
Simple data cleaning, 37

Social information dataset, 178
Social information labeling, individual
    mobile phone user
    Bayesian network, 179—180, 180f
    data description, 177—178
    administrative border dataset, 178
    human mobility dataset, 177—178
    prior dataset, 178
    social information dataset, 178
    evaluation metrics, 181
    joint probability, 181
    marginal probability, 181
    framework and case study, 178, 179f
    methodology, 179—180
    results, 181—184, 181t, 182f
    sampling, 180
    social information matching, 179
Social information matching, 179
Social media data, 8
Superresolution, 143—144
Surveillance camera data, 8—9

T
Time horizon, predicting results on,
    86—89, 89f—90f
Traditional map-matching method,
    158—159
Trajectory, 4—5, 144
    completion, 142—143
    dataset, 145
    generation, 143
    prediction, convolutional neural network
        for, 150—151, 150f
    similarity, 16—25, 17f
        point-to-point distance metric, 17—19
        similarity function of trajectory, 19—25
Trajectory super-resolution methods
    baseline methods, 148—152
    attentional recurrent networks, human
        mobility with, 148—150
    DeepMove, 148—150, 149f
    trajectory prediction, convolutional
        neural network for, 150—151, 150f
    TrajVAE, 151—152, 151f
    computer vision (CV), 141—142
    data description, 145—148, 146t
    average displacement error (ADE), 147

data preprocessing, 146
    evaluation metrics, 146—148
    macroview metrics, 147—148
    microview metrics, 146—147
    experiments and results, 152, 152t—153t
    Generative Adversarial Networks (GAN),
        141
    global positioning systems (GPS), 139,
        140f
    preliminary, 144—145
    recurrent neural networks (RNN),
        140—141
    superresolution, 143—144
    symbols and descriptions, 145t
    trajectory completion, 142—143
    trajectory generation, 143
    TrajVAE, 151—152, 151f
Transfer learning, 82—86
Transforming distance-based, 29—31
    Levenshtein metric, 30—31
    Wasserstein metric, 29—30
Travel mode detection, GPS trajectory
    Artificial Neural Network, 125—126
    Bayesian network, 125
    case studies, 127—132
        training, 131—132, 131t
        velocity analysis, 127—130, 128f—130f
    ground truth data collection, 118—121,
        118f—120f, 122f
    Hidden Markov Model, 125
    method for, 121—127, 123t—124t
    random forest, 124—125
Travel pattern similarity, 26—27
Trip segmentation
    application, 103—114, 104f
    decoding, 102—103
    Hidden Markov Model (HMM), 98—100
        position state, 100
        transferring speed state, 99—100, 99f
    mode detection, 98, 98f
    model training, 100—102
        supervised learning, 100—101
        unsupervised learning, 101—102
    short trips, spatial distributions of,
        105—107, 106f
    walkability, spatial patterns of, 107—110,
        108f—109f

short-trip density index, linear
 regression, 110, 111f
short-trip density index, spatial lag
 regression, 110—114, 111t, 113f

U

Urban computing, 2—3, 3f
Urban data
 big data, 1—2
 CDR, 6—7
 definition of, 2
 environmental monitoring data, 8
 event record, 7
 human trip record, 5—6
 social media data, 8
 surveillance camera data, 8—9
 trajectory, 4—5
 urban computing, 2—3, 3f
 urban sensor record, 7—8
 value, 3—9
 variety, 3—9
Urban sensor record, 7—8

V

Vehicle flow estimation, 70
Velocity analysis, 127—130, 128f—130f
Visualization of data, 191—194
 line, 192—193, 193f

point data, 191—192
region, 193—194, 194f
Volume difference focused measure,
 27—28

W

Walkability, spatial patterns of, 107—110,
 108f—109f
 short-trip density index, linear regression,
 110, 111f
 short-trip density index, spatial lag
 regression, 110—114, 111t, 113f
Wasserstein metric, 29—30
Web-based spatio-temporal data
 visualization technology, 186—190
 advantages of, 186—187
 frontend and backend, interaction
 between, 189—190, 189f—190f
 GIS-based, 187
 HTML5 webpage standard, 187—188
 JavaScript framework, 188
 massive data, 186
 responsive interaction, 187
 various characteristics, 186—187
 web-based visualization tools, 190, 191t
 WebGL 3D graphics rendering, 188
Web-based visualization tools, 190, 191t
WebGL 3D graphics rendering, 188

Printed in the United States
by Baker & Taylor Publisher Services